Environmental Policy in an International Context

PERSPECTIVES ON ENVIRONMENTAL PROBLEMS

ENVIRONMENTAL POLICY IN AN INTERNATIONAL CONTEXT

EDITED BY
Pieter Glasbergen and Andrew Blowers
Open Universiteit, The Netherlands, and Open University, UK

PERSPECTIVES ON ENVIRONMENTAL PROBLEMS
P. Glasbergen and A. Blowers

ENVIRONMENTAL PROBLEMS AS CONFLICTS OF INTEREST
P. B. Sloep and A. Blowers

PROSPECTS FOR ENVIRONMENTAL CHANGE
A. Blowers and P. Glasbergen

Environmental Policy in an International Context

PERSPECTIVES ON ENVIRONMENTAL PROBLEMS

EDITED BY
PIETER GLASBERGEN AND ANDREW BLOWERS

Open Universiteit, The Netherlands, and Open University, UK

A member of the Hodder Headline Group
LONDON • SYDNEY • AUCKLAND

© 1995 Open University of The Netherlands

First published in Great Britain in 1995 by
Arnold, a division of Hodder Headline PLC,
338 Euston Road, London NW1 3BH

British Library Cataloguing in Publication Data
A catalogue record for this book is available from the British Library

Library of Congress Cataloging-in-Publication Data
A catalog record for this book is available from the Library of Congress

ISBN 0 340 65261 6

1 2 3 4 5   95 96 97 98 99

Typeset in 11/12 pt Times by GreenGate Publishing Services, Tonbridge, Kent
Printed and bound in Great Britain by
St Edmundsbury Press Limited, Bury St Edmunds, Suffolk and
J W Arrowsmith Limited, Bristol

Contents

BOOK 2: ENVIRONMENTAL PROBLEMS AS CONFLICTS OF INTEREST

EDITED BY
Peter B. Sloep and Andrew Blowers

BOOK 3: PROSPECTS FOR ENVIRONMENTAL CHANGE

EDITED BY
Andrew Blowers and Pieter Glasbergen

About the contributors

Andrew Blowers is Professor of Social Sciences (Planning) at the Open University, UK. His main teaching, research and publications are in the fields of environmental planning, politics and policy. He is particularly concerned with the politics of sustainable development and the problems of radioactive waste. Among the books he has written are *The Limits of Power; Something in the Air*; *The International Politics of Nuclear Waste* (co-author); and *Planning for a Sustainable Environment* (editor). As former Dean and Pro-Vice-Chancellor of the Open University, Andrew Blowers is currently Chairman of the Interfaculty Studies Board. He is also a member of the government's Radioactive Waste Management Advisory Committee (RWMAC), Vice-Chair of the Town and Country Planning Association and has served as an elected county councillor in Bedfordshire since 1973.

Ron J.M. Cörvers is a lecturer in Environmental Policy and Management at the Open Universiteit of The Netherlands. He is primarily interested in the relation between physical planning, environmental policy and water management, using nature development strategies. He is preparing a thesis on the feasibility of region-oriented intergovernmental projects that promote the conservation and development of nature. He recently published 'Forecasting land-use disputes. Network analysis of a nature development project', in P. Glasbergen (ed.), *Managing Environmental Disputes: Network Management as an Alternative*, Kluwer Academic Publishers, Dordrecht.

Pieter Glasbergen is Professor of Environmental Studies – Policy and Management at the University of Utrecht and at the Open Universiteit, both in The Netherlands. He specialises in planning and policy issues, particularly with reference to environmental policy, physical planning, water management, and policy for landscape and nature conservation. He has conducted research for various government bodies such as the Ministry of the Environment, the National Physical Planning Agency and the Ministry of Public Works and Water Management. Dr Glasbergen has (co)authored or edited 12 books. Recently he edited the fourth edition of Milieubeleid; een beleidswetenschappelijke inleiding (*Environmental Policy: A Policy Science Introduction*), Vuga Publishers, and *Managing Environmental Disputes. Network Management as an Alternative*, Kluwer Academic Publishers. He chairs the Section Environmental Policy of The Netherlands Institute for Physical Planning and Housing.

Mike Gordon, an economic development and environmental planning consultant, working in the UK and elsewhere in Europe, is mainly involved in science parks and related projects. As Environment Course Tutor for the UK Open University and part-time lecturer in Planning and Law and EIA at Anglia Polytechnic University, he has published articles about the interrelationship between development and the environment and is particularly interested in water resources and development.

Dr Menno T. Kamminga, senior lecturer in International Law at Erasmus University in Rotterdam, The Netherlands has published widely on questions of international environmental law and international human rights law, including *Inter-State Accountability for Violations of Human Rights*, University of Pennsylvania Press, Philadelphia.

Dr Angela Liberatore is a scientific officer in the Socioeconomic Environmental Research Unit of the Environment Research Programme of the Directorate General for Science, Research and Development of the European Commission in Brussels. The chapter she has contributed to this volume was drafted when she was a researcher at the European University Institute in Florence. She is interested in institutional and societal aspects of science/policy interactions regarding European and international management of environmental problems. She recently published a study on 'Facing global warming. The interactions between science and policy making in the European Community' in M. Redclift and T. Benton (eds.), *Social Theory and the Global Environment,* Routledge, London and New York.

David Potter is Professor of Political Science at the Open University in the United Kingdom. His current research interest is the advocacy work of NGOs in relation to the environmental policies of nation states and transnational corporations in Asia. He is editor of the *Journal of Commonwealth and Comparative Policies*. A recent publication is 'Democratization in Asia' in D. Held (ed.), *Prospects for Democracy*, Polity Press, Cambridge.

Dr Peter B. Sloep is a senior lecturer in Theoretical Biology at the Open Universiteit of The Netherlands. He is primarily interested in conceptual and modelling issues regarding ecology and environmental science. His most recent publication is a study concerning the relevance of the notion of sustainability for the interdisciplinary nature of environmental science, in G. Skirbekk (ed.), *The Notion of Sustainability*, Scandinavian University Press, Oslo.

Dr Maria C.E. van Dam-Mieras is Professor of Natural Sciences at the Open Universiteit of The Netherlands. Her fields of interest are biochemistry, biotechnology and cleaner production strategies. She recently was involved in the development of the BIOTechnology by Open Learning (BIOTOL) project. BIOTOL consists of a series of 33 books supported by seven computer programs providing an overview of fundamental principles and application areas of biotechnology. BIOTOL books are published by Butterworth Heinemann, Oxford; BIOTOL computer programs are avalaible from Greenwich University Press, London.

Dr Jan van der Straaten is a senior lecturer in Environmental Economics at the Department of Leisure Studies at Tilburg University, The Netherlands; additionally he is seconded as a senior researcher to the European Centre for Nature Conservation at Tilburg University. He is interested in the effects of economic theories on policies in the area of nature and the environment, particularly in a European context. He gives special attention to the problems of rural development as regards nature conservation, agriculture and tourism. He edited, with Jeroen van den Bergh, *Toward Sustainable Development: Concepts, Methods and Policy*, published by Island Press, Washington, DC.

Preface

Environmental Policy in an International Context or, to use its familiar acronym, *EPIC* is a course that developed as a result of discussions between the Dutch and British Open Universities in 1991. Eventually a collaborative project emerged which now consists of three textbooks, a workbook/study guide and six video programmes. The course has been written by an international group of experts able to bring together the latest thinking on a subject area that is relatively new but of immense importance to our future.

The course takes a critical and analytical look at contemporary environmental issues building up a discourse around four key questions. In Volume 1, *Perspectives on Environmental Problems*, the key question is, 'What are international environmental problems, and why have they become important politically?' The question is examined from the different viewpoints of the natural sciences, sociology, politics, law and economics. It is emphasised that a multidisciplinary approach is necessary if we are fully to understand environmental problems. Volume 1 covers various themes. One is that environmental problems have both physical and social aspects and that, therefore, the social context must be understood. A related theme is that environmental problem solving is both a scientific and technical and an economic and political matter. There is a need to assess the relationship between scientific evidence and policy. The scale of contemporary environmental problems is such that policy must be addressed through international arrangements. Volume 1 focuses on conceptual and theoretical analysis, illustrated by a range of environmental issues. Especially it adopts a critical perspective on the concept of *sustainable development*. It is stressed that sustainable development should be seen in terms of the conflicts of interest that arise out of development and distribution problems.

Volume 2, *Environmental Problems as Conflicts of Interest,* considers the interaction between political power, policy making and environmental consequences. The organising principle of Volume 2 is the question, 'What are the causes of international environmental problems, and what are the conflicts surrounding their definition and potential solution?' Volume 2 consists of case studies of specific environmental problems. The logic of the case studies is that they move from the local to the global, analysing the nature of problems in the western world, the former communist countries and the South, concluding with those problems that are truly global, such as the threat of nuclear proliferation, the onset of global warming, and the loss of biodiversity. In Volume 2 it is emphasised that conflicts of interest often have both local and global implications in relation to policy and that resolution of the conflicts must be related to the social context of the problems.

Volume 3, *Prospects for Environmental Change*, goes on to discuss the possibilities for influencing environmental policy at the international level. The question addressed here is, 'What are the major constraints and opportunities that influence environmental policy making in an international context?' The opening chapters consider the role of major international actors, the nation state, non-governmental organisations and the business community in setting the policy-making agenda. The following chapters examine the importance of international relations (trade; West and East; North and South) in setting the context for environmental policy making. From this analysis the book turns its attention to the prospects for achieving sustainable development. The key question here is, 'How far can international action achieve sustainable development and in whose interest is such action taken?' The problem of translating the concept of sustainable development into practical policy and its implementation is considered before, finally, the book speculates on the social changes that are necessary if a sustainable society is to be secured.

Although *EPIC* is designed as a course with integrated components, each of the course books is also freestanding so that it can be read by those who are not taking the course. The three books, both individually and together, are intended to provide a context and body of knowledge of interest and importance to both social and natural scientists and a wider audience beyond.

Andrew Blowers (Open University, Milton Keynes, UK)
Pieter Glasbergen (Open Universiteit, Heerlen, The Netherlands)
Course Chairs – April 1995

Acknowledgements

The present book is part of a course which is taught by the open universities of both The Netherlands (Open Universiteit) and the UK (Open University). The course has been developed by a joint course team from both universities.

Particular thanks go to the senior administrators and staff in both institutions who made this book possible by providing the necessary funding and administrative support to permit the venture to go ahead.

The editors wish to extend their thanks to the members of the course team and to the many others who have in some way or other contributed to the present book. Without wanting to seem ungrateful to those who contributed in small yet important ways, we would like to thank a number of people explicitly:

John Bennett, Dr John Blunden, Ron J.M. Cörvers, Dr Bernard Eccleston, David Potter, Dr Alan Reddish, Varrie Scott, Dr Peter B. Sloep, Paul Smith, René van Veenhuizen, Dr John Wright, Anke H. van der Zijl for their services as members of the core course team. Professor Michael Redclift, the course's External Assessor, is thanked for his comments, and assessments of the course materials. Also, the services of the Tutor Panel (Fenella Butler, Mike Gordon, Gordon Jones, and Miles Litvinoff) in the UK, and Dr. Wim Westera and the Student Testers in The Netherlands were invaluable and indispensable.

We further thank Miek A.M. Wierts-van Helden for logistics support, Ommo E. Smit for editing the manuscript, and Jan Klerkx for his editing of the English language. Finally we must thank Evelin B.A. Karsten-Meessen for typing up the manuscript, and all the secretaries who provided their services over the years.

This book, *Perspectives on Environmental Problems,* is volume one of the series Environmental Policy in an International Context. First published in 1995, it is part of the Open University course N.22.2.1.2.

The following photographs were provided by:
- Lineair/Derde Wereld Fotoarchief, Arhem, The Netherlands:
  1.1, 1.2, 1.3, 1.4, 2.1, 2.3, 3.1, 4.1, 4.2, 4.3, 5.2, 5.3, 6.1, 6.2, 7.1, 7.2
- Ministerie van VROM/Oerlemans van Reeken studio, Den Haag, The Netherlands:
  2.2, 3.2, 7.3
- Sunshine, Almere-haven, The Netherlands:
  3.3, 5.1.

1

Environmental problems in an international context

Pieter Glasbergen and Ron Cörvers

1.1 Introduction

Why are environmental problems international problems? Just a few decades ago, this question would not have been asked. Therefore why should we be asking it now? Before we can answer these questions, however, we need to have some idea of what 'environmental problems' actually are.

Given the huge number of environmental problems and their disparity, it is no easy matter to identify their characteristic features. The definition which we shall be using in this introductory chapter is a simple one, and we shall be elaborating on it in the next chapter. For the present, we shall consider environmental problems as constituting *those instances in which people's behaviour affects their physical environment in such a way as to place their own health, other people's health, the built environment or natural systems in jeopardy*. This is the case, for example, where pollution occurs, where natural resources are exhausted, and where natural features are damaged. Environmental problems are both physical and social problems. Although one can almost always point to certain scientific data as underlying the definition of environmental problems, it is not possible to see them solely in 'objective' (scientific) terms. The scientific data in question need to be qualified in the context of social norms and values. As we shall see later on (Chapters 3 and 4), both the definition of environmental problems and the ways and means of solving them are the subject of political debate involving large numbers of organised lobbies. All this means that any study of environmental problems has got to include their social context and the conflicts taking place within it.

Even many centuries ago, conditions occurred which, by modern standards, would be classified as environmental problems. One such example can be found in ancient Mesopotamia, where large-scale irrigation led to the salinisation of fertile agricultural land. This was one of the factors which ultimately brought about the decline of the Mesopotamian civilisation. In medieval times, too, many people living in towns and cities suffered greatly as a result of widespread smoke pollution and contaminated water supplies. Similarly, the Industrial Revolution, which started at the turn of the 19th century, had a dramatic effect on the quality of the physical environment, not only in terms of public health, but also of the disappearance of all sorts of age-old natural features. Again, the extinction of animal and plant species as a consequence of human behaviour is by no means a modern phenomenon.

In all these instances of environmental problems, certain changes took place in the physical environment which were either difficult or impossible to reverse. At a local and regional level, people nonetheless consistently managed to find a means of survival. In fact, the evolution of the human race could be described as a trend towards increasing control of natural systems and the constant improvement of the conditions on which life is dependent. It was not, in fact, until fairly recently that people began to acknowledge the presence of a new, modern, global environmental threat.

For a long time, the natural environment was treated as a boundless resource. Since the 1960s, however, the bottom of the well has gradually been coming into view. It is now clear that the increasing exploitation of the natural systems (in terms of both output and input, as well as the structural changes which are caused in the process) is undermining their capacity for use both now and in the future. Indeed, it seems increasingly likely that humanity is sowing the seeds of its own destruction, in some cases as a result of its material prosperity, and in other cases as a result of its poverty. In other words, we are seeing the emergence both of environmental problems which are associated with a high standard of living, and of those which are caused by its very absence. The interrelationships between environmental problems occurring in different areas are also becoming more and more evident.

A new perspective is emerging in which environmental problems can be seen in the light of worldwide ecological relationships. In this chapter this new perspective is discussed in relation to the concept of *interdependency*. Three types of interdependency have been identified for this purpose: *ecological, economic and political*. These interdependencies are interrelated but they are also closely connected with economic factors which create the problems and hamper their elimination. In order to solve the environmental problems, changes are needed in the political decision-making process.

In order to gain a clear insight into current and possible future environmental problems, we shall focus on each of these interdependencies in turn showing how they have changed in the course of time. We shall also discuss a fourth aspect, the role of technology which can be seen as both cause and solution for environmental problems.

1.2 Ecological interdependencies

Today's environmental problems are no longer incidental difficulties which can be resolved by means of ad hoc solutions. Our readiness to accept this as a fact of life has been largely due to the broadening of our scientific knowledge of the causes of human behaviour and its effect on natural systems. Our knowledge has improved in two respects.

In the first place, at the time when the environment first became an 'issue', we did not know much about it. Whilst knowledge is clearly relative and, as we shall see in later chapters, our knowledge of many contemporary environmental problems is still clouded in uncertainty, what was known about the environment in the old days was empirical knowledge gained from experience. Today, however, we are increasingly able to anticipate future environmental problems. In a number of areas, there is general agreement that new environmental problems will arise in the future if human behaviour is not changed in good time, even though these problems are not having any visible effects at the moment. Global warming is a good example of such a problem.

In the second place, our current knowledge is such that it is possible to reveal the relations between the various factors which are at work on natural systems. As a result, we have become more aware of the synergistic and cumulative effects (in terms of both scale and speed) of behaviour that takes place in totally different areas of the world. We are, for example, now familiar with the general effects in global terms of the felling of tropical rainforests. These effects were not known at the time when the European forests were cut down. In addition, the new knowledge is disseminated more freely. In other words, scientific research is revealing more and more of the secrets of the Earth as a natural system, as well as of the threats facing it.

For the purpose of this chapter, this particular development is referred to as the process of revealing 'ecological interdependencies'. Although these have always existed, changes in the relationship between human beings and the natural environment have given them features which are characteristic of the time in which we now live. A number of these features will be discussed in the remainder of this section.

Crucial changes in ecological interdependencies

What changes have there been with regard to ecological interdependencies? A comprehensive analysis, assuming that this is feasible, would go beyond the scope of this chapter. For this reason, we shall concentrate on a number of crucial changes.

The first crucial change lies in the fact that the natural environment is now used more widely and more intensively than it used to be. This is due not only to population growth but also to new technological developments, and to new applications which have been discovered in the course of time. As a consequence, certain elements of the natural environment which were previously assumed not to have any economic value are now regarded as possessing a certain value in use. This has been the case, for example, with minerals, for which new applications have been found.

A second crucial change has been the development of new materials (such as plastics) which cannot be broken down directly by natural processes. Here too, new technologies have played an important role. As a result, certain substances are now entering the natural system which were not previously present. Other substances are now entering the natural system in much larger quantities than was previously the case. Both these trends may disrupt or even irreversibly damage the natural regeneration mechanisms.

The problems caused by these changes are the depletion of natural resources and environmental pollution (as a consequence of waste materials). These problems have characteristics which are specific to the time frame in which they are placed and which introduce two further crucial changes.

The third change is that, because many environmental problems cannot be solved on

3

a local or regional basis, it is no longer possible for people to cut themselves off from such problems. Even if the appropriate measures are taken in certain areas, they will not prove effective if similar measures are not taken at the same time in other areas. Many of today's environmental problems are international or even global in essence; acid rain and the depletion of the ozone layer are two good examples of these. Only international action can solve them.

A fourth change is that certain key effects of today's environmental problems are only felt in the long term. The process of increasing acidification is a clear example of this: even though it has been going on for a long time, the damage it causes to forest, for example, has only recently become apparent. It has now also become clear that it is a difficult process to reverse. Even if there is no further acidification in the future, it will be a long time before we manage to control the effects caused by the process of acidification in the past. The future effects of other environmental problems (such as global warming) can only be estimated by means of projections based on models. If no action is taken now, the victims of such problems will be tomorrow's generation.

It could be said that these developments have made the world smaller. Box 1 illustrates the increase in the scale of environmental problems from three different viewpoints.

Plate 1.1 Ecological interdependence: dramatic effects of acidification in Karkonosse Park, Poland. Photo: David Drain/Lineair

Increase in scale of environmental problems

Trends in air pollution
- air pollution in towns and cities
- acidification of large areas
- depletion of the ozone layer
- climatic change on Earth

Build-up of phosphates and nitrogen in the soil
- eutrophication of surface water
- presence of fertilizers in soil and surface water
- global disruption of nutrient cycles

Concern about state of the environment
- disappearance of rare plants and animals
- preservation of ecosystems
- preservation of biodiversity around the world

Links between environmental problems

As was noted above, today's environmental problems connect the lives of people in very distant regions of the Earth, connect the Earth with the atmosphere and affect very diverse communities. With the aid of two detailed examples we shall examine this particular point more closely. In doing so, we shall highlight a further characteristic feature of present-day environmental problems: the unequal distribution of causes and effects.

Deforestation is a good example of both the scale on which and the rate at which we are changing our natural environment. During the period since 1850, the area of the Earth which is covered by forest has declined from 6 billion to 4 billion hectares. There has been a particularly sharp increase in the rate of decline during the past few decades. The tropical region, where some 60% of the world's remaining forests are located, has suffered most in this process. For example, whereas just 40 years ago 30% of Ethiopia consisted of forest, today only 1% of the country is covered by forest.

At the beginning of this century, more than half of India was covered by forest. Today, the figure is just 14%. Although there are plenty of other, similar examples, the trend is clear: the tropical rainforests are rapidly disappearing. It is estimated that 20 million hectares are lost every year. The process has both a local and a global impact. Among the local effects are increasing erosion, the silting up of rivers and the flooding of farmlands. On a global scale, the consequences include a loss of habitats for species and an accelerating and irreversible destruction of genetic diversity. The effect of the latter is to deprive future generations of genetic material which they may need for developing medicines and disease-resistant food crops. The same effects may also be felt by whole ecosystems, which could be thrown out of balance as a result. Finally,

5

deforestation also results in a net release of carbon dioxide, and hence contributes to the greenhouse effect.

The greenhouse effect provides the second example. Although natural sources are the primary producers of greenhouse gases, anthropogenic sources are becoming ever more important in this respect. Carbon dioxide accounts for approximately half of all the gases which we introduce into the atmosphere, and the amount involved has increased dramatically in the course of time. Until around the middle of the last century, the amount of carbon dioxide in the atmosphere represented about 275 parts per million (ppm). This amount has risen during the intervening period to 350 ppm, with the rate of increase being currently estimated at 1.8 ppm (or 0.5%) per annum. The concentration of other greenhouse gases, such as methane, CFCs and nitrous oxide, is also on the increase. The probable result of this process will be a rise in the temperature on Earth and hence a rise in the sea level. This will have a disastrous effect not only on the climate but also on the suitability of large parts of the world for human life. On the one hand, there is considerable uncertainty as to the precise effects. Although there is now proof that the volume of greenhouse gases is increasing, the effects can only be predicted with the aid of models. On the other hand, it is too risky to wait and see whether the predictions actually come true. If they do, and nothing has been done in the meantime, it will no longer be possible to turn the clock back.

These two examples of environmental problems show that there may be a link between what seem at first sight to be unconnected problems. The felling of rainforests, which is restricted geographically to a number of tropical regions, has an impact all over the world. The same applies to global warming, the sources of which are not evenly distributed over the world (see Table 1.1).

The two environmental problems have different backgrounds. In the case of the rainforests, it should be pointed out that these represent vital ecological capital to developing countries. They need – generally for financial reasons – to exploit the rainforests in order to produce exportable goods. In this way, the richer, predominantly Western countries acquire a natural resource which they themselves do not possess. For both parties, however, the benefits are merely of a short-term nature. In the long term, this ecological capital will become exhausted. The same situation holds for many other natural resources in the developing countries: out of economic necessity, natural resources are over-exploited to the advantage of the more powerful, i.e. richer, market players, who consume the ecological capital which in many cases originates thousands

Table 1.1 *Total emissions of greenhouse gases*

Regions	World population (%)	Responsibility for global warming (%)
The West	15	46
Central/Eastern Europe	7	19
Third World	78	35

Source: *New International,* April 1990. Adapted from Elliott (1994), p. 42.

The 'shadow ecology' of an economy

2

Western nations rely heavily on resources spread around the globe and should be aware of their shadow ecologies and the need to pursue policies that will sustain them. Some countries, of course, are more dependent on dispersal resources than others. Japan is a case in point. Being a resource-poor country, the world's second largest economy has to import most of its energy and renewable resources as raw materials and export them as finished products. Japan's vast population also depends on access to its shadow ecology. Seventy percent of all cereal (corn, wheat, and barley) consumption and 95% of soyabean consumption are supplied from abroad. Poor crop yields in exporting countries due to environmental degradation or bad weather could have a grave impact on Japan's food supplies. Japanese imports of roundwoods account for one-third of the world total ... .

Source: MacNeill *et al.* (1991), p.59.

---

of miles away from their own countries. MacNeill *et al.* (1991) have referred to this phenomenon as the 'shadow ecology' of an economy (see Box 2).

Global warming, on the other hand, has a different background to that of deforestation. Global warming is primarily the result of an increasing level of prosperity, and of the use of fossil fuels in particular. The concentration of the sources of CO_2 emissions in the most prosperous countries is a clear indication that those countries have been the main economic beneficiaries of this form of environmental degradation. This places an extra burden of responsibility on them in terms of achieving the necessary reductions in emission levels. The reductions which are needed simply in order to prevent the concentrations of greenhouse gases in the atmosphere rising above present levels are estimated to be in the range of 50–80%. Yet these reductions, even if they are attainable, may be counteracted by the effects of the economic growth which the developing countries are struggling to achieve. This growth is based on an increasing consumption of fossil fuels. If no counter measures are taken, CO_2 emission levels in the developing countries in the course of the next century could actually exceed those now recorded in the industrialised countries. This particular environmental problem clearly highlights the need for international co-operation in an area in which all sorts of different interests are at play.

Environmental problems in different parts of the world

Today's key environmental problems (two examples of which have just been discussed) cannot be regarded in isolation, without reference to the main forms of development. They are the result of population growth, the development of technology and a desire to achieve economic growth that is highly dependent on intensive energy consumption and an intensive exploitation of natural resources. These various factors have led to fundamental environmental changes. Environmental problems which were once restricted to a small area, and may in many cases still have localised origins, are now proving to have an impact all over the world. Environmental problems which

7

initially seemed to be of concern only to the present generation are now proving to constitute threats to future generations as well. It should also be borne in mind that the world population will double during the course of the next 50 years. This is a process which is difficult to control: one-third of the world population are under the age of 15. Similarly, the degree of economic growth to which countries aspire remains dependent on the same natural resources, all of which will ultimately either be consumed in their entirety (as is the case with minerals) or be changed in such a way that they may even form a threat to human existence (e.g. the atmosphere).

This line of reasoning should not necessarily be seen as simple doom-mongering. Its object is rather to produce a sense of realism and a desire to identify the characteristic features of the problems in question. One of these features has already been touched upon in relation to the examples we have given: environmental problems differ from region to region. One popular dividing line which is often used in the analysis of environmental problems is that between the North and South. The North is in turn divided into the former socialist countries of Eastern and Central Europe on the one hand, and the capitalist countries known as 'the West' on the other (consisting of the USA, Canada, the European Union, Japan, Australia and New Zealand). The South is taken to consist of the developing countries. Although these distinctions are by no means absolute, they are useful in that they cast some light on the relationship between political ideology, the level of development and environmental problems. This relationship may be described in the following terms.

The industrialised Western countries are characterised by a high level of economic activity. Some of them, for example Japan and The Netherlands, have achieved this on a relatively limited land area with a limited local supply of natural resources. Others, notably the USA, have based their development initially on an abundant resource base. A third group, Canada and Australia, continue to export some of their natural resources. Over time in all these countries to a greater or lesser degree, rapid development has been founded on two cornerstones: the exploitation of natural resources increasingly imported from elsewhere (usually from developing countries) and technological innovation. The environmental problems are thus closely linked with the continuing process of economic growth, and may be considered as a consequence of the lifestyle in the West. The problems in question are all adverse effects of economic behaviour which is widely regarded as a benefit rather than a problem. Economic development is determined primarily by forces of supply and demand exerted by relatively autonomous market forces. Government policy is aimed at rectifying any harmful effects (which are taken to include any detrimental impact on the environment) caused by the interplay of these forces. It is in these countries that environmental policy has been most finely tuned as a remedial mechanism. On the other hand, policy makers are generally reluctant to take much account of long-term considerations. In the light of their wealth, these countries bear a certain degree of responsibility for the environmental problems in other parts of the world. Although this responsibility is indeed widely acknowledged, it has, so far, not led to any great amount of practical action.

Compared with the Western world, the countries of Eastern and Central Europe are characterised by a low level of economic activity. Most of them possess a reasonably large local supply of natural resources. The dominance of a communist ideology in these countries, however, has meant that the existence of environmental problems was denied for a long time and as a result, environmental policy was undeveloped. For a considerable period during the past, Nature was regarded as an obstacle to progress which had to be surmounted. The recent political revolutions have now revealed the environmental consequences of the mismanagement which took place under the communist regimes. There was enormous wastage in the use of the natural system: not only were far more raw materials and energy used per unit in the extraction, transport and production of natural resources than is the case in the West, but large parts of the region have now become so badly polluted that the situation is actually life-threatening. These countries are now going through a process of economic reconstruction. Whilst this offers an opportunity for 'building in' the necessary environmental measures, it has become clear that these countries are not capable of bearing the costs involved, including the ecological clean-up costs, on their own.

The patterns shown by the countries of the South are extremely diffuse. In general terms, however, it could be said that they have a very low level of economic activity (as defined in Western terms) and a wealth of natural resources. The environmental problems experienced in most of these countries are largely the result of a struggle for life which, in many areas, has thrown the local population into a vicious circle. As a result of poverty, people are compelled to overexploit natural resources, for both agricultural purposes (with soil exhaustion, desertification and deforestation as the consequence) and industrial purposes (leading to the exhaustion of mineral supplies). This overexploitation leads to the disappearance of the natural resources on which the sustenance of future generations depends. This, in turn, creates further poverty. The process is aggravated by population growth. It should also be pointed out that, in many countries in this part of the world, it is only a very small, rich elite which actually feels the benefits of overexploitation. Economic growth on Western lines is the explicit target of the political ideologies. In a number of countries, this has led to rapid economic growth and consequently to additional environmental pollution. Without outside assistance, many of the countries in this part of the world will not be capable of combining environmental protection and development. For them, economic development is the prime – and essential – target, and environmental protection is neglected.

1.3 Economic interdependencies

Scientific research has made it possible not only to identify both existing and potential environmental problems, but also to establish their causes. What we get, however, is only part of the picture. The definition of the term 'environmental problem' which we proposed at the beginning of the chapter makes clear that environmental problems are inextricably bound up with human behaviour. Various aspects of human behaviour have already been referred to in the preceding section. They may be described in more abstract terms as productive and consumptive behaviour, and referred to collectively as economic activity. In order to understand the background to present-day environmental problems, we therefore need to know something about the characteristics of, and the changes which have occurred in, this activity. This is the domain of the social sciences.

Social scientists, like natural scientists, have witnessed changes in the knowledge which is needed in order to gain a better insight into environmental problems. It has become increasingly clear, for example, that today's environmental problems are caused by global socioeconomic relationships. Certain aspects of these relationships can be used to explain not only how environmental problems arise, but also why they are not solved. The problem of deforestation is, for example, explained by social scientists in terms of conflicts of interest between the rich and the poor, financial dependencies and international trade relations. For the purpose of this chapter, we shall use the term 'economic interdependencies' to refer to the trends in socioeconomic relations which are relevant to environmental problems.

The relationship between the environment and the economic process is a reciprocal one. On the one hand, the environment has an effect on the results of the economic process. Natural resources are, after all, one of the key factors behind production decisions. On the other hand, the results of the economic process have an impact on the environment. Production and consumption may lead to a decline in the environmental quality that is needed in order to safeguard the continuity of the economic process. Within the scope of this chapter, our interest lies primarily in the second aspect of the relationship: the role of economic behaviour as a cause of environmental problems.

While there can no longer be any doubt that economic behaviour does indeed lie at the source of many environmental problems, societies have yet to convert this awareness into action by instigating the necessary process of economic restructuring. The issue basically consists of three vital elements:

○ Not enough attention is paid to the potential for environmental degradation inherent in economic processes.
○ Setting economic growth as a policy target encourages environmental degradation.
○ Environmental degradation is sustained by international economic interdependencies.

The environment as an external economic factor

In a capitalist economic system, a price mechanism is used to regulate the use of products and services. In theory, the prices of goods reflect their actual cost of production. This does not, however, apply to the environmental costs associated with production and consumption. The costs of more environmental degradation are not reflected in higher prices. Environmental degradation is – in economic terms – an external effect, passed on from those who produce the effects to society as a whole. Those responsible for the external effects of acidification (for example, motorists, farmers, the oil-refining industry) are not compelled to pay for the resulting damage caused to nature, drinking water supplies or buildings.

This insight has led some economists to the idea that price stimuli should play an important role in the prevention of environmental problems. Prices must tell the social truth about the cost of environmental degradation. Scarcity should be reflected in higher prices, which should in turn encourage people to review their priorities. When there is a change in relative prices (scarce resources and polluting activities are priced higher), people do what they have always done: they adapt their behaviour accordingly, become more inventive, and look for environmentally-friendly alternatives.

How much does the market cost?

3

'The assessment in monetary terms of the benefits of avoided environmental damage poses particularly large problems. These benefits should be weighed against the costs of avoiding environmental damage. Estimates for the latter can be made easily and quite accurately. For example, the cost of reducing the pollution level of a river that contains heavy metals from the effluent produced by a firm, equals the cost of treating the polluted river plus the cost of adapting the polluting production process. Problems arise when the benefits of a clean river have to be estimated. Some benefits can be expressed in market prices, such as the lower cost of producing drinking water and the higher revenues from fishing. Many benefits, however, cannot be expressed in market prices, simply because there are no markets for public goods like ecosystems and landscapes. What is, for example, the price of a square mile of wetlands?'

Source: Dietz and van der Straaten (1992a), p.31.

The 'creation of a market', however, is not an easy task. Higher prices might be capable of preventing a shortage of finite resources. If certain finite resources become increasingly scarce, their market prices will gradually rise. And even though many of these markets are imperfect, so that they do not respond immediately to price stimuli, rising prices may act as a warning signal and lead to certain adjustments. In the case of renewable resources, it is difficult to use the market to avert a decline in the quality of the resource. In many cases (e.g. air or water quality), these resources are either unpriced or difficult to price (see Box 3). Consequently, an increasing scarcity of these resources will not necessarily make them any more expensive and hence reduce their consumption (there is more discussion about this topic in Chapter 6).

How much does the environment cost?

At present, the quality of the environment is not a factor which plays a role in the economic decision-making process. As we said above, environmental costs are passed on to society as a whole. For this reason, environmental economists claim that the indicators which are used to define the level of a country's material welfare (such as the national accounts) are not a genuine reflection of the actual standard of living. Indeed, it is even possible that figures which ostensibly suggest economic growth could conceal what is in reality a decline in living standards. This would be the case where one sector of the population suffered substantial damage which was not accounted for as a result of certain environmental impacts produced by another sector of the population.

It may be argued that any loss of function of natural systems should be translated into monetary terms and treated as a loss of income. It is this principle which is behind proposals which have been put forward for instituting 'green national accounts'. Unfortunately, there are enormous difficulties, both economic and technical, in producing such accounts. Another proposal is to introduce changes in the tax system,

4

Market forces and pricing

In a free market, prices are the result of the interplay of supply and demand. Generally speaking, prices are determined by:

○ production costs (i.e. the costs of raw materials, energy, capital investment, labour, etc.)
○ the profit anticipated in the light of demand and the level of competition.

The price of a product does not, however, include the additional costs incurred during production and use and upon disposal, as a result of environmental pollution, damage caused to public health, waste processing, etc. Until now, these costs have been borne neither by the manufacturer nor by the users of the product. They are either passed on to society in general or – as is often the case – passed down to future generations.

An ecotax could therefore be based on the following principles:

○ The polluter should pay the full social and ecological costs of a product.
○ A polluting product should be made more expensive than an environmentally-friendly substitute which is available for it, so that consumers are encouraged to buy the latter instead.

In this way, the production of new, environmentally-friendly products would be stimulated, market opportunities for them would be improved, and sales of polluting products would decline. The revenue earned by the government from the proposed ecotax could be used for lowering the tax and social security contributions payable on human labour. This would have the additional effect of allowing human labour to compete more effectively with machinery, leading in turn to an increase in employment and hence a decrease in the numbers of unemployed.

Source: Van Arkel and Strohalm, (1992) (translated).

imposing levies on energy and resource use, on polluting emissions and on products with a high environmental impact (see Box 4). According to those in favour of such tax reforms, they will not necessarily lead to an increase in the overall tax burden provided that taxes on labour, savings and investment are lowered at the same time. For the time being, however, the proposals for an 'ecotax' remain proposals. The problems are not only technical but also political, for the imposition of an ecotax could have an undesirable effect on the distribution of income in society. And because any tax reforms would also affect the relative competitiveness of industry, they could only be instituted within an international framework. Only if it is clear that they will be applied across the board in all countries is there any likelihood of such measures being accepted.

Economic policy and the environment

The quality of the environment has both a direct and an indirect effect on the standard of living. It is clear from the above that, as a result of the pressure of international competition, these effects have little or no role to play in economic behaviour.

Environmental degradation is not, however, simply a byproduct of economic activity. It is also the consequence of the priorities set by states in their economic policies. These policies are aimed at stimulating production and tend to ignore its environmental consequences. Economic policies may actually have more impact on the quality of the environment than those policies explicitly designed to protect the environment (see Box 5).

These 'perverse interventions in the market' occur both in developing countries (see, for instance, Bojö *et al.*, 1992, p.32) and in industrialised countries. They are sustained by the interests of powerful lobbies, and have disastrous effects, not only ecologically but also economically, given that inefficient use is made of scarce resources. Again, change is only possible if a vital process of economic reorientation takes place within an international context and is subject to international control.

The environment and economic development

The environmental problems in different parts of the world formed the subject matter of Section 1.2, in which we touched briefly upon the relation between environmental problems and the level of economic development. This is in fact one of the most fundamental issues highlighted by an analysis of environmental problems in an international context. It is also an issue with many facets. Our natural environment may be considered as an indivisible ecosystem, as the planet Earth in relation to the atmosphere. The threats to this system are, however, interlinked by processes relating to differences in economic development. The various stages of economic growth achieved in the various regions are of vital importance. In Central and Eastern Europe, for example, environmental problems are interwoven with a low standard of living and a highly inefficient economic process. In the developing countries, on the other hand, whilst these problems are also closely connected with a low standard (but not necessarily quality) of living, they are equally the result of a need to create a basic means of sustenance for large numbers of people. In the West, finally, environmental problems follow largely from a high material standard of living. This unequal distribution of wealth is in itself one of the greatest threats to the Earth as an ecosystem.

Whilst there is on the one hand a need to move away from modern forms of economic development characterised by high levels of energy use and an intensive exploitation of natural resources, the presence on the other hand of widespread poverty forces many communities to aspire to short-term economic growth at any cost. In many cases, there is no other option but to treat the control of environmental degradation as a lower priority. The results of this trend have begun to make themselves felt over the past few years. We have seen, for instance, a tendency for companies to relocate to developing countries, where the environmental requirements which they have to meet are not as strict as in other countries. Some firms which have been set up in developing countries are so 'dirty' that they would not even be tolerated in other regions (see Box 6).

A country at a low level of economic development will find it practically impossible to take the necessary measures to prevent environmental degradation. Not only does it not have the financial means for buying the necessary technology and creating the right infrastructure, but its economic priorities are also different. There are two other factors which exacerbate the problem.

5

Economic policy and environmental degradation

Some examples from the agricultural, forestry, transport and energy sectors

Agriculture
Virtually the entire food cycle in North America, Western Europe, and Japan attracts huge direct or indirect subsidies, at a cost to taxpayers and consumers of over $250 billion a year. These subsidies send farmers far more powerful signals than do the small grants usually provided for soil and water conservation. They encourage farmers to occupy marginal land and to clear forests and woodlands, make excessive use of pesticides and fertilisers, and waste underground and surface waters in irrigation.

Forestry
The pressures on forests throughout the world vary greatly but in both developed and developing countries these pressures are reinforced by government policies. The logging and forestry industries attract a wide variety of direct and indirect subsidies. The Brazilian taxpayer has been underwriting the destruction of the Amazon with millions in tax abatements for uneconomic enterprises. The Indonesians do the same. So do the Canadians. American taxpayers are subsidising the clearing of the Tongass, the great rainforest of Alaska. Perverse incentives that encourage the overharvesting of temperate as well as tropical forests also mark world trade in forest products.

Transport
This sector, especially motor vehicles, also 'benefits' from policies that are ecologically perverse. Fuel taxes in many jurisdictions, for example, still fail to distinguish between the environmental effects of different types of fuel (petrol or diesel, leaded or unleaded). The tax and tariff structure, and direct and indirect subsidies, encourage heavier and more energy-intensive vehicles and road freight as opposed to rail transport in many countries. In some countries, private vehicle expenses can be deducted from taxable income.

Energy
The major obstacle to energy efficiency is the existing framework of incentives for energy exploration, development, and consumption. These incentives underwrite coal, shales, oil, and gas; they ignore the costs of polluting air, land and water; they favour inefficiency and waste. In the United States alone, it is estimated that total energy subsidies, including tax abatements, amount to more than $440 billion annually. The figure for Canada is at least proportional, about $4 billion annually. Germany provides heavy subsidies for coal, as do China, India, and other countries. While industrialised countries have been spending billions to distort the market and consumer prices in ways that actively promote acid rain and global warming, they have been spending only a few million on measures to promote energy efficiency.

Source: MacNeill *et al.* (1991), pp.34–37.

The export of environmental problems

6

Every year, millions of tonnes of hazardous waste are traded on the world market. A large proportion of this is exported from industrialised countries to developing countries. Environmental legislation in many parts of the West is so strict that the processing of waste has become an extremely costly business. For the developing countries, on the other hand, the import of hazardous waste represents a source of income. These countries do not, however, possess the technology which is needed in order to process the waste in a safe manner involving minimal pollution.

A number of international agreements have now been made which are aimed at limiting this type of 'environmental exploitation'. What is still needed, however, is a good monitoring system for keeping check on waste flows, as well as a system of sanctions which would allow penalties to be imposed on those found to be acting in breach of the rules. In the absence of such systems, there is currently a flourishing black market which is estimated to be worth many hundreds of millions of dollars a year.

The first is the consequence of the worsening financial situation in which the developing countries now find themselves. Third World debt is currently estimated at over $1000 billion. Many countries spend all of their export revenues (and more besides) on paying off the interest on loans; interest payments are now in excess of $70 billion per annum. A watershed was reached in 1982 when for the first time, there was a net transfer of capital from the developing countries to the industrialised nations. According to current estimates, the net amount of capital which the poor countries transfer every year to the rich countries is over $50 billion.

The second factor is closely associated with the economic emphasis placed on policy aimed at improving the financial position of developing countries. The institutions responsible for this policy, such as the International Monetary Fund, place great emphasis on the need for increasing exports, attracting industrial investment and restricting government expenditure. This leads to an additional exploitation of natural resources, whilst at the same time no financial resources are available for conducting a programme of environmental protection.

Viewed from a global economic standpoint, environmental problems are primarily a matter of inequality. If we bear in mind the rate of economic growth which the poorest countries are presently experiencing, and the rate of growth which they hope to experience in the future, the combined effect could easily be to cancel out any positive impact which might be achieved by the environmental policies pursued in the rich countries. This places a dual international responsibility on the shoulders of the rich countries, who will need to be the key instigators of action in order to protect the global environment. The Western nations will need not only to assist the developing countries to realise their equitable aim of achieving economic growth, but also to give them the financial and institutional help which they require in order to carry out essential environmental protection policies. By linking economic development with environmental protection (and this is exactly what the developing countries themselves have

Plate 1.2 Economic interdependence: international economic relations affecting local economies, Harare, Zimbabwe. Photo: Ron Giling/Lineair

been urging in various international fora), the West can lay the foundations for a new, just and equitable international order. International trade forms an important aspect of this process (see Box 7).

1.4 The role of technology as a 'double agent'

An understanding of the ecological and economic interdependencies, as well as of the relationship between these two factors, may help give us a clearer insight into the contemporary environmental problems. It may also show us the way towards finding an answer to the questions which we asked at the beginning of the chapter. In anticipation of the discussion which follows below, we are now able to give a broad outline of the possible answer. Environmental problems are international problems in the first instance because they have an impact on a very large geographical scale, and in the second place because they are caused and sustained by economic relationships which also affect very large areas of the world. The global context in which current environmental problems – and their causes – should be seen makes them all the more difficult to keep under control. Unfortunately, this awareness does not bring us any closer to finding a solution to these problems. An understanding of a third area of knowledge is needed in order to do this: technology.

International trade and environmental problems

A key area of debate is the role which international trade should play in realising a more equitable and ecologically sound international order. International trade and the desire felt by developing countries to achieve economic growth are frequently incompatible with the needs of environmental protection. Current trading patterns and world market prices take no account of any excessive consumption of natural resources, and particularly of non-renewable ones, or of other external environmental factors. Nor do they attempt in any way to do so. Some 90% of world trade is regulated by the GATT (General Agreement on Tariffs and Trade), the underlying philosophy of which is that free trade is conducive to economic growth, and that, in order to achieve free trade, it is necessary to remove import and export restrictions, and other trade barriers. Viewed from the GATT angle, any restrictions placed on international trade for reasons of environmental protection are damaging to economic growth. GATT in fact prevents countries from imposing environmental safety requirements on imports, with the result that, where countries decide to impose them on their own exports, they undermine the competitiveness of their own industry. In other words, the interests of free trade are at the present time in conflict with those of countries who wish to ensure that environmental costs are included in the prices of their products.

At the same time, free world trade can stimulate economic growth in the developing countries. Thanks to the low price of labour there, they can often compete with the West once any Western trade barriers have been removed. This conflict of interests between the environment and development can be resolved only if all countries decide to charge polluters for the cost of adverse environmental effects.

In short, international trade is not a problem in itself. It can often stimulate greater productivity and consequent saving in the use of resources and improved technology which prevents waste and pollution. This positive effect on the environment can be enhanced with the aid of an enforceable system of internationally accepted environmental quality targets. At the same time, liberal trade policies should encourage efficient production through countries specialising in those activities in which they have a comparative cost advantage. Looked at this way, international trade may be seen as a means of helping developing countries not only to achieve economic growth, but also to realise environmental aims.

The role of technology in relation to environmental problems may be described as that of a double agent. On the one hand, it is technology which has enabled more natural resources to be exploited more intensively. In fact, technological developments are themselves one of the causes of environmental problems. On the other hand, new technology can help to solve these problems, for example by helping to create alternative sources for future energy supplies.

Technological solutions are regarded by some with great suspicion, and by others with great optimism. The former attitude is often adopted by environmental activists, who are afraid that society will pin its hopes on technological progress and close its eyes to the fundamental social changes which they consider to be necessary. In their

Plate 1.3 New technology: solar cooker in a school in Gujarat, India. A big pot behind a window collects the sun's focused rays. Photo: Sean Sprague/Lineair

view, a new economic order is needed in order to solve the problems. The optimistic attitude, on the other hand, tends to be the preserve of those who are interested in maintaining the status quo and therefore wish to block the adoption of any meaningful environmental policy. Both attitudes are, however, one-sided. Whilst it is true that technology can in principle offer certain solutions, these solutions cannot achieve success without social sacrifices being made.

Studies have shown that the potential for improvement is actually much greater than some environmental activists may suspect. Experiments conducted in The Netherlands, for example, have demonstrated that, if the technology already available was implemented on a large scale, it would be possible to achieve the national environmental targets (which are among the most demanding in the world) and at the same time still enable economic growth of 2–3% per annum to be realised. If all the available technology was now put to use in The Netherlands, the country could achieve the same level of output and yet reduce energy consumption and waste production by 50–60%. It would also be possible to bring about a sharp decrease in the deposition of acid substances (Maas, 1993).

The same situation holds for other countries, too. Turkenburg, for instance, has confirmed that it is technically possible to combine economic growth and population growth with the necessary reductions in CO_2 emission levels. He believes, however, that it will be difficult to bring this about in practice. On a global scale, there is a potential for achieving a 50% saving in energy consumption by around the year 2010. In the long term, the reduction could actually be as much as 80%. In addition, we have

8

Three factors play a role in the depletion of stocks of finite natural resources

Resource-saving technological progress
Technological progress has generated large savings in the consumption of natural resources. This applies both to mineral fuels and to other resources. To give three examples: the amount of energy which the OECD countries require in order to produce one unit of GNP is much lower than 100 years ago: the amount of glass used to make one milk bottle has been virtually halved in the course of 50 years; and the amount of aluminium used in the production of a can of beer has been reduced by over 80% over a 40-year period. In other words, the consumption of natural resources does not necessarily mean less production capacity for future generations. The same standard of living can be achieved on an ever-declining base of natural resources.

The presence of suitable substitutes
An increasing scarcity of certain natural resources can also be counteracted by switching to other, less scarce resources or to new materials. Such substitution processes have already taken place, and are still taking place. More and more metals, for example, are being replaced by silicon-based materials, supplies of which are abundant. In a more general sense, we are witnessing a tendency to restrict the use of scarce resources to relatively high-tech applications. As far as mineral fuels are concerned, the scope for using substitutes is (for the time being at least) far more limited.

Reuse of natural resources
Some natural resources, metals in particular, should not strictly speaking be regarded as being finite at all. In theory, metals can be fully reused without any time limit. Already, between 30% and 40% of all aluminium used in the OECD countries is recycled. At the same time, it has also become clear that the marginal cost of recycling is going to increase in the future. This does not alter the fact that an increase in recycling will be accompanied by a decrease in waste production.

Source: SER (1991), pp. 14–15 (translated).

the technology that is needed in order to produce more clean energy from sources such as the biomass. We even have the technological capability in the long term of getting all the energy we need from the sun, either directly or indirectly. These are, however, options which have not yet progressed beyond the planning stage, and which require a special institutional infrastructure, the presence of dedicated research centres and the funding of targeted research projects (Turkenburg, 1993).

It has also been demonstrated that technology can offer a solution in particular to the problem of the depletion of finite resources. We have already discussed in Section 1.3 the positive effects which market forces can have. This point is further elaborated in Box 8.

This discussion makes clear that there is no reason for rejecting out of hand all optimism about the potential benefits of technology. At the same time, we should remember that technology cannot solve every environmental problem (a case in point being the decline in biodiversity as a result of deforestation). Moreover, technology is not enough in itself. Like many other things, technological innovations need to be organised. Any innovation leads to all sorts of changes in the social setting in which it is framed. In other words, the problems will not be solved simply by relying on the innate resourcefulness of the human race. The right social conditions must be in place for stimulating the use of new technologies. One of the prerequisites is a framework for transferring technology to those countries which do not have sufficient financial means for gaining access to it without assistance. Here too, international co-operation is essential.

1.5 Political interdependencies

Whether solutions can be found to environmental problems depends primarily on whether people are both willing and able to change their behaviour. A key problem is how to organise the process of change. In the international context account must be taken of the role of sovereign states, their interrelationships, the international frameworks in which they are active, as well as their relations with organised interest groups (such as international companies and environmentalist groups). If today's environmental problems are to be tackled in an effective manner, a wide range of players will need to be brought into action. In essence, the issue is a political one. In order to gain a grip on these problems, the political decision-making process must be used as the channel through which the ongoing development of the socio-economic system must be controlled, so that it does not outstrip the capacity of the ecological system to support it.

The international nature of contemporary environmental problems means that international political action is needed in order to solve them. However, the international political system consists of a large number of countries, each of which claims its own sovereignty, and all of which are embedded in political and economic structures which are based primarily on a desire for (economic) growth, peace and security, and not (or to a much lesser extent) on any wish to solve environmental problems. The fundamental problem in this connection is that the environment, as a complex system whose many facets are closely bound up with each other, has to be controlled by a highly fragmented political system. Two important issues need to be considered in this respect:

○ Which countries/sectors/players are going to be required to play a pioneering role in finding a joint solution to environmental problems, and which countries/sectors/players are going to benefit more than others? This may be referred to as the 'distribution issue'.
○ What type of development, both political and economic as well as social and cultural, will provide the best basis for a successful, long-term coexistence between human society and its environment? This is referred to as the 'development issue'.

The resolution of the distribution and development issues is contingent on processes of change within the international political system. For this reason, a third category of interdependencies (in addition to the ecological and economic) which we shall discuss is that of the 'political interdependencies'.

Environmental problems on the international political agenda

In the early 1970s, the environment for the first time achieved a prominent place on the international political agenda. There were, however, two important drawbacks: firstly, the key contemporary issues of peace, security and development were also fighting for a place on the same agenda, and secondly, there was no institutional framework within which environmental problems could be discussed effectively in an international context. Nevertheless, three crucial events resulted in the environmental issue ultimately taking its definitive place on the international political agenda. They were:

○ the United Nations Conference on Human Development, which was held in Stockholm in 1972
○ the publication of *Our Common Future* (generally known as the Brundtland Report) by the World Commission on Environment and Development in 1987
○ the United Nations Conference on Environment and Development, Rio de Janeiro, 1992.

The Stockholm Conference

A first important step was taken with the first world environment conference, the United Nations Conference on Human Development, which was held in Stockholm in 1972. The Stockholm Conference became a key symbol for political acknowledgement of the growing worldwide awareness of the environment. Delegates from 113 countries, in both the northern and southern hemispheres, attended the Conference. The Conference resulted in the publication of the Stockholm Declaration, which enumerated 26 joint principles relating to human rights and responsibilities for the global environment, as well as a Plan of Action consisting of 109 recommendations. The Conference did not, however, lead to the formulation of a common strategy for solving environmental problems. This was largely due to the fact that most of the environmental issues addressed by the Conference affected only the Western world, and very little time was allocated to discussing the problems affecting the South. The developing countries were disappointed, and disassociated themselves from what they regarded as the 'Stockholm problems'. They felt that environmental pollution was a problem which only the rich Western countries could afford to have, which they had caused, and which they therefore should solve. These feelings were reinforced by the West's desire to point to economic growth as the source of environmental problems, and hence to adapt growth across the world. The countries of the South, on the other hand, considered growth to be vital if they were to eliminate poverty, and hence environmental problems. The Eastern bloc, finally, was taken up fully with its ideological conflict with the West, and had no time for environmental problems. Any such problems which were regarded as being caused by command economies were dismissed as being incidents of a temporary nature. The time was clearly not yet ripe for adopting an international approach to environmental problems.

International strategies for dealing with environmental problems were devised only sporadically and were generally restricted to a small number of countries (i.e. to combat the effects of acid rain, river pollution, etc.). Even the setting up of the United Nations Environment Programme (UNEP) in 1972 in the wake of the Stockholm

Conference failed initially to give an impetus to international co-operation to combat environmental problems. This was chiefly because the UNEP did not have enough resources to take the appropriate initiatives. Moreover, the United Nations impact on international relations between countries and regions in any event was only marginal in the 1960s and 1970s.

Our Common Future

In the absence of any adequate measures taken on an international political scale, the environmental problems simply grew even further. It was not until the mid-1980s that the politicians 'discovered' the scientific evidence for the international nature of the environmental problems, and the issue was placed at the forefront of international political debate (see Box 9).

The establishment of the World Commission on Environment and Development (WCED) during the United Nations assembly in Nairobi in 1982 was a further important step towards international political awareness of environmental problems. In 1987, the WCED published a report entitled *Our Common Future* (generally known as the Brundtland Report), the most frequently quoted part of which is undoubtedly the passage describing the concept of 'sustainable development': 'Sustainable development is development that meets the needs of the present without compromising the ability of future generations to meet their own needs ... . In essence, sustainable development is a process of change in which the exploitation of resources, the directions of investments, the orientation of technological development, and institutional change are all in harmony and enhance both current and future potential to meet human needs and aspirations' (WCED, 1987, p.43 and p.46). The report had a great impact and was well received all over the world (see Box 10).

The WCED concluded that world issues such as the environment, development and peace are all closely connected, and that there has been a growing realisation among national governments and other institutions that it is impossible to separate economic development issues from environmental issues. This relationship was explained in Section 1.3, in which we saw on the one hand that many forms of development erode

9

Nothing new about international environmental problems

'The greenhouse effect and the possibility of climatic change taking place have been known since the beginning of this century. The depletion of the ozone layer became obvious in 1974. The acidification of forests and lakes in Scandinavia and Canada has been a cause for concern since the Second World War. The destruction of tropical rainforests was already raised as a nature conservation issue in the 1940s.'

Source: CLTM (1990), p.5 (translated).

10

Reasons for Brundtland's worldwide popularity

○ It was targeted at the long term, and dealt with both environmental and developmental problems (introducing the concept of sustainable development for the latter).

○ It emanated from the United Nations, and was therefore regarded as being authoritative and impartial. This was demonstrated at the United Nations conference in Rio de Janeiro in 1992, where the question of how to achieve sustainable development was one of the topics of discussion.

○ It was based on the premise of economic growth, which meant it was acceptable to the developing countries.

○ It was published at a time when environmental problems which affect the whole world (e.g. ozone layer depletion, the greenhouse effect) were becoming plain for all to see. The environment was no longer a regional issue.

○ It was published at a time when the rich countries were starting to take an interest in the environmental problems in the poor countries (e.g. the destruction of the tropical rainforests and the international trade in hazardous waste).

Source: CLTM (1990), p.7.

the environmental resources upon which they must be based, and on the other hand that environmental degradation can undermine economic development. It is therefore futile to attempt to deal with environmental problems without widening the perspective to encompass the economic system. In addition, the whole notion of security, in terms of political and military threats to national sovereignty, has to be expanded to include the growing impact of environmental problems.

The years at the end of the 1980s and the beginning of the 1990s seemed to herald a new era in international politics. The collapse of the socialist system in the East created a need for new relations between the East and West. The security issue was transformed from a global political problem (centring on East versus West) into a question of regional conflict management (as in the Middle East, Somalia, the former Yugoslavia, etc.). The problems relating to the environment and economic growth, on the other hand, appear to have become, to a much greater extent, matters of daily concern. The failure of the socialist system has thrown the environmental problems in the East into true relief. The desire to transform the economies of the former socialist countries into more capitalist-orientated systems has added a new dimension to the world's environmental problems. Whether a decision is taken to develop a more market-based system of production and consumption or to leave things more or less as they are, in both cases there is a risk of damage being caused to the environment. The Eastern countries are now seeking the help of the West in getting through this transitional period, and this in turn requires a fundamental change in the Western attitude to international relations. It is also becoming increasingly clear that the South (and particularly countries such as China, India, Brazil, Mexico and Taiwan) will play a more and more important role as an origin of global environmental problems.

Population growth, economic growth and technological progress are key factors in this respect. The first step has now been taken on the road to an international political debate on a new world order in which environmental issues will play a much more pivotal role than before and which will accommodate the institutional framework needed for this.

The Rio de Janeiro Conference

The concern about the environment, poverty and social and economic inequality led to the calling of the United Nations Conference on Environment and Development (UNCED) in Rio de Janeiro in 1992, the third of the key events referred to above. More than 150 countries took part in the Conference, the chief benefits of which were agreement that 'peace, development and environmental protection are interdependent and cannot be seen in isolation of each other' (Principle 25 of the Rio Declaration) and a growing awareness that the North and South depend on each other to ensure that the planet continues to be a life-sustaining ecosphere. The Conference resulted in the promulgation of the Rio Declaration, in which 27 principles are listed for the sustainable development of the world community. Although the Declaration is not legally binding, most countries have stated their willingness to use it as an important guideline for their own national policies.

A further outcome of the Conference was the signing of Agenda 21, a plan of action for the 21st century incorporating more than 100 different programmes in the field of sustainable development. Despite the fact that agreement was reached on a wide range of issues, however, the funding of Agenda 21 (representing a figure of around $675 billion per annum) remains clouded in uncertainty. An important achievement of the UNCED was the signing of a Climate Treaty, a Biodiversity Treaty and a Forests Declaration (see Box 11).

Limitations of the international political system

The fact that certain agreements were reached at the UNCED does not necessarily mean that all the countries in the world decided to give absolute priority to solving environmental and developmental problems. Although the principle of sustainable development was formally adopted during UNCED and the Conference accentuated the interrelationship between the environment and development, the countries of the North seemed nevertheless to regard environmental protection as forming the chief problem, whereas the southern countries regarded underdevelopment and poverty as the key issues. The issues preoccupying the North were climatic change and the depletion of the ozone layer. The South, on the other hand, were exercised by poverty, food supplies and desertification. In addition, the North wanted the South to tackle the problem of population growth and to halt the decline in the quality of the 'global commons' (such as the tropical rainforests). The South for its part claimed that the North was largely responsible for the world's environmental problems (e.g. climatic change and the depletion of the ozone layer), and insisted that the North should supply it with the resources and technology which were needed in order to eradicate environmental problems caused by underdevelopment. The South was making these demands

UNCED: Climate Treaty, Biodiversity Treaty, Forests Declaration

11

Climate Treaty

The Climate Treaty, the signatories to which committed themselves to limiting the increase in the emission of greenhouse gases, was signed by 154 countries.

A number of Arab countries decided not to sign the Treaty in the light of their oil interests. Malaysia refused to sign because the Treaty, in accordance with the explicit wishes of the USA, did not impose any firm obligations on the rich countries. The Climate Treaty is indeed less far-reaching than had originally been hoped. A number of countries, including The Netherlands, have agreed to go beyond a straightforward implementation of the Treaty based on a literal interpretation of the text. The Climate Treaty is binding.

Biodiversity Treaty

The Biodiversity Treaty was signed by some 150 countries. The Treaty is aimed at the protection of flora and fauna, and contains agreements on the accessibility of genetic material and the costs associated with gaining access. To the dissatisfaction of the developing countries, the USA refused to sign the Treaty, which is binding on signatories.

Forests Declaration

Major disagreements arose between the developing countries and the industrialised countries over the management of the forests in the various parts of the world. The question of national sovereignty played an important role in this connection. The developing countries were unwilling to enter into commitments which could be construed as permitting violations of their sovereignty, which many of them had in fact only recently acquired. The industrialised countries for their part did not show any generosity in offering help in the form of forestry expertise to countries with rainforests in their territories. As a consequence, hardly any commitments were undertaken in relation to this field. The Conference did not progress beyond a non-binding Forests Declaration; a Forests Treaty proved to be an unattainable target.

Source: 'Relatie Noord-Zuid nieuw leven ingeblazen' (A new life for the North-South relationship). In: *Internationale Samenwerking*, September 1992, pp.42–43. Publication of the Dutch Ministry of Foreign Affairs (translated).

at a time when global environmental problems had created a situation in which, for the first time in history, the North found itself dependent on the South.

The question remains whether the current international political system is capable of dealing adequately with today's environmental problems. There are a number of grounds for doubts.

Firstly, the international political system consists of many countries all of which claim their own territorial sovereignty. Generally speaking, countries are very wary of surrendering any of their sovereignty. Joint initiatives are normally started on a voluntary basis, and in just about every instance the participating countries have let their own interests take precedence. As long as there is no authority which has the power where necessary to order countries to join such initiatives, it will remain difficult to promote any joint action at an international level. Joint action can, however, be encouraged if those countries which bear most of the responsibility for the origins of environmental problems take the initiative in drawing up plans for concrete action. For example, if the USA, as the world's largest producer of CO_2, is not willing to take the first step in reducing emission levels of greenhouse gases, no other countries will take any action because whatever they do will not ultimately solve the problem.

Secondly, although all sorts of collaborative ventures have come into being at an international level, few, if any, of the political and economic structures now in place are based on the concept of sustainable development. The existing institutions, such as the European Union, the World Bank, the International Monetary Fund (IMF) and the General Agreement on Tariffs and Trade (GATT), however, have taken environmental problems on board, even though they were not originally designed to deal with such issues. But integrating environmental policy into their other policies is a far from easy matter. The number of organisations which have been set up specifically to deal with certain environmental problems is small. The International Whaling Commission is an example of such an organisation.

Thirdly, international institutions do not generally have much power in relation to sovereign states. The European Union is an exception to this rule. However, in order

Plate 1.4 Political interdependence: United Nations headquarters in New York. The United Nations is the only international political organisation with almost universal membership of nation states. Photo: Ron Giling/Lineair

to prevent the EU as a supranational body from acquiring too much power, the member states have adopted the principle of subsidiarity. This principle has a bearing on environmental problems because the member states are able to use it (in addition to the principle of sovereignty) in order to prevent the EU from interfering in their 'domestic' affairs. The subsidiarity principle means that decisions are taken as closely as possible to the citizen. Under the terms of the EU's fifth Environmental Action Programme, 'the Community will take action, in accordance with the principle of subsidiarity, only if and insofar as the objectives of the proposed action cannot be sufficiently achieved by the Member States and can therefore, by reason of the scale or effects of the proposed action, be better achieved by the Community' (Commission of the European Community, 1992, p.73).

Whilst the member states of the EU have surrendered some of their sovereignty on the one hand, the principle of subsidiarity is intended on the other hand to prevent a situation from arising in which all matters are regulated at a supranational level. The decision as to when and where the principle can be applied will depend largely on the political will of the individual member states. In order to ensure that adequate action is taken to counteract environmental problems, the EU has also introduced a further concept: that of 'shared responsibility'. Shared responsibility requires a much more broadly based and active involvement of all economic players (such as public authorities, public corporations, the private sector and the general public). The objective in the involvement of and interplay between these economic players is to strike a new balance between the short-term benefits to individuals, companies and governments, and the long-term benefits to society as a whole.

Fourthly, the structure of government in virtually every country is not designed for dealing with environmental issues. The environment and the economy are still regarded as two separate domains. As a result, it has been more or less impossible to integrate environmental targets into all other policy fields. In addition, politicians are used to thinking on a short time-scale (there is little credit to be gained from long-term goals given that there will always be an election coming up in the short or medium term) and do not like to take decisions in an atmosphere of uncertainty. Both these aspects are frequently involved in decisions affecting environmental issues. A further complication lies in the fact that international policy planning is regarded as falling under the competence of the Foreign Ministry. This policy evolved against a background of trade and security, and is defined in terms of 'getting the best possible result for the country'.

Finally, it should be pointed out that a lot of decisions which have an impact on the environment are taken outside the jurisdiction of governments. Multinationals and financial institutions play an important role in this, with non-governmental organisations (NGOs) often performing a corrective role. If all the relevant parties are to be involved in the decision-making process, a political system will need to be created that is relatively accessible at both national and international level.

Clearly, radical changes will have to be made before national and international politicians can start to act in terms of sustainable development. The most vital processes of change will be needed in the area of the strategic competence of the state apparatus, i.e. the capability of the apparatus of government to set comprehensive long-term policy targets, to co-ordinate the implementation of policy, and to see it through to the achievement of the targets set. These are prerequisites for sustainable development. The implication is that national governments will have to surrender part of their sovereignty to international institutions (many of which do not yet exist), and that NGOs and multinational firms should become much more closely involved in decision making. Governments and international bodies must be prepared to allow the other parties to play a role in the process; this will be a test case for the quality of democracy all over the world. In addition, international networks will need to be created which cross the present demarcation lines between today's institutionalised structures. The first cases of such international co-operation have involved NGOs which have formed international alliances, in some cases even with native tribes. Governments will have to join forces with all other parties in order to turn the concept of sustainable development into concrete action.

1.6 Conclusion

Changes in the physical environment have created a new political challenge: the question of how to deal with the maintenance of the world's basic stock of natural capital. This chapter has shown that this problem is closely linked to the more general social issues of economic interrelations and economic development. It is also clear that a great deal depends on the attitude taken by the developed countries. It is these countries which must take the initiative in tackling global environmental threats. And it is these countries which will have to assist the poorest countries in solving their environmental problems, which have both local and international effects. And in doing so, the developed countries will need to foster the development of the developing countries, for environmental problems are also a matter of international inequality. The problems must be tackled within the context of a world system that is characterised by great cultural, political and economic heterogeneity.

No one would claim that there is a simple solution to environmental problems. This might perhaps be the case if there was outright opposition to solving them. There is, however, no point in trying to name possible culprits: the problems are much too complex for this, and indeed much too firmly rooted in international economic and political relations. The question is more one of how to start a process of change which can bring a solution closer to hand (Glasbergen, 1995). The internationalisation of environmental problems in an ecological, economic and political sense has created a need for a fundamental change in the social structures in both the North and the South. 'Sustainable development' is the concept which underlies the nature of the change. The concept has already brought about an important change of thinking, in that a large number of countries are now united on its significance, i.e. the linking of the environment and development as the basis for a new, just and equitable international order.

Yet this political acknowledgement of the importance of sustainable development is not in itself enough. Sustainable development implies processes of change not only in human behaviour vis-à-vis the environment, but also in the way in which people behave towards other people. International cultural diversity may not only provide opportunities for people to learn from each other, but may also place the whole process in jeopardy where 'different' is taken to mean 'underdeveloped', 'inferior' or 'undesirable'. The recent international recognition of environmental problems is, however, a sign of change. Countries have taken the first cautious steps towards sustainable development. The next question is whether fine words are going to be translated into (more) action.

The following chapters discuss in further detail the problems we have just outlined. As a methodology for the book we took the position that the natural environment and the social environment should be studied as interrelated entities.

The problems addressed are not of the simplest. Furthermore, international environmental problems constitute a relatively new area of research, and an area which, by its very nature, is a highly complex one. Both the natural and social sciences contribute to our understanding of the environment. Comprehensive and more or less complete theories are not yet available. Environmental studies as it has developed is applied science and is problem-driven. Many disciplines have only recently developed partial approaches to environmental problems but even within one and the same discipline there are often various theoretical approaches. In social sciences, environmental problems even constitute a relatively new challenge, the challenge to develop an understanding of the 'material' aspects of society and how they relate to social processes and relations. These are aspects that the founding fathers simply excluded from their theories. In addition to this, attempts are being made to bridge the gap between the partially developed theories from the natural sciences and those from the social sciences.

The state of the art can best be typified as one of perspectives. These starting points for developing theories are used to analyse and to understand the relation between society and nature. Each of these perspectives represents a different method of conducting a critical analysis of environmental issues in an international context. The present variety of theoretical perspectives will be used in this book for a first conceptual and theoretical analysis, which is illustrated with a wide range of concrete environmental problems.

We start with a natural science view of environmental problems, after which some chapters look at the issues from the perspectives of a sociologist, a political scientist, a legal expert, and an economist. The final chapter brings some lines together, focusing on the concept of sustainable development again. This concept is most frequently used for the integration of theoretical approaches on the way towards a more multidisciplinary or interdisciplinary environmental science.

2

Science on environmental problems

Peter B. Sloep and Maria C. E. van Dam-Mieras

2.1 Introduction

In the previous chapter environmental problems were discussed in terms of their interconnection with other problems that our modern world faces. Here we look at environmental problems from the vantage point of the natural sciences. In particular, we shall attempt to assess how the natural sciences may further our understanding and control of environmental problems.

Two rather extreme stances are sometimes taken on this matter: that science is totally irrelevant or that it is sufficient on its own. The science sceptic claims that, ultimately, political compromise is all there is to environmental problem solving (see Glasbergen, 1993, who briefly discusses this position), whereas the science diehard believes that science is all you need. We believe the sceptic's position to be wrong, even though politicians may sometimes seem to act according to it. To us, science has genuinely useful insights to offer that can only be ignored at everyone's peril. But we do not side with the science diehards either. That position is an almost arrogant overestimation of the capability of science.

Both positions err in that they entertain much too simple a notion of our environmental predicament. First and foremost, environmental problems are social constructions. Notwithstanding this, any environmental problem also has an objective side, something which cannot be altered at will, through social consensus or otherwise. This leads us to believe that scientific knowledge is necessary but not sufficient to solve environmental problems. This is the perspective that the present chapter has to offer.

The chapter is divided into five major parts. The next section (2.2) provides relevant background knowledge as it attempts to outline a scientific, that is, ecology-based, view of our world. It does so by regarding the biosphere – the collective ecosystem of our world – as a machine. In particular, the importance of energy transport and of material cycles needed to keep the machine running will be discussed. An environmental problem, one might say, is anything that obstructs the machine's proper functioning. In our view, however, this machine metaphor is naive, perhaps even to the point of being misleading. Why this is so and what would be a better definition of an environmental problem is the subject of the next section (2.3).

Having discussed in a general way the nature of the environment and of environmental problems, section 2.4 discusses actual environmental problems. A concise overview is given of the historical changes in our society that led to our present-day problems. Emphasis will be put on the impacts of the Industrial and Green Revolutions in the developed countries of the North as these might fulfil an exemplary role. The next section (2.5) is devoted to the problem of solving and preventing environmental problems. It discusses a scheme for bringing scientific knowledge to bear upon environmental problem solving. This results in a multidisciplinary view of environmental problem solving and hence environmental decision making. The final section (2.6) draws our main conclusions.

2.2 The environment in the eyes of a natural scientist

It almost amounts to a truism to say that the environment is of vital importance to living organisms. And indeed, organisms of all species, including *Homo sapiens*, live in continuous interaction with their environment. They import from it the energy and raw materials needed for growth, development and reproduction. Because of the intimacy of the interaction with the environment, the environment also constitutes a threat to organisms. This is true for the non-living parts of the environment (the so-called abiotic factors) such as extreme humidities or temperatures, fluctuations of humidity or temperature, acidity, lack of oxygen, etc. It also holds for the living part (the biotic factors), i.e. other organisms, which may act as infectants, parasites, predators or competitors. After all, these organisms use their environment for their own survival, thus affecting the survival of others. Organisms, of course, have evolved strategies to ward off these threats, and maintain themselves in the 'struggle for life'. Most of the time these strategies work well, but there are limits to their efficacy. Certain changes in the environment, whether biotic or abiotic, pose insurmountable problems to organisms. Changes may be so novel, emerge so suddenly or fluctuate so wildly that they exceed the (genetically determined) physiological limits of adaptation of organisms, ultimately leading to their demise. Furthermore, if the changes occur sufficiently rapidly, the process of coping through evolution, that is, through changes in the genetic make-up of organisms, is simply too slow. In such cases entire species may end up becoming extinct.

Natural disasters are good examples of such drastic environmental changes. Extensive floods or fires and volcanic eruptions are eventualities that hardly any organism can prepare itself for. But such accidents, one might say, are among the natural risks of life. Recently, however, a new class of threats has emerged, for which organisms cannot prepare themselves either. We are referring here to *environmental problems*.

Before discussing environmental problems, however, we need to know a little more about the exact ways in which organisms cope with their 'normal' environment. As environmental problems are our ultimate interest, we can afford to limit our discussion to those modes of interaction that are particularly relevant to our topic proper.

Ecosystems and food webs

Tracing all the nutritional relationships in some ecosystem (see Box 1) would effectively amount to outlining a *food web*. Food webs are not haphazardly put together by nature, but display an intricate organisation. Although no ecosystem is identical in its details to another, some general rules exist that apply to most of them. Barring some exotic ecosystems (such as those near thermal vents deep in the ocean or those in secluded caves) all food webs have plants as their most important primary producers. Through a process called *photosynthesis*, plants capture solar energy and store it as chemical energy. Plants are eaten by animals and other organisms, collectively called herbivores. Being eaten means that not only matter is transferred 'one level up' but also the energy stored in the food. The herbivores, in turn, are eaten by animals of a higher level called predators, who in their turn may be eaten by yet other predators. The predators again transfer matter and energy. It thus appears to be the 'function' of food

Food webs

Organisms do not occur in nature in haphazard collections; they are to some extent organised. Although dichotomising easily leads to oversimplification, we will assume for the sake of our argument that there are two fundamentally different, though complementary ways of looking at these organised collections of organisms.

The first approach, called *ecosystem* ecology, focuses on functional groups of organisms (herbivores, predators, prey, etc.). Organisms within such groups belong to different species but are grouped together because they perform the same functional role in the ecosystem. (The concept of an ecosystem is hard to define as it is always used in a rather loose way; roughly, an ecosytem encompasses the organisms that live in an area and the abiotic, physical aspects of that area affecting the organisms.)

The ecosystem approach investigates the transfer of energy and matter between the functional groups within the ecosystem. The second approach, called *community* ecology, focuses on populations of organisms. A population is a group of organisms that inhabit a particular area and belong to a particular species. The community approach mainly investigates competitive relations between and within populations.

The present chapter takes the ecosystem approach because it focuses on energy relations and nutrient cycles. Had the focus of interest been nature conservation and biodiversity issues, the community would have been chosen as this lends itself better to a discussion of these issues. In the ecosystem approach, food webs play a crucial role. One of the earliest examples of a quantitative analysis of food webs was that by the late American ecologist Raymond Lindeman. Figure 2.1 derives from his classic paper on the subject and aptly illustrates the concept of a food web (Lindeman, 1942).

webs in an ecosystem to transfer energy and matter, and the various organisms in the ecosystem play their different roles in sustaining this transfer. We shall now look a little closer at the process of transfer.

The transfer of energy and matter

Apart from a few exceptional cases, the sole energy source for plants is solar radiation (see Figure 2.1; the exceptions include parasitic or saprophytic plants, plants that live at the expense of other living or dead plants). Plants store this energy in carbon compounds. The carbon needed for this is derived from carbon dioxide, which is abundantly available in the atmosphere. During photosynthesis, solar energy is converted to chemical energy and stored in the bonding energy (roughly the energy needed to keep the molecule together) of molecules of sugar, a carbon compound. For similar reasons, petrol is also an energy source. These sugar molecules can be regarded as the plant's reservoir of both raw materials and energy. The sugar molecules are

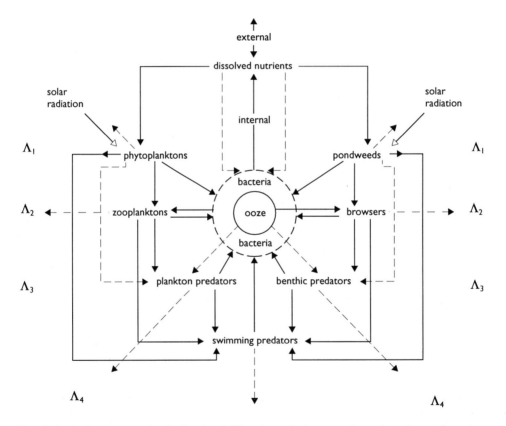

Fig. 2.1 A classic example of a food web. The phytoplanktons and pondweeds are the primary producers, the zooplanktons and browsers, the herbivores and the organisms called plankton, benthic, and swimming predators the predators. The role of the bacteria is somewhat complicated and therefore left out of consideration. Source: after Lindeman (1942).

transported to all of the plant's cells and converted to other compounds by the various reactions in the plant's metabolism. These compounds make up the various components of plant cells, which consist mainly of the elements carbon, hydrogen, oxygen, nitrogen, phosphorus and sulphur. In addition to these, there are small amounts of other elements. The role of these so-called trace elements is to catalyse ('speed up') cellular metabolism; they are taken up from the soil by the roots of the plant. Nitrogen, phosphorus and sulphur-containing compounds are also absorbed from the soil.

In short, plants absorb a variety of nutrients from their environment and trap the energy of sunlight in the form of chemical energy. They need both nutrients and energy for their growth, maintenance and reproduction.

Because plants are eaten, they serve as a source of energy and nutrients for other organisms, particularly the herbivores. Plants are a source of nutrients (food) because all organisms, in spite of their tremendous diversity, are largely composed of the same four main groups of molecules (carbohydrates, lipids, proteins and nucleic acids). Hence, herbivores are not confronted with completely foreign substances. Also, the major metabolic pathways in organisms, i.e. the chains of chemical reactions which various compounds in the cells of organisms undergo, are remarkably similar. Therefore, to the extent that chemical conversions are required, they are well within the capacities of the herbivores. Indeed, with the exception of plants, which need the sun as their energy source, all organisms can potentially use each other as sources of energy and raw materials. It is because of these similarities in substances and in reaction chains that herbivores can live off plants, and predators can make a living out of preying on herbivores and other predators.

Both herbivores and predators absorb their food in basically the same way. During its passage through their alimentary tract (stomach(s), intestines), the nutritional source is degraded into smaller molecules, which are taken up by cells of the alimentary tract. In turn, these molecules may be further transported via the blood and imported into the cells of other organs of the body. Within these cells, the molecules are degraded further until they are fit for the biosynthesis of cellular compounds. At the same time, some of the compounds obtained are used to generate energy in a form that can be used by cells (adenosine triphosphate, ATP for short, is the common energy currency). Some predators – the so-called top predators – are not themselves preyed upon. When they die they are eaten by micro-organisms, collectively called decomposers, as is all organic material that is not otherwise consumed. The micro-organisms break down – degrade – complex organic molecules into the simple ones that they can use for their own metabolism. Once again, the similarity principle reigns.

The above description of the biosphere-machine is very sketchy. We have left out all sorts of complexities such as the role of scavengers, the existence of non-photosynthetic primary producers and photosynthetic micro-organisms, the role of certain fungi (higher organisms that are able to degrade complex molecules), etc. The discussion, however, has highlighted two important principles that govern the biosphere.

The first principle states that there is a flow of energy within ecosystems from photosynthetic plants (or, generally speaking, autotrophs) to non-photosynthetic organisms (generally speaking, heterotrophs). The energy flow is essentially *linear* in that it is a one-way flow, from autotrophs to heterotrophs. Furthermore – and this is a fundamental law of physics – only part of the energy remains available in usable form in each step; the remainder is lost (as non-usable heat) to the ecosystem. The number of transformation steps in an ecosystem or, in other words, the number of levels in the food web is therefore limited. The situation may be likened to travelling through the European Community, exchanging money for the local currency at every border. Not only does the initial sum diminish because money is spent on the way on food, lodging, etc., but at every border a fraction of the remaining sum is lost in the exchange process. Indeed, given enough crossings, any sum will dwindle to nothing because of the exchange fees alone. In much the same way, energy is not only used for 'living', but a fraction of the energy is also lost at any transfer step, because it is turned into non-usable heat. This degradation of the quality of energy, as it is sometimes called, is as much a law of nature as is the conservation of its total amount.

The second principle says that there is a flow of matter in all ecosystems. Unlike the flow of energy, this flow is *cyclic*. Plants are dependent upon autotrophic organisms to regenerate carbon dioxide (which the latter 'exhale' when 'breathing') and minerals. Plants need these in order to carry out photosynthesis and build their own cellular constituents. The same is true for many other elements, such as nitrogen and sulphur. The cyclic flow of carbon and other elements within the biosphere is well documented. The cycles are usually referred to as *geochemical cycles*. As the organisms in the ecosystem carry out the transport by eating and being eaten, it is photosynthesis and, in the final analysis, solar energy that provides the power input driving the mineral cycles.

Ecosystem functioning and malfunctioning

The general overview of the natural or, more precisely, ecological order just given may suggest that we are dealing with a system that is able to sustain itself indefinitely. The

Plate 2.1 The natural order: an ecosystem without human interference, Isavo, Kenya. Photo: Fred Hoogervorst/Lineair

continued energy input from the sun – needed to compensate for the losses – and the cyclical flow of elements would seem to suffice to keep the machinery running for ever. But the truth of this conjecture depends on what exactly we mean by it. If we refer to the ability of ecosystems – and even of the biosphere as a whole – to persist over a prolonged period of time, we are basically correct. Life on Earth is already about 3.5 billion (thousand million) years old. If, however, we interpret it as an unaltered persistence, we miss an important point.

Current life forms only remotely resemble the earliest ones. Organisms have evolved over time and continue to do so (see Box 2). They evolve in response to changes in their environment. The metabolic capabilities of organisms, for example, change continuously; their efficiency in collecting food and ability to cope with parasites and predators change too, as do their defences against unfavourable abiotic changes in environmental conditions. As an ultimate consequence of all these changes, some species become extinct and others emerge. Thus, over evolutionary time, we witness all kinds of shifts in the biological components which take part in the geocycles. Notwithstanding this dynamic feature, the overall picture of (re)cycling materials and linearly transferring energy has remained unaltered. In the absence of large-scale infringements that are forced upon this slowly evolving system, we could indeed safely claim that it will continue to exist for aeons to come.

Unfortunately, the present day indeed witnesses infringements large enough to upset the ecosystems of the world. The development of modern technology – in a broad sense – has, on the time-scale that evolution operates on, taken place in a very short time indeed (decades or centuries rather than thousands or millions of years). The natural world, largely reliant upon the evolutionary mechanisms for its adaptation to changing environmental circumstances, requires significant periods of time to adapt. To what extent the present interferences with the biosphere, caused by human activities, pose threats to the ability of the biosphere to sustain itself remains an open question. There is no doubt, though, that notable changes in the biosphere's functioning are to be expected. Indeed, many argue that such changes have taken place already. They point to the growing percentage of solar energy that flows into agricultural ecosystems rather than natural ones (see Vitousek, 1986) or to the increased concentration of greenhouse gases such as carbon dioxide and methane. Sooner or later, these changes will significantly alter current patterns of the transfer of energy and the recycling of materials. When that occurs, grave problems are to be expected for the entire biosphere, affecting us human beings too. For example, climate change, one of the best known consequences of the increased concentrations of greenhouse gases, is likely to occur. For its part climate change will have all kinds of unwanted consequences, droughts here, excessive rainfall elsewhere, flooding, etc.

The upshot is that we should examine closely the infringements that we humans inflict upon the biosphere, investigate their disruptive effects, and determine how best to repair them or avoid them in the future. After all, although we can afford mentally to step outside the biosphere, physically we are animals among the animals, organisms among the organisms.

The sections to come will be devoted to looking at the nature of environmental problems. In them we will take the perspective of a natural scientist. Before embarking upon this task, however, there is an important preliminary concern to be dealt with. The

Evolution

2

Life on Earth is the result of a long and slow process of non-directional change. Starting with very simple organisms, a great diversity of organisms, both complex and simple, has arisen in the course of about 3.5 billion years. However, it is not only the bewildering diversity of organisms which requires explanation, but also their remarkable adaptation to the environment. The process responsible for the adaptations is called *natural selection*. It only occurs if the following three conditions have been fulfilled.

First, organisms of the same species differ in their characteristics, physical, behavioural or otherwise. This is called the *principle of variation*. Secondly, this variation is heritable, i.e. parents transmit to their offspring the characteristics that set them apart from their conspecifics (*principle of heredity*). Thirdly, parents leave different numbers of offspring, the numbers reflecting their ability to cope with the threats – both biotic and abiotic – the environment poses: the better they are able to cope, the longer they live and the more offspring they will produce. This is the *principle of natural selection*. Evolution thus takes place because there is heritable variation in coping abilities that natural selection works on. It results in organisms that are ever better adapted to their environment.

Evolution, however, is slow because its measure is the generation time of a species. Bacteria are thus able to react more quickly to a changing environment than, say, humans, because bacteria might produce a new generation within 25 minutes, whereas it takes humans about 25 years. There is thus an upper limit to the speed with which species can adapt to a changing environment by evolutionary means.

But organisms adapt to their environment not only through natural selection but also by physiological means. They may grow a thicker fur in winter, adjust their skin colour, hibernate, shed leaves, etc. All these adaptations take place within the lifespan of an organism and are hence referred to as changes at an ecological time-scale. This offers organisms an alternative way of coping with environmental changes. However, here too possibilities are limited.

The very abilities to grow a thicker fur, adjust skin colour, hibernate, shed leaves, etc. are themselves products of a process of natural selection: they are themselves evolutionary adaptations. Although ecological (physiological) adaptations are thus much faster than evolutionary ones, they are also limited in their possibilities, limits which are set by evolution.

But why not be highly flexible then, one may ask.

After all, this seems to offer the best chance to cope with a quickly or erratically changing environment. Research, however, has revealed that flexibility comes with a high price. Being flexible in some respect always means being rigid in some other: one person cannot win both the marathon and the 100 metres in the Olympics. One way or the other, a too rapidly changing environment always endangers species survival.

notion of an infringement as used in the previous section is very much a scientific one: a disruption of natural ecosystems. As such it seems unproblematic. The question arises, however, of how it is related to the cognate notion of an environmental problem. After all, as we saw in Chapter 1, environmental problems have similar features. Clearly, not all infringements automatically qualify as environmental problems; but which ones do? Might one say, for instance, that once infringements have caught the public eye they qualify as environmental problems? Or is there more to it? As we shall see, it is indeed necessary to probe for the exact connection between the notions of an infringement and an environmental problem, as there are important consequences for the ways in which we should solve and avoid environmental problems. That is what the next section will do.

2.3 What constitutes an environmental problem?

The physical dimension

So, what then is an environmental problem exactly? We will tackle this question in a stepwise fashion: suggest a definition, discuss its limitations, and refine it accordingly, until a satisfactory answer has been obtained (see also Sloep, 1994).

First, any definition should restrict environmental problems to changes in the physical environment and rule out changes in our social environment. This follows from our discussion of infringements above: they are infringements of *natural* systems. But the restriction is useful on independent grounds too. Not many, for instance, would argue that the hindrance caused by, say, drug dealing in some neighbourhood should count as an environmental problem; nor would many insist that the misery of having to live under a totalitarian regime is to be considered an environmental problem. Yet both are human interferences with our environment. The point that disqualifies them as environmental problems is that they are changes *solely* of our social environment. If, on the other hand, we look at something like the depletion of the stratospheric ozone layer (the so-called hole in the ozone layer) – commonly seen as a genuine environmental problem – we are dealing with a change in the physical environment. (Later on we will discuss the ozone case in some depth.) Admittedly, this has consequences for our social environment. A case in point would be the dramatically altered attitude of Australians and New Zealanders towards sunbathing (see Figure 2.2).

It should be noted that it is the change in the physical environment that has prompted these responses. It is thus appropriate to describe ozone depletion as an environmental problem and the change in people's attitudes that it prompts as one of its consequences. Keeping these elements apart is crucial, since they have different roles to play, as we shall see shortly. It can be provisionally concluded that:

○ an environmental problem is a change of state in the physical environment.

The social dimension

But this characterisation is not sufficiently specific. Not all changes in the physical environment are environmental problems. Consider natural disasters. A case in point would be the damage believed to have been done to the ozone layer by the ashes shot into the air in the June 1991 eruption of Mount Pinatubo in the Philippines (see Kiernan, 1993, and Pitari *et al.*, 1991).

Clearly, this is an infringement of the physical environment, but should it count as an environmental problem? We do not think so. Natural disasters, and other changes

Fig. 2.2 The same advertisement for a suntan lotion in an Australian and a European newspaper. Source: *New Scientist,* 16 May 1992.

not caused by humans, should be disallowed, for including them would cloud the issue of responsibilities and liabilities. An industrial plant using large quantities of ozone-destroying chlorofluorocarbons (CFCs) can be held accountable for damaging the ozone layer. However, Mount Pinatubo cannot possibly be held responsible for obstructing stratospheric ozone production, nor can the inhabitants of the Philippines, for that matter. The crucial difference is that in the former case voluntary human action is to blame, whereas in the latter case it is Nature's exigencies. Since the possibility of legal action is an important element in developing policies for solving environmental problems, a distinction needs to be drawn between human-induced problems and natural disasters.

Of course, one could decide to call both kinds of physical changes environmental problems since, obviously, both concern problems in our environment. But since we wish to retain the possibility of discerning between environmental problems that result from deliberate human intervention and those that do not, this would necessitate the introduction of two new categories: human-made and natural environmental problems. Although this certainly could be done, we have chosen not to, partly because we feel that it is common usage to employ the more restrictive notion.

In passing, it is worth noting that this classification does not automatically relegate all catastrophes to the category of natural disasters. Floods would be a case in point. Often, floods that at first sight appear to be natural disasters turn out to be environmental disasters or problems. Closer inspection reveals them to be ultimately brought about by human actions. Extensive deforestation, for instance, is known to be responsible for many floodings as the water-retaining capabilities of forest soils greatly exceed that of the denuded soils. If such is the case, the apparent natural disaster actually is an environmental problem. These considerations lead us to make the following change to the above definition:

○ An environmental problem is any change of state of the physical environment which is brought about by human interference with the physical environment.

The normative dimension

A crucial element is still lacking, however. A moment's reflection shows that environmental problems essentially carry what may be called a *conventional element*. Let us be more specific. Not all human-made physical changes in the environment should be dubbed environmental problems; only those should be allowed whose consequences are somehow deemed unacceptable. To put some flesh on this rather abstract statement, consider the case of the depletion of the stratospheric ozone layer, mentioned briefly earlier. It is not so much the diminishing of the amount of stratospheric ozone itself that bothers us, but rather its consequences: the increased UV-B radiation which causes a higher incidence of skin cancer, a faster degradation of plastics or altered migratory behaviour or even death of plankton, lowering primary production of coastal shelves and open oceans (plankton constitutes the primary production). And these consequences are unacceptable for various reasons. The increase in skin cancer is unacceptable because it will cause unnecessary suffering and more costly treatments; the shorter lifespan of plastics is unacceptable because it is uneconomical; the diminished primary production is unacceptable because it messes up food webs and reduces fish stocks, which has grave social and economic consequences. Thus, human conventions – agreed upon norms – are crucial in calling some issues environmental problems.

True as this may sound, it is only so up to a point. Closer inspection of the ozone example reveals that matters are a little more complex. Asked to lower immediately the release of ozone-damaging CFCs, the US and Europe reacted in markedly different ways. While in the US non-essential CFCs were banned relatively quickly, the then European Community was slow to act and only recommended a regulation of the production capacities of some CFCs. Although at present no significant differences exist, the interesting point for our discussion is that the US and the EC reacted differently in the face of the same scientific information. The grounds for their different attitudes may be located at two different levels. The first is the level of ethics, the second that of sociology.

First, the norms of what constitute acceptable consequences or effects of an environmental infringement may differ, and this may result in different policies. It is entirely imaginable that the EC and the US have different norms for what constitutes an acceptable increase in the incidence of skin cancer, an acceptable reduction of the economic life of plastics or an acceptable decrease in marine primary production. And even though these are rather technical norms and do not themselves constitute ethical principles, ultimately they are grounded in such principles. This is clearest in the case of the increased incidence of skin cancer. That some people are allowed to have a more pleasant life (because they can afford aerosol cans, fridges, and what have you) at the expense of the suffering or even death of others runs counter to very basic normative, indeed moral principles. And similar cases can be made for social or economic damage, particularly for the peoples of the developing world, where economic damage often is a matter of life and death. So there is no doubt that ethics matter. But there is more, and this relates to the second level mentioned.

Apparently, if differences in (technical) norms exist, different policies could well follow. But this is not a foregone conclusion. More significantly, perhaps, even if the norms are identical, different policies could still arise. The reason for this is that neither ethical principles nor technical norms can be translated into policies in a straightforward manner. The sociopolitical arena decides what shape this translation takes. Conflicts of interest usually abound, compelling one to set priorities between norms. Thus short-term economic prosperity can come to eclipse 'environmental concerns', which was probably the real reason behind the EC's hesitation in the case of the CFC ban. Also, social processes have their own dynamics, leading, for instance, to privileges for the powerful. This is probably the reason why environmental issues in the formerly communist, eastern European countries never made it to the political agenda: the ideology of the power elite prevented this from occurring. In later chapters, starting with the next, this sociopolitical dimension will receive ample attention. We will therefore not go into it any further here. Let us conclude by saying that, alongside ethical considerations, the sociopolitical arena needs to be taken into account when contemplating a definition of environmental problems.

Summarising the discussion, we arrive at the following definition:

○ An environmental problem is any change of state in the physical environment which is brought about by human interference with the physical environment, and has effects which society deems unacceptable in the light of its shared norms.

This definition shows that all environmental problems result from actions that, to some extent, alter the biosphere's functioning. After all, that is what a change of state in the physical environment boils down to. It also points out that not all such infringements automatically qualify as environmental problems. The ones which do are those whose effects society considers unacceptable. Although in the paragraphs to come we will go into the causes of environmental problems without explicitly mentioning the latter proviso any further, this does not detract from its urgency. Chapters to come, indeed, will pay ample attention to the non-scientific dimensions of environmental problems. Two more observations regarding the definition are in order.

First, it is important to note that incorporating a reference to (shared) norms in the definition of an environmental problem allows us to escape from the commonly made charge of anthropocentrism. This charge holds that our concerns for the environment are ultimately grounded in concerns about our own well-being and that this is much too myopic a point of view. Our definition does not take sides in this debate and we consider this a virtue. It says that ethical norms should feature, but leaves open the question of what norms specifically. Whether one takes an anthropocentric stance or an ecocentric one depends on the system of norms one entertains. If the norms are anthropocentric and framed in terms of, for instance, human health and well-being, so will the notion of an environmental problem. If, however, the norms refer to the well-being of animals, ecosystems or the entire biosphere, anthropocentrism is avoided and replaced by some form of ecocentrism.

Secondly, and for the rest of our discussion most importantly, the definition is an essentially holistic one, one that points out that environmental problems arise out of the interplay between actions belonging to the domain of the natural sciences – the change of state in the physical environment – and those belonging to the domain of the social sciences – society and its norms. The definition thus also reflects what should have been obvious anyway, that environmental problems require a multidisciplinary approach for their solution. We shall turn to an analysis of how such a multidisciplinary approach might help to solve environmental problems, but only after we have examined in some detail the origins of our current environmental predicament.

2.4 How did our environmental problems arise?

From the Neolithic Revolution to the dawn of the Industrial Age

Section 2.2 discussed in admittedly schematic terms the way natural ecosystems operate, i.e. the way in which energy and raw materials are transported through food webs. How do human activities fit in with this? Human hunting and gathering societies pose no problems. After all, hunter gatherers alternately play the parts of herbivores, predators and prey. It has been calculated that had humanity continued to live this way, the total human population would have consisted of about 10 million people. In 1990, however, the human population was an estimated 5321 million. Such a hugely increased population size immediately prompts us to ask the following two questions: 'What allowed such a tremendous population growth to occur?', and 'What are the limits to the human population the Earth can support?'.

In order to find answers to these questions we need to go back in time and examine the development of human society. It is over 10,000 years ago that humanity changed from a hunting and gathering lifestyle to agriculture. The driving force behind this development is largely unknown. Some archaeological sources suggest that the increasing scarcity of large animals may have contributed. In addition, climatological changes occurring after the end of the last Ice Age (about 18,000 years ago) probably played a part. As these developments took place in the Neolithic period, the transition from a hunting and gathering lifestyle is sometimes described as the Neolithic Revolution. This revolution probably continued for thousands of years and did not take place simultaneously everywhere on Earth.

The most ancient farms have been found in the Middle East, in a region where wild wheat grew naturally. It is likely that people started to collect grains of corn and to use part of the harvest as sowing-seed for the next growing season. In Mexico, beans and maize were already being cultivated 8000 years ago. Societies also started to develop cattle breeding by letting tamed, wild animals reproduce in captivity. Together with agriculture and cattle breeding, the need to develop techniques for food conservation arose and this most probably stimulated pottery. In the same period, humanity also invented the wheel – which facilitated transportation – and started to use metals like copper and bronze for tool making. The use of these new tools, of course, further improved agricultural techniques.

The Neolithic Revolution is usually not regarded as a severe threat to the ability of the biosphere to sustain itself. Even though soil erosion, pollution, deforestation and land degradation did occur where human settlements arose, sunlight still provided the primary energy source and people and their crops still neatly fitted into the natural

Linear versus exponential growth

3

Suppose you have a sum of money (say, ECU 100.00) that you do not immediately need. You therefore decide to put it in a savings account with your bank. Rather than offering you the regular deal of a fixed interest rate (say, 5%), the bank makes you a special offer: a fixed annual sum (ECU 10.00) which in the first year exceeds the sum you would obtain had you chosen the regular deal (ECU 5.00). Asked to consider the offer you wonder whether this indeed is a good deal. The correct answer is 'it depends'. It will be intuitively clear that, profitable though the deal initially may be, after a number of years you will lose on it as the interest on your growing sum exceeds the fixed amount you receive (in this case, after 28 years). So whether it is a good deal depends on how long you plan to leave your money in the bank.

This example illustrates the difference between linear and exponential growth. The ordinary deal with a fixed interest rate makes your capital grow exponentially as each year a fixed fraction is added; the special deal is an example of linear growth as each year a fixed sum is added. However large this fixed sum, at some point of time exponential growth is bound to overtake linear growth. The reason is that with exponential growth the amount of increase in a certain period of time itself becomes eligible for growth. You get 'growth on top of growth', so to speak.

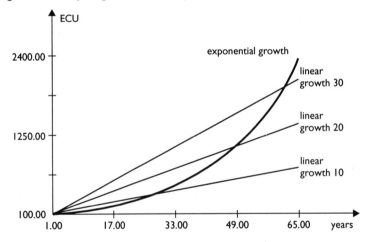

Exponential growth is fast, much faster than most of us intuitively expect. The trick of it is that it gets faster as it goes (see the curved line in the accompanying graph). This is why exponentially growing processes are so deceptive. Doubling the fixed sum of ECU 10.00 to 20.00 makes a difference. But it only helps for an ever shorter while: now after 22 more years the point is reached where an ordinary, interest rate deal is the better one (compare the two lower straight lines). And if ECU 30.00 were to be offered 12 more years would suffice to reach that point (top-most straight line). So the time needed for the exponentially growing sum to overtake the linearly growing one increases, but less and less so.

Malthus was one of the first people to appreciate the distinction between exponential and linear growth.

geocycles. What infringements did occur had a minor and non-lasting impact, owing to the relatively small size of the human population. They could be accommodated, it is believed, by the biosphere's inherent abilities to adapt and restore. This does not apply to the second revolution, that originated in Europe.

In the beginning of the Christian era, about 37 million people were living in Europe. By about 1500, Europe had 70 million inhabitants and after 1650 the population rapidly increased. The reason for this rapid population growth was that, as a result of improved agricultural techniques, a relatively large amount of food was produced. Therefore, a product like wheat was cheap, people were better nourished and thus had an increased resistance to disease. As a result, population growth increased rapidly. This implies that a growing number of people needed food, clothing and housing. In addition, a growing number of people needed employment in order to earn a living. However, agriculture did not offer sufficient employment because of low prices, and trade only provided work for a limited number of people. Thus the perspective in those days was not rosy. According to the English clergyman and economist Thomas Robert Malthus (1766–1834) it would be impossible to provide the ever-increasing population with food. In his essay *The Principles of Population and its Effects on Human Happiness* (1798) he argued that there was a tendency for the population to increase exponentially, to double about once in every 25 years, while the means of supporting the growing population, growing linearly, could never keep up with this pace (see Box 3).

War, famine and catastrophes, however, would continually reduce the size of the population to a level which could be supported. According to Malthus, this mechanism would mean that the standard of living of the majority of individuals would never surpass mere subsistence. Others argued that the advance of science and technology would bring humanity prosperity and opportunities for personal development. The jury is still out on whether indeed science and technology will in the end bring prosperity for all. However, the optimists at least have proved to be correct to some extent in that science and technology have been able to suspend or alleviate Malthus' doomsday scenarios. In the countries of the North, the Industrial Revolution of the 18th century and the ensuing Agricultural Revolution have been successful in banishing famines almost completely. In the developing world, the Green Revolution of the 1960s was instrumental in providing food for many more than previously, thus ridding a country like India entirely of famines.

The Industrial and Green Revolutions

In the English society of the middle of the 18th century, spinning and weaving were mainly cottage industries, carried out in the countryside during the winter season. The products made by spinning and weaving were sold to travelling merchants. The increasing demand for textiles arising from the increasing population size resulted in an interference with the textile cottage industry by these merchants. First the merchants started to provide the cottage workers with raw materials. The products made from these materials were collected after an agreed period. Later the degree of organisation of their activities increased still further. The merchants (entrepreneurs) started to hire buildings and made textile labourers work under supervision and for fixed periods of time in factories.

At first, the most important source of energy in the factories was muscular strength, sometimes supplemented with water and wind energy. This situation dramatically changed after the development of the steam engine by the Scottish engineer James Watt. Its development resulted in an increasing demand for machinery, coal and iron. Industrial production necessitated transport and stimulated both the development of means of transport and the associated infrastructure (such as roads, warehouses, etc.). An industrial development was set in motion which has continued until the present day. Thanks to this development, the primary necessities of life such as nutrition, clothing, housing and medical care are increasingly provided for, at least in the prosperous countries mainly located in the northern hemisphere. In addition, luxury products, leisure time and opportunities for travel have increasingly become available, again predominantly in the prosperous countries. The lifestyle in these countries is now completely different from that of the 18th century European citizens and hardly bears any resemblance to that of our hunting and gathering ancestors.

Since the Second World War there have been revolutionary changes in agriculture. These have centred on the development and cultivation of new, high-yield hybrid crop varieties. There are many such varieties which have vastly improved yields and productivity in Europe. Cultivation of these new varieties goes hand in hand with the use of fertilisers, irrigation and herbicides, fungicides and other pesticides. New crop varieties and accompanying technological changes were also introduced to many developing countries (for example, new rice strains in South East Asia or maize in Latin America) in a process called the Green Revolution, though, in many areas, these changes had adverse environmental impacts.

These agricultural changes have been more successful in delivering food in areas where an infrastructure already existed and could be stimulated than in areas where these favourable conditions were absent. The increased yields resulted in economic and social developments within these agricultural societies and created employment in the food industry and distribution services. People's lifestyles were dramatically changed also, particularly in the rural areas. Essentially the agricultural and industrial changes altered the natural transportation routes of energy and the natural geochemical cycles. The question of prime concern to us here is what the environmental consequences of these changes have been.

The impact of social changes on natural processes

In order to answer this question properly we need to appreciate that the Earth is a closed system. A closed system is one that exchanges energy with its environment but not matter. The Earth is such a system because it exchanges energy with its surroundings (outer space) but the total amount of matter on the planet for all practical purposes remains constant. The description of the biological model of living Nature in section 2.2 revealed how solar energy was trapped and converted into chemical energy by the process of photosynthesis in autotrophic organisms (mostly plants). Solar energy is 'stored' in biomolecules and released when necessary. Release can take place not only in the plant itself, but also in an organism that has directly or indirectly fed on the plant. Thus, all living organisms use solar energy, directly or indirectly. Living organisms are very skilful at converting energy from one form to another.

Industrial production processes also convert energy. The efficiency of these energy conversions, however, is (still) a far cry from that of natural processes. It is not only the efficiency of natural energy conversions which deserves our attention; we should also consider their economy. Living organisms only produce the materials they need in order to function, and hence use energy in a highly economical way. When the energy balance is positive, energy is stored in compounds such as starch, glycogen and lipids. Each living organism degrades biomolecules that have fulfilled their biological function to smaller units and subsequently uses these for the production of new biomolecules or as a cellular fuel. Moreover, the biomolecules present in an organism can, after the death of this organism, be used by other organisms, especially micro-organisms. Industrial production processes tend to be much more wasteful.

While the efficiency with which energy is converted and the economy with which it is used constitute a significant difference between natural and industrial processes, both processes also differ in the kinds of materials and energy they use. Natural production processes mainly use the elements carbon, hydrogen, oxygen, nitrogen, phosphorus and sulphur, in addition to very small amounts of other elements. Processes designed by humans, mostly aimed at fulfilling social desires, use practically all elements present on Earth and also ones outside the natural geochemical cycles. This often implies that, when a product is no longer needed, degradation of dumped material by micro-organisms, Nature's janitors, is difficult or even impossible.

Even in producing materials, involving the elements commonly found in biomolecules, we often use processes which make the products virtually non-biodegradable. For example, the polymerisation of molecules (creating chains of the same molecules) using free radicals (highly reactive chemicals) to produce plastics, and the halogenation (addition of fluor) of organics to produce pesticides involve processes alien to biological systems. Free radicals, for instance, are highly damaging to living systems because of their reactivity. The use of such molecules in production processes, particularly in unnatural reaction conditions (for example, very high temperatures and pressures), leads to products that are completely 'unknown' to living systems. Unlike bioproducts, these products often are effectively untouched by geocycling, which leads to their accumulation in the environment. As we all know, accumulation of dangerous substances poses various environmental problems, to put it mildly.

The types of energy used in industrial production processes also differ from those in natural processes. As was explained above, solar energy is directly or indirectly converted to chemical energy in Nature. Biomolecules thus contain a certain amount of energy stored in a huge variety of compounds of the element carbon. The energy can be released again from the carbon compounds by oxidation. This oxidation principle is used by living organisms during the biologically controlled energy-yielding reactions of metabolism. On a large scale it is applied during the combustion of fuel in human-made production processes. Not only is the efficiency of combustion far lower than that of natural 'combustion', but unwanted side reactions take place that do not occur in living Nature. The products resulting from such side reactions often have negative effects on the environment.

The environmental consequences of human intervention

When a living organism dies, it stops converting and storing energy, but the reduced carbon compounds still exist. They can be used by other organisms. This does not, however, always happen. Under favourable geological conditions, this organic material can be converted into gas, oil or coal. In this way huge amounts of solar energy have been stored in these three fossil energy sources. What humanity began to do on a large scale around the middle of the 18th century was to maintain human society at the expense of these energy reserves. We are, however, rapidly exhausting our energy resources and the adverse environmental effects are becoming more and more evident. In satisfying its needs and wants, humanity uses practically all elements present on Earth and the Earth's energy resources. Matter is thus converted from one form into another, usually at the expense of much energy. Matter is not lost during conversion and can, in principle, be recycled, but again at often considerable energy costs. But the situation is completely different as far as the energy resources are concerned; fossil energy is simply being exhausted.

Plate 2.2 Exploitation of non-renewable energy resources: winning of natural gas in the North Sea off the Dutch coast. Photo: Rob de Wind

So even if at present we can keep 5321 million individuals alive on Earth, this situation cannot last forever. Problems may arise in two fundamental areas. Given that the total amount of matter on Earth is constant, the production of materials which are not easily recyclable (either biologically or by human activity) means that the pool of resources is being depleted. If, at the same time, the accumulated products have undesirable properties (for example, in that they are toxic or carcinogenic or cause the climate to change), then their production, use and dispersal become key environmental issues. These problems are exacerbated through population growth, because more materials are produced, resources are more rapidly depleted, etc. Important though these issues are, the more crucial issue is ultimately that we should not use more energy than is entering the system. How can we trap, convert and store the energy that is entering the Earth's system and how much of it can we trap? The use of autotrophic organisms – i.e. plants, algae, etc. – would at first sight seem to be a viable option. It means that agriculture should redirect its mission from primarily food production to food and energy production. This would mean a revolutionary change in agricultural practice.

Interestingly, the last four to five decades have already witnessed an agricultural revolution that has greatly increased food production. But for all these benefits, there have been and still are negative effects. Although they are not our primary concern here, some of these are negative social effects. The development of new high-yielding varieties is expensive and, in the absence of international aid, remains beyond the reach of poor farmers in developing countries. This further widens the gap between the rich and poor countries. Our prime concern here, however, is the negative environmental effects. The modern agricultural revolution owes its success to a large extent to the abundant use of fertilisers and crop protectants (herbicides, fungicides and other pesticides). Insects and pathogens, through evolutionary changes, may develop and have developed resistance against crop protectants. Their use thus makes the fight against pest animals even more difficult and often also more expensive. This effect is further exacerbated by the trend in modern agriculture to produce ever larger monocultures, thus reducing genetic diversity and increasing the vulnerability of crops to diseases and pests.

Modern agriculture also consumes much fossil energy. The production of herbicides, fungicides and other pesticides requires energy, as do irrigation and mechanical treatment of the soil. The manufacture of the machines used to plough soils, deliver fertilisers, and apply crop protectants also requires energy, as does their transportation. The result is that agriculture is now responsible for about 5% of world energy consumption. This energy use has negative environmental effects, as we have already discussed above.

In summary, both the Industrial and Agricultural Revolutions have brought prosperity to the developed countries and, though to a much lesser degree, to the developing countries. They could only achieve this by significantly altering the natural environment. Not all these changes were for the better, though. Indeed, there is a general consensus that many changes prompted grave environmental problems, in both the developed and developing countries.

Mineral resources were and still are being used in a wasteful way. Hence they will be depleted, and so will our fossil energy resources, even though in some cases new resources are discovered at a faster rate than existing ones are depleted. Metaphorically speaking, we are living off the dowry the Earth has provided us with and pretty soon nothing of it will be left for our children to inherit.

Even worse, perhaps, we are rapidly polluting the environment, making it less habitable for us humans, for our fellow creatures and for our and their offspring. And to make the picture yet grimmer, developing countries justly claim their share of the developed countries' prosperity. Were they to obtain it the way the developed countries have, an environmental disaster is inevitable; on the other hand, were the developing countries to be denied their share – if that is at all conceivable – a social disaster looms large.

2.5 Environmental problems: preventing and solving them

Overcoming our environmental predicament means no less than abandoning wasteful and polluting behaviour in a way that is fair to both the developing and developed world. What this boils down to is achieving a sustainable development on a worldwide scale.

The question of how exactly one might do that is a large one, too large indeed for this chapter (but see Chapter 7 for more on this subject). Scientific knowledge, however, should play a part in its answer. How, in general terms, it does so is the subject of this section.

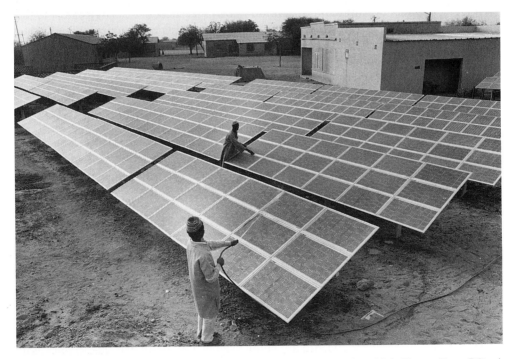

Plate 2.3 Renewable energy: solar energy for a hospital in Gao, Mali. Photo: Ron Giling/Lineair

In section 2.3 we concluded that environmental problems arise out of the interplay between actions belonging to the domain of the natural sciences – the change of state of the physical environment – and actions belonging to the domain of the social sciences – society and its norms. Similarly, solutions for environmental problems need to tap into both scientific and sociopolitical knowledge, while looking for guidance from the norms that society entertains. Understanding this tripartite interaction requires the adoption of a decision theoretical framework. What this amounts to is best understood through the examination of a concrete example first. We will therefore return to the ozone example, touched upon in section 2.3.

The depletion of the ozone layer

It is almost universally agreed that the release into the atmosphere of chlorofluorocarbons, CFCs for short, is by far the greatest cause of the depletion of the ozone layer. CFCs are widely used as coolants in air conditioners and refrigerators, but also as cleansing agents for electronic circuitry. They are cheap and chemically almost inert, two factors that explain their wide use. The story changes, however, in the upper stratosphere (see Figure 2.3). At that level, there is a thin layer of ozone, a highly reactive form of oxygen. It is formed through the action of solar radiation upon ordinary oxygen molecules. Ozone is also formed in the troposphere, the lowest stratum of the atmosphere, but at that level it reacts instantly with other molecules and hence disappears quickly. In the stratosphere, however, there are not many molecules to react with, resulting in the build-up of a thin layer of ozone. This layer is of great importance for life on Earth in that it prevents nearly all harmful solar radiation, the so-called UV-B radiation, from reaching the Earth.

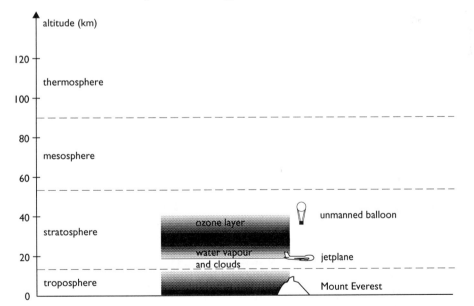

Fig. 2.3 The layers of the atmosphere. The ozone layer is confined to the lower stratosphere, with the ozone concentration peaking at an altitude of about 25 km.

However, the CFCs introduced by humanity in the lower atmosphere have slowly leaked into the upper stratosphere and have affected the ozone layer's protective potential dramatically. The chloride in the CFCs reacts with ozone and changes it back into ordinary oxygen, which is a much less effective absorber of UV-B radiation. To make things worse, the chloride acts as a catalyst, that is, after having reacted with an ozone molecule it is still available to engage in reactions with yet other ozone molecules. The net effect of all this is that the 'thickness' of the ozone layer (more precisely, the concentration of ozone molecules) will be reduced for years to come, the more so as it takes about 15 years for CFCs released in the atmosphere to reach the upper stratosphere.

What we have described so far, solely in chemical terms by the way, are the first order effects of the human introduction of CFCs into the atmosphere. We have traced effects up to an increased intensity of UV-B radiation. But the story does not end there as the increased UV-B in turn causes its own effects. Exposure of the skin to UV-B radiation may lead to the emergence of skin cancer; the more intense the radiation the higher the probability. At the level of an entire population, this translates into an

---

4

Modelling the ozone hole

Any mathematical model that seeks to show, for example, the damage done to the stratospheric ozone layer by CFCs should start with a description of the normal situation. Once the adequacy of such a model has been established, one may incorporate CFCs into it and try to explain and predict their effects.

A description of the normal situation is already quite complex. First of all, it should incorporate a large number of chemical equations. Because of the reactivity of ozone one cannot restrict one's attention to oxygen (out of which ozone is formed) alone, one also has to take into account the effects of molecules that occur in small concentrations only (hydrogen, nitrogen, naturally occurring chlorides). Secondly, some of these reactions are photochemical reactions, others are thermal reactions. Photochemical reactions depend on the intensity of the light and, as light intensity varies seasonally, diurnally (daily) and by latitude, the model has to take into account these three variables too; thermal reactions depend on the temperature and, as temperatures are altitude and latitude dependent, models should also consider these variables. Thirdly, reaction products are often transported, vertically and horizontally. Effects of such transports should therefore also be accounted for in a model.

A model that takes heed of all these complications becomes unmanageably complex. Simplifying assumptions therefore have to be made and are being made. It has been proven that such simplified models are quite well able to describe the natural ozone concentrations at various altitudes and longitudes. Such models have also been shown to be able to incorporate the effects of humanly released CFCs, although specific situations such as those occurring at the poles require specific models.

Sources: the above description is based on the moderately technical treatments found in Phillips (1988) and Sherwood Rowland (1988). More accessible but nonetheless comprehensive treatments can be found in Chapter 5 of Meadows et al. (1993) and RIVM (1992).

increased incidence of skin cancer, as indeed it has in Australia and New Zealand (see Figure 2.2). Another effect of the increased intensity of UV-B radiation is a more rapid degradation of plastics; yet another is the altered migratory behaviour of planktonic algae, affecting primary production in coastal waters and ultimately the size of fish stocks. It is these ultimate effects that for various reasons – ethical and economic – we deem problematic.

The world community has reacted with amazing speed to the threat of increased intensities of UV-B radiation. In 1987, a protocol was signed at a conference in Montreal, with the intent of taking measures to protect the ozone layer. The protocol demanded levels of the major CFCs to be kept at 1986 levels until 1993. After 1993 a gradual reduction was to take place. However, model predictions soon revealed that the levels of CFC emissions admissible according to the Montreal protocol would not sufficiently protect the ozone layer. In fact, calculations showed that chlorine concentrations would keep rising, as a consequence of which the ozone layer would probably end up being entirely depleted. Under the guidance of UNEP, the United Nations Environmental Programme, a new, more stringent agreement was signed in London within a year after the Montreal protocol. Under this agreement, chlorine levels should start falling around the year 2000, which is when the current amount of tropospheric ozone will reach the stratosphere and start to leak away from there.

Decisions and models

Clearly, the decision to cut back on CFCs was taken on the basis of model predictions fuelled by the broadly felt unacceptability of increased UV-B radiation intensities. How did this decision come about?

We will not provide a sociopolitical analysis – such is left to chapters to come. Rather, we will try to understand how in a formal sense scientific models and public norms interact to produce decisions. For this we need some elementary decision theory. The benefit of such an admittedly unrealistic approach is that it provides the backdrop for actual policy making. Of course, our treatment here will be elementary and only aimed at elucidating the principles at work.

In decision theoretical terms, then, cutting back on CFCs is an *action*. Actions have particular *outcomes*, depending on the kind of system acted upon; in the CFC case some local ozone concentration would qualify as an outcome. (Actually, things are a bit more complex as it only makes sense to talk about an ozone concentration at some altitude and latitude at some specific point of time; we shall ignore these complications; see Box 4.) A *model* of the system allows one to figure out what outcome some action will have (see Figure 2.4). Depicted this way, decision processes look quite simple: given a particular agreed upon outcome, the model at hand dictates which action to take. This picture, however, is too simple in at least two ways.

One should never consider singular actions. Different actions usually will have different outcomes and one should evaluate and compare several actions with respect to their outcomes. After all, the first action considered need not be the best one. When one considers the Montreal and London protocols as actions – and one may justifiably do so even though their outcomes were evaluated consecutively rather than simultaneously – they aptly illustrate the principle.

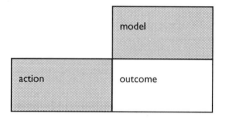

Fig. 2.4 A simplistic decision matrix. An action results in a particular outcome, given some model. Choose the action in such a way that it produces the outcome desired.

Evaluating outcomes with respect to their desirability, however, presupposes the existence of some yardstick. Outcomes in and of themselves are unfit for this; they are just particular states of the system under consideration, such as particular local ozone concentrations. In decision theory, outcomes are evaluated with respect to each other by attributing *utilities* to them; the outcome with the highest utility is the one most preferred. So the outcome of actions taken under the London protocol has a higher utility than the outcome under the Montreal protocol, precisely because we value higher ozone concentrations more than lower concentrations.

We will not delve too deeply into the question of how exactly one arrives at utilities for outcomes. Two observations need to be made, however. First, and not surprisingly, different outcomes should have different utilities. Otherwise, the utility scale chosen would be unfit for comparing outcomes. Second, and more importantly, in the final analysis all comparisons between utilities are founded upon some normative stance. In section 2.3 we already argued that environmental problems contain an element of convention: agreed upon norms are essential in calling some issue an environmental *problem*. Now the time has come fully to deliver on this qualification: what utility scale one adopts in the effort to solve some environmental problem ultimately depends on the particular normative stance one takes.

As we saw, in the ozone case norms used may be premised upon such diverse considerations as unnecessary human suffering or excessive economical damage. Much as in the phase of a problem's definition, how basic ethical rules get translated into utilities is subject to a process of negotiation that takes place in the sociopolitical arena. In democracies this is usually formalised and often cumbersome; in dictatorial states hardly any negotiations take place. Even so, whether for the benefit of all or for that of the powerful only, ethical considerations (or the lack thereof) play their part. Indeed, some argue that the quality of such processes of translation would benefit greatly from a more explicit incorporation of ethical principles (for more on the subject of the role of 'practical' ethics, see Shrader-Frechette, 1991, 1994). This is an important conclusion as it undermines the often-voiced conception that science alone would suffice to solve environmental problems. As we shall see shortly, this conception is to be criticised on yet other grounds.

So far, the impression has been given that *one* model would do to predict the outcomes of actions. This, however, is seldom the case. More often than not, a variety of models are in use and scientists disagree over their reliability, applicability, validity, accuracy, etc. This is hardly surprising. By their very nature, models capture reality

The limits of scientific knowledge

5

Knowledge about the world is generally captured by models (or theories, laws, hypotheses). Such empirical knowledge is fallible, as the philosophy of science has established beyond much doubt. Models, however well confirmed, may turn out to be mistaken, as the history of science amply illustrates. This implies that the prediction that some action results in an outcome is only as good as the models used to generate the prediction. Models, furthermore, need data in order to connect actions with outcomes. Models use functions in which parameters feature for which in turn numerical values are needed. Also, the state which the model is in at some particular starting time, say t_0, has to be characterised, meaning that numerical values for the state variables (the variables characterising the model's behaviour) are required at t_0. These values could either be measured directly or inferred through other models which in turn rely on data that are either measured or inferred from models which …. Such data are not absolutely reliable.

If they have been inferred, they result from computations that may employ mistaken models. If they have been measured, measurement errors may have occurred. Indeed, one may justifiably claim that *all* data are in a sense inferred, because knowledge of the functioning of measurement devices rests on models. It may now seem that scientific knowledge is hardly useful in environmental decision making but such a conclusion would be a serious mistake. The above lines of reasoning apply to all empirical knowledge, from natural or social science or other sources. Hence, whether we like it or not, our powers of control over the world are limited in a fundamental, epistemological sense.

There are, however, also more prosaic reasons why our knowledge of the world is limited. First, some perfectly deterministic models – models in which no chance effects occur – may yet not allow one to know their future states at all. The reason is that such models exhibit chaotic behaviour, meaning that an ever so slight imprecision in their initial state implies an almost total ignorance of that system's future states. Secondly, stochastic models, i.e. those that do harbour chance effects, involve predictions about future states which take the form of probability distributions over the system's set of possible states.

Both these reasons constitute limits to our powers of control that operate at the theoretical level, but there are also limits that operate at a more pragmatic level. First, as was already argued above, data are needed in order to specify numerically parameter values and initial conditions. However, there could be problems in obtaining these data. Perhaps the necessary experiments are unethical, perhaps they are too costly, perhaps they take too long. Any one of these limits may imply that one has to work with estimated or, even worse, guessed data. Second, when models also make assumptions about the social behaviour of people – and models that include the implementation of measures always do – the possibility has to be included that people react to measures taken. That is, the very measures that a model recommends may prompt people to behave in certain ways that differ from the way the model in the first place assumed them to behave. Unless one alters the model accordingly, such reactions invalidate the model. However, incorporating reactions is notoriously difficult. Doing it tends to complicate models beyond control; not doing it seriously affects their value. Unfortunately, there is no easy way out of this dilemma. The upshot is that scientific knowledge, whether social or natural, has its limits, epistemological, theoretical and pragmatic. But that, of course, should not keep us from using the models in which such knowledge is embedded.

Source: Doucet and Sloep (1992).

only in part. They make all kinds of simplifying assumptions, and they have to, otherwise they would become unmanageable (see also Box 4). An issue for discussion, of course, is what simplifying assumptions to make and how these affect the model's performance. Also, one may argue over parameters. In principle, they are constants needed to do the calculations (arrive at numerical predictions). However, their exact values are often disputed. Indeed, one may challenge the assumption that some parameters are constants at all and argue that they actually should have been incorporated in the model as variables. Sometimes, the very structure of a model is under dispute. Particularly, when the implementation of measures is incorporated in a model and social structures therefore are to be taken into account, many alternatives may be considered (see Box 5 for an elaboration). All in all, there seems to be ample room for disagreement over models. In almost all decision processes, therefore, various models will be considered.

This may have far-reaching consequences, depending on the kind of decision situation at hand. One makes decisions in complete certainty, limited uncertainty, and complete uncertainty. The first category poses no problems as, in fact, one is dealing with a one-model decision problem. The second category hardly ever obtains in environmental decision making, as it seldom occurs that one has the required numerical estimate of the likelihood of application of the models involved. The third situation occurs frequently and we will illustrate it here through the ozone case. Unfortunately, this case does not lend itself optimally to illustrating these matters as alternatives were considered consecutively rather than simultaneously. Discussions about the suitability of the models used therefore did not really arise. (It was effectively a decision problem with complete certainty.) We will use it nevertheless by making some counterfactual assumptions.

Decision rules

Suppose, for the sake of argument, that the Montreal and London protocols were considered simultaneously and that two models, based on two different data sets, were available at the same time. Furthermore, suppose that one had no way of deciding which one of the models was the better one. Figure 2.5 illustrates this situation. In it, utilities have been ranked with number 1 as the most preferred outcome and number 4 as the least preferred outcome.

The utilities are awarded according to the following two rules, rule 1 taking precedence over rule 2 (outcomes are assumed to be in the form of ozone levels):

○ *Rule 1*: the ozone level which is on target gets the highest rank; ozone levels above target get higher ranks than ozone levels below target. The rationale behind this is that, once a target ozone concentration has been agreed upon, higher ozone concentrations are better than lower ones in terms of the damage done by the UV-B radiation.
○ *Rule 2*: all other things being equal, ozone levels achieved under the Montreal protocol receive higher utilities than those achieved under the London protocol. Here the rationale is that, as the London protocol demands more extensive actions than the Montreal protocol, it is the economically more expensive one.

Presumably, outcomes (1,1) and (2,2) (see Figure 2.5 for the numbering convention) have identical ozone concentrations and hence identical utilities according to rule 1; rule 2 now makes (1,1) preferable over (2,2). Rule 1 also tells us that outcome (2,1) is to be preferred over outcome (1,2).

Now, notice that action 1 leads to outcomes with both the highest and the lowest utility rank (1 and 4 respectively), while action 2 leads to the intermediate ranks. However, no action is uniformly better than the other in that it gives the better result whatever model obtains: if model 1 obtains, action 1 is the better one, if model 2 obtains, action 2 is the better one. In cases like this one has to follow one of the following rules. Either *play it safe*, take no risks and choose the action that minimises the losses; that would be action 2 as it avoids the worst outcome. Or *gamble*, hope for the best, and maximise the gain; that amounts to action 1 as it picks the best outcome (and runs the risk of losing a lot).

What rule to pick is a matter that is external to the particular decision problem. One has to agree on it beforehand on the basis of some normative position one adopts with respect to the question of whether it is OK to gamble with the environment or not. In our present rendering, one might decide to stick to the original Montreal protocol and gamble that the model 2 predictions do not apply. No doubt, this would save industry – and hence us all – money. However, if the model 2 predictions turn out to be correct after all, we would suffer severe damages. There is a reason then why one might decide to play it safe and go for the more restrictive London protocol.

In actual fact, model 2, which is based on newer and better data, has replaced model 1. As we have said, the actual decision problem thereby has become one of complete certainty rather than complete uncertainty. Therefore, it suffices to look at the cells in the righthand column of the matrix only. And clearly then, action 2, the London protocol, is the better one.

But the ozone case is atypical. More often than not much battering goes on over the question of which model applies. Although lack of space prevents us pursuing this matter, the climate change case exemplifies this situation exactly. Cases like that typically conform to the decision problem depicted by Figure 2.5.

	model 1	model 2
action 1 Montreal protocol	1 (1.1)	4 (1.2)
action 2 London protocol	3 (2.1)	2 (2.2)

Fig. 2.5 A decision matrix for the adapted ozone case. Actions are protocols, models are models, outcomes are ozone concentrations. The large numbers represent ranked utilities for outcomes, 1 being the most preferred and 4 the least preferred outcome; the small numbers in brackets are used to identify outcomes.

In summary, the scientific knowledge embedded in models is crucial for reaching decisions. The present section has described why. However, it has also revealed the crucial importance of norms. Without norms it is impossible to attribute utilities to outcomes; and if the decision situation is one with complete uncertainty, it is furthermore impossible to choose between decision rules.

2.6 Conclusion

The ground covered by this chapter may conveniently be summarised by citing two dichotomies. In discussing environmental problems and the relevance of science for them, we have mixed specific facts and problems (sections 2.2 and 2.4) with general models and issues (sections 2.3 and 2.5); and we have contrasted the roles of science-based models and facts with ethics-based norms and values.

In conclusion we may say that, on the whole, science certainly has a solid contribution to make to understanding, preventing, and solving environmental problems. This conclusion holds irrespective of the normative character of environmental problems. At the same time, we should beware of putting too much faith in the natural sciences. Science-based recommendations have to be implemented, for which knowledge of society and its policy-making processes is indispensable. Chapters to come, starting with the next, will go into these matters.

Finally, the question of which policies to adopt willy-nilly reflects an ethical stance. Such ethical matters, implicit though they may be, are too important to be left to either scientists or politicians. They affect all of humanity, indeed the entire biosphere, and should therefore be the concern of all of humanity.

3

The social construction of environmental problems

Angela Liberatore*

3.1 Introduction

As was discussed in Chapter 2, science plays a crucial role in identifying problems related to the functioning and deterioration of ecosystems. It also became clear that apparently purely physical problems need to be understood in social terms.

In this chapter we develop the idea that environmental problems are not pure and self-evident physical facts. Certain steps and conditions are needed before, for example, global warming can be conceived of as a risk to be dealt with. Global warming is not (or not yet) a visible phenomenon; one does not see incremental increases in temperature and for the time being there is no scientific consensus about the view that phenomena such as certain floods or drought observed in recent years are due to global warming. Nevertheless, it is regarded as a problem by many scientists, politicians and non-governmental organisations (NGOs). Why?

The factors of relevance include the widespread perception that certain 'things' are negative – because of their impact on human health, ecosystems, certain aesthetic or ethical values, and so on – and the conviction that something should and could be done to deal with them. In turn, perceptions are based on several societal factors such as the relative importance of certain problems in different socioeconomic contexts, and the public's trust (or distrust) in the political and scientific institutions that are responsible for addressing the problems at hand. In other words, environmental problems are not given per se but are socially constructed and the way this construction process develops is influenced by the prevailing cultural, economic and political conditions in different social contexts.

In this chapter special attention is paid to the analysis of the processes through which certain physical events become (or do not become) environmental issues. The interaction between science and policy, including the 'translation' of scientific findings into economic and political terms, is addressed too. This is regarded as an important component of the process of definition and selection of environmental issues.

This chapter provides a sociological perspective on the question of 'What are international environmental problems and why have they become important politically?'. It is composed of two 'theoretical' sections (illustrated with examples) and two 'empirical' ones, followed by some concluding remarks. The theoretical sections focus, first, on the interface between science and policy (section 3.2) and, second, on the social construction of environmental issues (section 3.3). The empirical sections that follow illustrate the theoretical arguments in the context of two specific examples of international environmental problems. The first example discusses how the depletion of the ozone layer came to be defined as a policy issue in the US, the EC, the former USSR and developing countries (3.4), while the second considers the different definitions of and responses to the Chernobyl fallout in Italy, Germany and France (3.5).

3.2 The interaction between science and policy

Questions such as how dangerous for human health and the environment a certain substance is and what alternatives are available, or what is the carrying capacity of ecosystems and what are the causes of human-made pressure on the global environment, involve the need for scientific investigation of biological, chemical, physical and social processes. These questions are thus viewed as matters to be solved by experts, that is, people competent in specialised fields of knowledge. Experts are frequently asked by politicians to provide scientific evidence that can be used to make scientifically sound (or at least scientifically justifiable) policy decisions. In order to develop 'sustainable' policies it is in fact necessary to have some knowledge of the actual and potential environmental impacts of certain activities and some knowledge of the technical characteristics, economic costs, social acceptability and possible side effects of alternative policy options. However, disagreements between experts often emerge over data-gathering methods or over the interpretation of a particular body of evidence. Moreover, even scientifically uncontroversial evidence can be used in various ways by policy makers. The complex interface between science and policy therefore needs to be researched in order to deepen our understanding of how environmental issues are constructed. This in turn influences the way those issues are dealt with in practice. Some examples may illustrate the points to be analysed.

In 1985, *Nature* magazine published an article by J. Farman and other researchers of the British Antarctic Survey, presenting the first scientific evidence of the 'ozone hole'. This evidence had been provided by ground-based measurements in two measuring stations in Antarctica. At first, most scientists were sceptical. The British Antarctic Survey was not yet well known in the scientific community involved in ozone research. It was thought that if huge ozone losses were occurring, satellites would have picked them up. Scientists of NASA's Goddard Space Flight Center reviewed the satellite data that could have detected a large ozone loss, and realised that they had overlooked the computer data that showed the ozone hole. This was owing to the fact that, since instruments sometimes gave measurements known to be anomalous, the Goddard scientists had programmed their computers to throw out any measurements of ozone below 180 Dobson units, which was considered impossible (Roan, 1989). This example clearly shows how data-gathering and selecting methods, and the status of certain scientists within the relevant expert community, may stimulate or prevent certain data being regarded as evidence.

The second example refers to a controversy between scientists over the construction and interpretation of estimates. In its 1990–1991 report on the global environment, the World Resource Institute (WRI), a well-known US environmental research and lobbying organisation, published some estimates of net emissions and sinks of greenhouse gases for various countries. This provoked strong criticisms by scientists of India's Center for Science and Environment, who argued that the estimates provided by WRI were biased because net emissions depend on where natural sinks are located and because CO_2 and methane emissions from deforestation in developing countries had – in their view – been overestimated by WRI (Agarwal and Narain, 1990). More generally, the Indian scientists argued that WRI's estimates seemed to be intended to blame developing countries for global warming and to perpetuate global inequalities. This case indicates that, on the one hand, well-known scientific sources are not universally trusted and that, on the other hand, scientists in different social contexts and countries may look at data from different perspectives, perspectives that are influenced by – among other things – concerns regarding the implications and uses of evidence for policy purposes.

Many other examples of the construction of scientific evidence and the social determinants of scientific controversies could be provided. Among these are the controversies over the health risks of low doses of radiation or over the carcinogenic properties of chemical substances such as aldrin and dieldrin or the environmental damage caused by the transboundary impact of acid rain. For the present let us look at some of the main points arising from case studies which help us to interpret the relationship between science and environmental policy making.

The social embeddedness of science

Studies on the sociology and history of science emphasise the embeddedness of science in its social and historical context. In particular, they argue that all observations and statements of fact are theory – and value-laden. Scientists are socially situated reasoners rather than bearers of universal truth. Specific orderings are constructed – rather than revealed – in sequences of activity which, however attentive to experience and to formal consistency, could nonetheless have been otherwise and could have had different results.

Even more specifically, several sociologists and philosophers of science point out that what is 'seen' and selected as relevant evidence, and how such evidence is interpreted, is conditioned by a variety of factors. Among them are the organisation of laboratory practices and scientific work; the influence of previous theories and schools of thought; the impact of peer review and criticism of relevant expert communities; the constraints imposed by financial resources allocated to research and the technical equipment available; and the value attributed to scientific knowledge in different cultural and political systems (see Barnes and Edge, 1982; Hesse, 1974; Knorr-Cetina, 1981; Kuhn, 1962; Ravetz, 1971).

Scientists are in many cases aware of these issues, as is proved by the debates within the scientific community on the limits of science, the social responsibility of scientists, and so on. However, the diffusion of these debates is constrained by two factors. On the one hand, certain scientific institutions continue to defend the absolute objectivity and neutrality of science, in order to preserve a status of 'bearers of truth' they might otherwise lose. On the other hand, this attitude is reinforced by policy makers who ask scientists to provide 'certainties' that can guide or justify policy decisions.

The social embeddedness of science reveals itself rather clearly in the provision and use of policy-relevant evidence. In analysing the process of standard-setting, Giandomenico Majone (1983) notes that such processes can be regarded as a microcosm reflecting conflicting epistemologies, professional values, regulatory philosophies and national cultures. Moreover, Sheila Jasanoff (1987) emphasises that the very border between science and policy is often controversial and socially determined. It is in fact difficult to define where science stops and politics starts in order to determine, for example, which air or water quality standards would best protect health and the environment. Always value judgements must be made regarding the degree of protection to be achieved.

With regard to this last point another important element, stressed by Brian Wynne (1987) and other scholars, is the credibility of scientific experts (see Box 1). Only if experts are credible can they influence policy decisions and provide advice that will be listened to by governmental and non-governmental actors. In turn, the credibility of experts is based on social relationships by which trust or distrust is developed and through which the authority of experts is at the same time institutionalised (in research, professional and advisory organisations) and challenged (for example, in cases of major technological accidents that challenge experts' ability to deal with the unintended effects of the products of their own knowledge).

Trans-science, half-knowledge and the management of uncertainty

The influence of expert advice in the policy process is documented by other case studies that reveal not only the power of expertise in defining problems and identifying possible solutions, but also the use of specialised knowledge by policy makers to legitimise their decisions (see Barker and Peters, 1993). The potential legitimating function of science in the policy-making process is addressed by the concept of 'half-knowledge' first introduced by Lazarsfeld (1967) and developed by Marin (1981). According to these authors, decision makers do not necessarily try to obtain all the information which is or could be made available and is relevant to the problems and the identification of solutions; rather, they select the information they need on the basis of their goals and resources. In other words, they look for a half-knowledge that can be safely organised into politics, avoiding the knowledge that could provoke embarrassment and conflicts. The attempts made to underplay the impact of major technological accidents or the long-term and transboundary consequences of pollution problems such as acid deposition are cases in point. At the same time, the selection of half-knowledge is not completely arbitrary. For example, politicians cannot pretend that certain data do not exist if these data are widely known within and beyond scientific communities or national borders. In other words, the available knowledge

---

Experts' credibility and the protection of the Mediterranean

An illustration of the importance of expert credibility in the definition of environmental problems is offered by the case of the protection of the Mediterranean Sea. Expert groups, mainly ecologists and marine scientists, have played a crucial role in defining the problem. In fact, they were the ones to suggest that the Mediterranean is a vulnerable ecosystem to be protected as a whole. Moreover, the lobbying by experts – or by 'epistemic communities' as Peter Haas calls them (Haas, 1990) – through scientific advice to governments and international organisations was instrumental in launching the Mediterranean Action Plan of the United Nations Environment Programme.

The concept of the epistemic community may be regarded as problematic, since it seems to take for granted the objective nature of the 'episteme' knowledge and the legitimate role of expert 'communities' in proposing camps of action. The point of interest here is, however, the major influence of experts in the policy process. The Mediterranean case shows that if the experts involved had not been credible, both within the respective professional communities and in the eyes of policy makers, they could not have had this influence in defining the problem and suggesting actions aimed at coping with it. At the same time it must be stressed that other extrascientific reasons, particularly the economic and strategic interests of some coastal states in the Mediterranean area and the interest of some international agencies in playing a leading role with regard to environmental issues, favoured the emergence of the idea of developing international co-operation to protect the Mediterranean.

---

limits the discretion of politicians in the choice of half-knowledge. Such discretion appears to be greater in cases where the knowledge available is controversial and uncertainties are more evident.

With regard to this last point, a concept that must be taken into consideration in analysing the interaction between policy making and controversial science is the concept of 'trans-science'. This concept was introduced by Alvin Weinberg (1972) to characterise those questions that can be stated in scientific terms but that are, in principle, beyond the proficiency of science to answer. Following Weinberg, questions such as the risks of low doses of radiation transcend science. Getting answers to such questions would be prohibitively expensive. In any case the matter might be too variable to enable research to proceed according to the generally accepted methods of scientific inquiry. A further problem, and one which was debated in the previous chapter, is that questions often involve moral or aesthetic judgements to be made in seeking answers.

The distinction between science and trans-science points to the important issue of the limits of science and the need to live with scientific uncertainties and controversies. At the same time, such a distinction is problematic. It assumes in fact that a clear-cut distinction can be made between facts and values, object and subject and this is at least controversial. Furthermore, the distinction between science and trans-science raises the problem of institutional power, that is, who should determine where the line between science and trans-science is to be drawn and, once a line has been drawn, who should decide the controversial trans-scientific issues.

The discussion on half-knowledge and trans-science brings us to a crucial aspect of the interaction between science and policy in defining environmental issues and formulating possible solutions, that is, the management of scientific uncertainties. As Jerome Ravetz and Silvio Funtowicz (1989) write, 'We now face "hard" policy decisions (involving huge investments and the fates of many people) for which the necessary scientific inputs will be irremediably "soft", uncertain and contested'. The debate on climate change is a highly significant example of this situation. Scientific uncertainties characterise the identification of the causes and, even more, the understanding of the mechanisms and the forecasting of the scale, timing and impact of climate change. At the same time, the development of policies aimed at stabilising or reducing the emissions of greenhouse gases would require huge financial investments – including financial aid to assist developing countries in controlling their emissions – and the restructuring of entire economic sectors such as energy production and transport. Uncertainties also characterise the assessment of the various policy options in terms of their economic costs, social acceptability and political implications at the global, national and local levels. In other words, social science uncertainties, as well as natural science ones, must be dealt with.

An examination of how uncertainties have been managed in the context of the debate on climate change helps us understand the interaction between the framing of environmental issues and the way decisions on environmental matters are made.

In the face of uncertainty three possible courses of action can be identified. Decision makers may either:

❍ decide to wait for more information
❍ take a decision while taking uncertainty into account
❍ take decisions while neglecting or even hiding uncertainties.

The first two alternatives were those most commonly advocated in the climate change debate. The Bush administration in the USA strongly advocated – especially during the negotiations of the climate change convention that took place before and at the UNCED Conference – the need to reduce scientific uncertainty before deciding upon stabilisation and reduction targets (option 1). This would enable the US to evade or delay the actions needed to meet targets. The European Community, the Scandinavian countries and the Alliance of the Small Island States advocated instead the need to take precautionary action (option 2), that is, setting targets and developing policies on the basis of the available evidence and uncertainties. They argued that postponing action could mean starting to act when it is too late.

In spite of the reference to opposing principles, 'wait-and-see' versus the 'precautionary principle', most of these governments agreed that 'no-regret policies' should be developed, that is, policies that may help combat global warming and at the same time are beneficial to the economy. In this context emphasis is put on energy efficiency measures. In other words, what is economically and politically more feasible and palatable determines the way uncertainty is actually dealt with. In this respect it is worth stressing the interaction between issue framing and decision making. On the one hand, the way a problem is framed influences the way that problem is dealt with. In our case, the definition of the problem as a global environmental issue mainly caused by greenhouse gas emissions, but characterised by many uncertainties, influenced the formulation of policy actions. But the opposite is also true: the feasibility of certain actions influences the way a problem is framed. This is reflected, for instance, in the emphasis on energy efficiency measures to stabilise CO_2 emissions in the climate change debate.

This last remark points to the fact that natural science findings need to be 'translated' in political and economic terms to become policy issues. It was only when climatological models and theories started being translated in terms of the economic costs of possible impacts, and of the (economic and administrative) feasibility and social acceptability of policy options, that the risk of climate change became a policy issue as well as a research issue (see Liberatore, 1994).

3.3 The social construction of environmental problems

The example of 'risk'

We turn now to a second theoretical issue of concern to sociologists, the argument that environmental problems are socially constructed. A good way of discussing this issue is to take the notion of 'risk', a notion that is widespread in debates and policies in the field of environment.

Within the framework of risk assessment studies, risk is seen as a measurable phenomenon. It is often defined as the predicted magnitude of a loss or damage multiplied by the probability of its occurring. In spite of this precise definition, several aspects can be identified that make risk assessment a far from objective procedure.

Subjective elements are first introduced in the selection of population samples, extrapolation functions and so on (see Fischoff *et al.*, 1981; Renn, 1985). What is more, studies in risk perception show that whether something is regarded as a risk, and as a more or less acceptable risk, depends on several social factors. The list of these factors includes considerations such as whether the risk is taken voluntarily or not; whether the risk is controllable; whether exposure is a necessity or a luxury; whether the consequences may affect especially sensitive groups of the population, like children; whether the possible effects are immediate or delayed; whether they are reversible; and so on (Lowrance, 1976; Slovich *et al.*, 1982). Cultural studies also emphasise that the way people perceive risks cannot be separated from their position within society and from the way they experience and judge social relations and institutions (Douglas and Wildawsky, 1982; Reyner and Cantor, 1987) (see Box 2).

According to the reasoning presented above it can be stated that what is (or is not) regarded as a risk is a matter of perception, and this in turn is conditioned by social relations. In other words, risks are not objective entities but social constructs. This does not mean that risks are imaginary and that the probability of actual damage arising is just a matter of perception. Rather, to say that risks are social constructs means to acknowledge that a discussion of the risk of global warming or the extinction of certain species is the result of a complex process, involving the selection and interpretation of

---

Societal perceptions of risks

2

Issues such as waste disposal and the control of high-risk technologies like nuclear power and biotechnology provide useful illustrations of societal definitions of risks. Opposition to the siting of waste facilities (especially in the case of toxic and nuclear waste) often involves arguments regarding the unfair distribution of health and environmental risks over different sectors of society – those who live nearby and those who live far away from the site – and/or different generations. Those arguments in turn imply judgements – in this case judgements based on the category of fairness – about social relations. Likewise, perceptions of the controllability of high-risk technologies (see Perrow, 1984) involve judgements about the capabilities and the accountability of the relevant scientific and political institutions in dealing with the risk of serious, widespread and irreversible damages. In both cases, and in many others, different perceptions and judgements can emerge across societies and within the same society, depending on the prevailing social values and relations.

---

evidence, the emergence and diffusion of environmental awareness, and the willingness of certain actors to deal with the risk as a matter of environmental, economic, energy or other sectoral policies, international negotiations and/or media coverage.

A more detailed discussion of the construction and management of risks in a specific context is provided later in this chapter in the section on Chernobyl (3.5).

The framing of issues

The line of argument suggested with regard to the notion of risk also applies to the notion of *issue*. Several sociologists point to the social construction of issues, that is, the way certain events and experiences are interpreted according to 'cognitive frames'. Such frames include perceptive abilities – such as memory – and judgements based on previous experience and/or socialisation processes. According to one of the most influential sociologists in this field, Erving Goffmann, some 'primary' cognitive frames are needed to render what would otherwise be a meaningless aspect into something that is meaningful (Goffmann, 1974). Cognitive frames are, in turn, developed through the interactions between actors living in a specific society.

With regard to environmental issues it is especially important to look at the way Nature and the interactions between Nature and human beings are perceived. According to Michiel Schwarz and Michael Thompson (1990) it is possible to distinguish four main 'myths of Nature': Nature benign, tolerant, capricious or ephemeral. These views influence the way actors frame environmental problems. For instance, if someone regards Nature as ephemeral, they will consider any form and quantity of pollution as dangerous and to be prevented or eliminated. By contrast, if someone thinks that Nature is benign, they will view certain forms and quantities of pollution as unimportant, since Nature will be able to cope with them.

It must be stressed that these myths of Nature are the result of social conditions. For example, the view of Nature as benign appears to be related to industrialisation processes characterised by the use of environmental resources as a mere basis of and

Plate 3.1 Issue framing: 100 years ago whaling was common practice. Nowadays, public opinion has changed. The photograph shows a slaughtered Minke whale being hauled aboard a Norwegian whaling boat on the Barents Sea. Photo: EIA/Lineair

material for production. Such views are mainly held by business actors or by low-income social groups interested in limiting the environmental constraints on economic activities in order to make profits or preserve jobs. The alternative view of Nature as ephemeral appears to be related to environmental movements, especially, though not exclusively, in industrialised countries.

According to Inglehart (1977) the adherence to 'post-materialist values', i.e. values that pay greater attention to 'quality' – including environmental quality – than 'quantity', characterises contemporary Western societies. This focus on quality must be understood as largely shaped by changes in economic structures (decline of heavy industry, growth of the services sector, diffusion of information technologies), and by social and political processes (such as education and democratisation) that favour the emergence of social movements, including environmental movements (see Box 3).

However, the attention paid to 'post-materialist values' in industrialised countries should not lead to the underestimation of consumerist attitudes and behaviour in these countries, nor should it lead to the assumption that people of lower-income countries are concerned only with material values and cannot be mobilised for environmental protection. It is true that poverty and economic development are the main concern of developing countries. It is worth stressing, however, that attention to environmental quality and opposition to instrumental views of Nature characterise citizens' movements, like the Chipko movement in India or the Green Belt movement in Kenya, both mainly composed of women.

Green movements and environmental attitudes

3

The emergence and evolution of green parties and environmental movements as new and often influential social actors at the local, national and international levels have been extensively analysed (see, among others, McCormick, 1989; Rudig and Lowe, 1992). Green parties are generally seen as political actors that introduce not only new – environmental – topics but also different organisational forms and practices into the traditional political system. This also partly applies, but in a more 'diffused' way, to the role of environmental movements. Apart from parties and movements, the environmental attitudes of the broader public are being scrutinised through opinion polls and other means. The resulting data represent useful indicators of the spread and/or depth of concern about certain environmental issues in selected sectors of the 'public'. However, the reliability and significance of these data are obviously very much dependent on the methods used and on the selection of samples. Therefore, the gathering as well as the interpretation and use (for example, by the media) of data on 'public' environmental attitudes is more problematic than the interpretation of more focused studies on green parties or environmental organisations.

These two movements point to the fact that environmental issues are framed not simply on the basis of the emergence of physical phenomena (like the depletion of certain natural resources) or according to objective cost–benefit calculations. They largely depend on the prevailing cultural values within different societies (such as the holistic view of Nature and the consideration of humans as components of Nature in certain cultures) and on the prevailing social relations, including the social conditions of women and their role as daily managers of the living environment (see Dankelman and Davidson, 1988; Shiva, 1988).

Another example of the way environmental issues are framed in different social contexts might be the way people look at trees and the deforestation issue (see Box 4).

The different framings of the deforestation issue mentioned in this example are the result of several factors, including the different social conditions, geographical location, economic interests and main values of the relevant actors. These different factors also contribute to making certain cognitive frames prevail in certain societies or in certain social groups. An 'ecological cognitive frame' will thus interpret the deforestation issue mainly in terms of environmental protection, such as the need to preserve biodiversity, combat climate change or prevent desertification and soil erosion. A 'human rights cognitive frame' will emphasise the view of deforestation as a danger for and crime against indigenous populations. An 'economic growth cognitive frame' will instead favour the emphasis on deforestation as an economic issue to be dealt with in terms of cost-benefit calculations, trade conditions, and contributions to the gross national product.

Why trees are not only trees

Trees are such concrete and obvious things that it may seem strange to realise that trees are almost never simply trees but may be timber for export/import to one person, carbon sinks to someone else, sacred symbols or aesthetic objects to others, and so on. If trees are viewed differently by different people, 'what happens to trees' is also a matter of different perceptions and evaluations. Cutting down or burning trees can be viewed as a terrible attack on the preservation of biodiversity or on the beauty of landscapes, as a factor that contributes to the risk of global warming, as an action required for the building of infrastructure or for decreasing the debt burden through timber exports, as a direct threat to the survival of populations living in the forest, and so on.

Changes and learning

The way issues are framed is not a static phenomenon. Changes occur all the time, a particular issue becomes more or less important, urgent or problematic, and more or less linked with other issues. At the same time, new issues enter the agendas of governments, international organisations, mass media, business organisations, environmental groups and other collective actors or individuals. These changes require certain conditions. For instance, for an issue to enter the political agenda of governments or international organisations it is necessary that someone pushes to get that issue there. In this respect, John Kingdon (1984) points out the important role of 'policy entrepreneurs', that is, persons who dedicate time, energy and financial resources to advocating the importance of a certain issue. Moreover, several feasibility conditions decide whether or not an issue enters the political agenda as well as the agendas of the mass media, environmental groups, business organisations or scientific communities. These conditions include the resources that can be allocated to addressing a certain issue, and whether the issue clashes with or meets the interests of the most powerful actors in the various contexts. Also, as was mentioned above, certain structural conditions like the transformation of the economy in certain countries and periods of time influence the emergence of new values and issues.

In addition to those conditions that influence the emergence of new issues within the agendas of different actors and within societies at large, the changes in the framing of issues and the very development of new frames involve learning. It is by learning from experience, from new information and knowledge, and from each other's views that new ideas emerge and old problems are looked at in a different way.

Learning is an intrinsically social process. As was pointed out by sociologists like Klaus Eder (1985) and Max Miller (1986), learning can only occur through the communicative experience that takes place in given social and historical contexts. Learning does not necessarily lead to improvements, since one can learn erroneous lessons and negative behaviours, as past and contemporary events (such as wars) have demonstrated. Moreover, learning can be constrained by several factors, such as the resources of the potential learners. For instance, one cannot learn from new scientific evidence or from the experience of others if information is not accessible because of

> **5**
>
> # Learning and 'sustainable development'
>
> The evolution of the 'sustainable development' frame can be schematically summarised as a process in which the opposition between environmental protection and economic growth that was conceptualised in the early 1970s (especially in the 1972 Club of Rome report) is substituted by the idea that environmental protection and economic development are interdependent. Such processes have involved the participation of many organisations and individuals and have been marked by a number of important events, such as the Stockholm Conference on the Human Environment held in 1972 (where the core of the sustainability concept was advanced in the Action Plan), the work of the Brandt Commission and then the Brundtland Commission, the circulation of the Brundtland Commission's report *Our Common Future* (suggesting the most influential definition of sustainable development) and the Rio Conference on Environment and Development. These events represented fora of communication where the individuals and organisations involved learned several, and often different, lessons.
>
> In broad terms it can be said that environmentalists (see, for example, *Caring for the Earth* by WWF) learned that a clear-cut opposition between environment and development was neither acceptable – especially for people in developing countries – nor viable; nobody in fact seemed to be prepared to renounce economic prosperity for the sake of protecting the environment, even though some may be willing to limit it. Economic actors (such as the Business Council for Sustainable Development) learned that environmental concerns had to be taken into account and that the sustainability concept could be used as a means to tackle these concerns without too radically questioning certain economic activities. Policy makers learned that it was necessary to link environmental and developmental issues in order to develop feasible policies and conclude international agreements. A case in point would be the link between CFCs reduction and the transfer of CFC substitutes to developing countries in the context of the international negotiations on the convention for the protection of the ozone layer.

costs or political constraints. Still, learning must be taken into consideration when analysing changes in the framing of issues.

With regard to environmental issues, an especially significant case of 'reframing' that involves learning is represented by the emergence of the concept of 'sustainable development' (this concept is focused on in Chapter 7) (see Box 5).

While the reframing of the relations between environment and development in terms of sustainability represents a remarkable conceptual change with important practical implications, it has not yet led to visible improvements. In fact, putting into practice the idea of sustainable development requires an integration of political will, economic and technical resources, knowledge of natural and social processes and changes in social values and behaviours that is very difficult to achieve.

The theoretical sections have focused on the interaction between science and policy and on the social construction of environmental issues and policy making. We go on now to look at two examples of policy making in order to put some of these theoretical principles into an empirical context.

3.4 Why did the depletion of the ozone layer become a policy issue?

This section and the next attempt to decide whether the suggested theoretical discussion helps us understand why something becomes an environmental policy issue. The examples analysed are drawn from larger and more in-depth case studies on the responses in different countries and by different actors to ozone layer depletion and the Chernobyl accident. Of course, the short accounts and discussions offered in the following pages are necessarily selective. Readers can find more detailed accounts in texts included in the reference list and in other contributions to this book.

The discussion of the ozone layer depletion issue focuses on the cases of the United States, the European Community and the former USSR; moreover, reference is made to the position of some developing countries.

The USA case

In the USA the risk of ozone destruction was first addressed as a policy issue in a Congressional debate on supersonic transport aircraft (SSTs). Following this debate the Department of Transportation formed an advisory panel on atmospheric problems from SSTs. The risk of ozone depletion from SSTs (already indicated in studies by J. Hampson who worked on the possible impacts of nuclear weapons on the ozone layer) was discussed in the influential MIT-based Study of Critical Environmental Problems

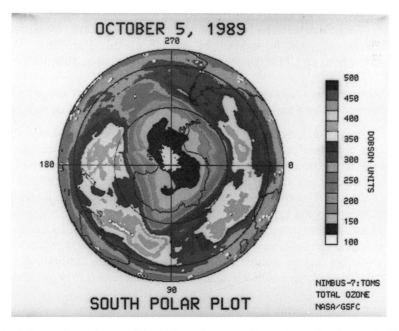

Plate 3.2 Scientific evidence of the hole in the ozone layer above the Antarctic, October 5, 1989. Photo: NASA

(SCEP) of 1970 as well as at Congressional hearings. At the same time, the development of the supersonic Concorde aircraft in Britain and France provided the practical issue to be dealt with; as was mentioned above, that issue was explicitly included in the transport policy agenda. Limitations on or even a ban of Concorde flights and the blocking of funds for SST development in the US were suggested (by governmental agencies and environmental NGOs as well) and were approved in the mid-1970s. In the subsequent years the risk of ozone destruction due to SSTs faded from the US governmental agenda. The fading out can be explained by new research that refuted the hypothesis of the impact of SSTs on stratospheric ozone depletion. It is worth noting that such results coincided with strong economic interests both within the US and abroad (mainly Britain and France).

While the impact of SSTs slipped down the agenda, the risk of ozone destruction due to human intervention did not fade away as a policy issue. In December 1974, a first bill on banning aerosols was presented to Congress. This happened a few months after the publication in *Nature* of the article by M. Molina and S. Rowland, which was the first to point out the role of CFCs in depleting the ozone layer. Besides scientific reviews, Congressional hearings were held on this topic. Since 1974, the depletion of the ozone layer due to CFCs – and other substances discovered later to have an ozone-depleting potential – remained an important policy issue on the US domestic environmental agenda. Local and state bans on CFCs, advocated by, among others, Rowland, were passed in 1974 and 1975, and a Federal ban on 'non-essential' CFC uses was jointly issued by the Environmental Protection Agency, the Food and Drugs Administration and the Consumer Product Safety Commission in May 1977. It also emerged as an important issue in the US external relations environmental agenda (the US led the adoption of the Vienna Convention and its protocols aimed at protecting the ozone layer). These measures had been enthusiastically supported by environmental NGOs and were not strongly opposed by the US chemical industry. (While still lobbying against bans on CFCs, Du Pont announced research on substitutes for CFCs as early as 1976.)

On the basis of this schematic account, the following points can be made with respect to the process by which ozone layer depletion became a policy issue in the US:

○ Scientific models and theories played an important role in 'pushing' the risk of ozone layer depletion onto the US policy agenda; but a difference can be noted between the SST case and the CFC case. In the case of SSTs, it is likely that US economic interests in the transport sector favoured or even determined the introduction of the SST/Concorde issue into the (transport) policy agenda, which means that the reference to and appreciation of scientific evidence can be regarded as functional and ancillary to economic interests. In the case of CFCs, by contrast, scientific input appears to have been the main source of cognitive change, since powerful economic sectors had an interest in preventing, rather than facilitating, the depletion of the ozone layer becoming a policy issue at that time (i.e. before the development of alternatives to CFCs).

○ The importance of scientific inputs cannot be separated from the communication patterns between the relevant actors in producing, selecting and using those data. Policy makers could learn from data because they could and were willing to learn from scientists. This can be explained in terms of the authority and credibility of the relevant scientists, the reliance on science that characterises the US regulatory system, and the nature of a policy making process that involves not only experts and governmental actors but also the mass media – covering the scientific 'news' – and NGOs. These actors referred to scientific evidence to support the call for action.

○ Another point worth stressing is that regulatory experience regarding the control of other health and environmental risks facilitated the transformation of ozone layer depletion into a policy issue. Particularly important in this respect was the previous experience of the Environmental Protection Agency and the Food and Drug Administration with policy instruments such as the banning of certain dangerous substances. An important element enabling a problem to become a policy issue is the possibility of doing something about it. Previous experience with certain instruments represents a valuable source of policy lessons.

○ Finally, as regards the impact of the cognitive transformation of the atmosphere into a policy issue, two main elements are worth noting. First of all, the persistence (and related influence) of ozone layer depletion due to CFCs as a US and international policy issue can be partly explained by the strength of the scientific hypothesis first advocated by Molina and Rowland and then confirmed by monitoring data. Moreover, this persistence was also facilitated by the activism of Rowland himself and other scientists, several environmental NGOs, members of Congress and governmental agencies (and then international organisations, etc.) as 'policy entrepreneurs'.

Secondly, the timing and weight of the policy actions taken in the US to protect the ozone layer once this had become a policy issue can be explained in the light of the viability (administrative, economic, political, social and technical) of the actions proposed. The reasons why those actions were viable in the US context and not in others require explanations in terms of interest, power relations and institutional structures as well as social perceptions and cognitive change. The USA case is explored in more detail in Dickson *et al.* (1992).

The EC case

The first emergence of ozone layer depletion as an EC policy issue was the EC Commission's proposal for a Council Recommendation on 'Fluorocarbons in the Environment', issued in August 1977, that is, a few months after the US ban on non-essential uses of CFCs. In this document the Commission proposed to regulate production capacities of CFCs. In May 1978, the Council issued a Resolution (a non-binding EC measure) based on the Commission proposal. In 1979, a new proposal for a Council Decision on the same subject was made by the Commission. This proposal became the basis of the Council Decision of 1980 on CFCs and the environment, the EC's first binding regulatory action on the subject.

Unlike the US ban, the EC Commission's proposals and the related Council Resolution and Decision focused on limits to the production capacity of fluorocarbons. This was mainly a result of pressure from chemical industries based in EC countries and organised at the EC level, which opposed strict measures. References to the US ban were avoided in the Commission proposal; reference was made instead to actions taken within EC member states (such as voluntary agreements on the reduction of CFCs in aerosol cans adopted in the FRG in 1977). Moreover, the international scientific debate – and especially the existing scientific uncertainties – on the risk of ozone layer depletion from CFCs (including its impact on human health) was mentioned by the EC institutions. Reference was made to studies published by the World Health Organisation and UNEP, and later on to various assessments made in the US and UK on ozone layer depletion (the second questioning the reliability of the first). EC-sponsored research activities relating to ozone layer depletion followed, rather than anticipated the emergence of the ozone issue on the EC policy agenda (unlike the US case and the EC context with respect to other issues such as climate change). The first EC scientific conference on the ozone problem was held in 1981, and EC-sponsored research in the area started in the late 1980s.

The pressure by environmental NGOs on EC institutions with respect to the ozone issue also followed rather than stimulated the start of work on an EC ozone policy. Criticisms and pressure on the EC Commission by groups such as the European Environmental Bureau started in the mid-1980s, especially on the occasion of international events such as the Vienna Convention.

Interesting differences between the EC and US cases emerge from the reconstruction outlined above:

○ First of all, it can be argued that ozone layer depletion became an EC policy issue as a reaction to previous policy actions in the US, in other non-EC countries and in some EC member states. Existing economic interests and the link between the ozone issue and the EC trade policy, rather than reliance on and learning from scientific evidence, appear mainly to explain the emergence of the atmosphere as an EC policy issue. Scientific evidence was referred to in order to justify the response to previous regulatory actions rather than to learn about the nature and seriousness of the risk.

○ At the same time it must be noted that exchange of information and communication between scientists and between governments at the international level favoured the emerging of an awareness of the problem (as the EC Commission proposal of 1977 expressed it, the Commission 'feels that something has to be done' about the ozone layer depletion problem) and the consequent evolution of the EC response. International fora such as scientific and intergovernmental conferences diffused information about the actions taken or planned in some countries regarding CFCs, and spread the scientific, political and/or economic arguments used to support those actions. In this way these channels of communication contributed to the modification of the perception of the interests at stake for the EC countries and institutions, even though the EC initially remained sceptical about the seriousness of the environmental dimension of the ozone issue.

○ Another striking aspect is that, unlike the US case where environmental policy and agencies such as Environmental Protection Agency and Food and Drug Administration were rather well established, the comparatively recent development of EC environmental policy (the first EC environmental action programme was adopted in 1973) limited the EC's opportunities to draw lessons from previous regulatory experience. The as yet weak institutional structure of EC environmental policy (in terms of personnel, budget, etc.) also limited its bargaining power with respect to strong interest groups and the opportunities to make use of lessons that could be 'unpalatable' to those groups.

○ Finally, it must be stressed that EC policy making is a relatively closed process, based on bargaining within and between the different EC institutions, between them and the member countries, and between EC institutions and governments and powerful interest groups. Environmental NGOs, citizens' initiatives and the mass media have easy access to the public aspects of these bargainings, but limited access to and little influence on the informal negotiating process. This situation represents a constraint on the communication process and influenced the way the ozone issue was framed in the EC context. A detailed appraisal of the EC case is provided in Huber and Liberatore (1993).

The USSR case

It is interesting to compare the previous cases with that of the former USSR. Two questions must be asked: 'Why did ozone layer depletion not become a policy issue in the USSR in the 1970s?' and 'Why did it become a policy issue later on?'. These questions can help us improve our understanding of the conditions which allow something to become an issue.

In the USSR, the ozone layer failed to reach the policy agenda in the 1970s. One reason for this is that no one tried to get it there. Scientists studied the problem but did not advocate policy measures to cope with it as Rowland did in the US. Scientific research on stratospheric ozone had been conducted in the USSR since the 1930s, while theories about the risk of ozone destruction by nitrogen components and by freons were discussed in the early 1970s, and a book dedicated to the ozone depletion issue was published by Alexandrov and Sedunov in 1979. The latter referred to the views of those who denied the existence of an ozone layer depletion problem. The late 1970s and early 1980s can be regarded as the turning point in the attitudes of officials in the influential state committee on hydrometeorology, Hydromet. Previously sceptical risk assessments were being gradually transformed into a recognition of the seriousness of the risk and of the need for further research. While environmental protection laws were in place in the USSR at that time, a comprehensive environmental policy and specialised institutions did not yet exist. Thus, there was no governmental agency in charge of environmental protection which could pick up ozone layer depletion as a policy issue, as the EPA did in the US and the Directorate General for the Environment did within the EC Commission. Furthermore, in the 1970s (and up until the late 1980s) the Soviet press did not pay any attention to the ozone layer depletion issue, and environmental NGOs were not in evidence in the USSR in that period. Given this situation, ozone layer depletion was hardly perceived as a risk by large sectors of society. It mainly remained a scientific, 'abstract' issue, dealt with by experts.

On the basis of these remarks, three main elements appear relevant with respect to the framing of the ozone issue in the former USSR:

○ First of all, such framing was determined and constrained by the number and kind of actors involved in the debate on ozone layer depletion. As emerges from the case studies relied upon, the 'ownership of the ozone problem' – as Joseph Gusfield would call it (Gusfield, 1981) – was held by a specific actor group, government scientists. Such 'ownership' was in turn favoured by the hierarchical power structure and the very restricted communication channels (channels mainly linking party and governmental bodies, but inaccessible to most citizens). In other words, structural elements and the tendency on the part of the 'owners' of the problem to regard it as a merely scientific one blocked the transformation of ozone layer depletion into a policy problem in the USSR in the 1970s.

○ With respect to the debate within the scientific community, it can be argued that the competition between different well-established scientific traditions and communities in the USSR and the USA probably limited the willingness of Soviet scientists to acknowledge the importance of results originating in the US. At the same time, this element and some reciprocal diffidence between scientists in different locations limited the circulation of criticisms by Soviet scientists that could have been constructive in the international debate.

○ As regards the later emergence – in the late 1980s – of the ozone layer as a policy issue, the most important factor appears to have been that the new foreign policy agenda formulated by Gorbachev, Shevardnadze and others picked up global environmental issues as a component of the new collaborative view of *perestroika*. The perception and use of global environmental problems within such a context appears to be an interesting case of learning how to reframe and use an environmental problem in a foreign policy context. This process was not limited to the former USSR; it also happened in other countries (including the US and the EC) and characterises the development of an 'environmental diplomacy' worldwide. More detail on the USSR case can be found in Prokop (1990) and Nikitina *et al.* (1992).

Developing countries

The ozone issue was framed in a different way in developing countries like China and India.

During the negotiations on the Montreal protocol on substances that deplete the ozone layer, some Indian officials framed the problem as a 'rich man's problem – rich man's solution'. Chinese and Indian delegates argued that it was unacceptable for developing countries either to have to forego necessities such as the use of products containing CFCs for food preservation and air conditioning or to pay more for CFC substitutes and enrich the very chemical industries of rich countries that had created the ozone problem in the first place (see Benedick, 1991). It was only after a revision of the drafted protocol, a revision that included financial aid and technology transfer provisions more favourable to developing countries, that China and India announced they were ready to accede to the Montreal protocol.

It can be noted that the core of the debate during those international negotiations was the finding of solutions to the problem, rather than the existence of a problem per se. Chinese and Indian delegates did not question that ozone layer depletion was occurring and should be dealt with. What they questioned was a universalistic definition of a problem that in practice tended to be an 'industrialised countries-centred' definition. Ozone layer depletion is a global risk caused by CFCs and other chemicals, therefore everybody must stop using CFCs in the same way. Pointing to the differentiated responsibilities for causing ozone layer depletion and to the different resources available to cope with it, Chinese and Indian delegates pushed for the explicit inclusion of questions of equity in the framing of the problem and of its possible solutions.

Summary

The analysis of the way in which ozone layer depletion became a policy issue in different contexts highlights some general points that relate to the discussion offered in the previous, 'theoretical' sections.

With regard to the interactions between science and policy, the case studies indicate that the way scientific evidence is selected and utilised depends on factors such as the credibility of scientists, the features of regulatory systems, the openness of the scientific and political debate and the economic and political interests at stake.

Another element worth pointing out is that the perception that something could and should be done to combat the depletion of the ozone layer emerged soon after the first scientific hypotheses on this phenomenon were circulated. Regulatory actions and technological options were advocated and implemented at national and international levels. At the international level, the different evaluations of constraints and potentials for action represented a major point of negotiation between developing and industrialised countries.

The last aspect also indicates that, even when a certain problem is acknowledged, the perception of its urgency, priority and links with other problems may differ substantially in different contexts. This aspect is particularly clear in the Chernobyl case.

3.5 Why did the Chernobyl fallout become a policy issue?

The different responses to the Chernobyl fallout represent another interesting illustration of the interplay between science and policy in defining a certain event as a problem or a non-problem. The Chernobyl fallout also represents a transboundary environmental problem that had a 'regional' dimension in terms of actual health and environmental damage, but was global in nature as regards the management of nuclear risks.

During the night of 26 April 1986, an occurrence calculated as extremely unlikely by refined risk assessment studies nevertheless took place. The meltdown at the fourth reactor of the Chernobyl nuclear plant was the beginning of an unfortunately still ongoing story of actual illnesses and deaths, together with deep uncertainties about the longer term consequences of the fallout. Unlike the ozone layer depletion, the Chernobyl accident was an immediately visible event. But, while the catastrophic dimensions of the Chernobyl accident were evident with regard to the impact on the population and the environment in the area near the plant, the transboundary consequences of the fallout gave rise to different interpretations and responses in different countries. A brief account is offered below of the responses to Chernobyl in Italy, the Federal Republic of Germany and France, in order to illustrate the reasons why the same phenomenon was framed differently in these neighbouring countries. More detail will be found in Liberatore (1992).

Plate 3.3 The damaged nuclear reactor number 4 at Chernobyl after the accident on 26 April 1986. Photo: SIPA Press/Sunshine

Italy

The first news of the Chernobyl accident dominated the front pages of the Italian newspapers on 29 April. Data and comments from Scandinavian, Soviet and US sources were reported, together with some reassuring statements from the Italian Minister of Civil Protection regarding possible consequences of the accident in Italy. On the previous day – as the first data on abnormal increases in radioactivity levels in Sweden reached Italy – a meeting had been organised by the Ministry of Civil Protection with experts of the National Health Council (ISS), the Agency for Nuclear and Alternative Energy (ENEA) and its safety division (ENEA-DISP). In spite of some disagreements on the evaluation of the available data, it was agreed to monitor radioactivity levels over the entire national territory.

On 1 May, the newspapers announced that radioactivity levels were increasing in Italy. The following day, the first countermeasures decided upon by the Minister of Health were announced. These included prohibiting fresh milk for children, no selling of leaf vegetables, plus some restrictions on the import of foodstuffs from Eastern European countries. Starting from that day, controversies over the necessity and suitability of countermeasures arose between different Ministers (especially between the Minister of Health and the Ministers of Agriculture and Industry, with the Minister of Civil Protection taking a midway position) and between experts (both between different governmental experts and between them and scientists associated with the environmental movement). Furthermore, in some cases divisions and contrasts between central and local authorities emerged concerning the implementation of countermeasures. This arose partially as a result of the different levels of radioactive contamination detected in different areas, but it was also influenced by different attitudes (more or less prudent) of advisors and politicians in the various regions and municipalities.

Disagreements and conflicts among political authorities and among experts were reported by the mass media, which were, in turn, accused by some politicians and scientists of 'creating' confusion and of alarmism. The media also covered the initiatives taken by the environmental movement, like the mass demonstration (about 150,000 participants) held on 10 May in Rome.

In the meantime, Parliament also addressed the problem of the possible consequences of the Chernobyl accident in Italy and the actions to be taken. During parliamentary sessions in late April and May, leftist parties demanded inspections to verify the safety of the three operational Italian nuclear plants, together with a revision of the national energy plan. These parties, together with the Greens (who were not yet represented in Parliament) and various environmental associations, also promoted a referendum on nuclear power that was held the following year.

Controversies regarding the suitability of the measures adopted by the government at the request of the Ministry of Health continued over the entire period of emergency. The emergency was officially declared over by the Ministers of Health and Civil Protection on 20 May.

On the basis of this account, it can be noted that the Chernobyl fallout was framed in Italy as a national public health emergency. This 'frame' was proposed by some governmental experts (mainly those of Istituto Superiore di Sanità) and authorities (the Ministers of Health and Civil Protection). The antinuclear movement and 'counter-experts' supported it by stressing the danger of radioactive contamination and asking for countermeasures. The mass media covered extensively not only the news concerning the consequences of the accident in Ukraine but also the results of monitoring and the debate on the consequences of the fallout in Italy. In this way they contributed to the definition of the problem as a domestic, as well as foreign, emergency to be dealt with by the public authorities.

This 'emergency frame' was challenged by other governmental authorities (the Ministers of Agriculture and Industry), experts and interest groups (especially farmers). The reasons why it prevailed in spite of the opposition of powerful actors are to be found in several institutional and social factors.

As for the institutional factors, the Health Ministry had a clearly defined legal competence in the protection of the public against ionising radiation. This was very important, given that fallout due to a nuclear accident beyond the national borders was not provided for in the Italian legislation (nor in that of most other countries before Chernobyl). Besides having the legal resources, the Health Ministry also had the scientific ones, in the form of the ISS and the scientists of this institute persuaded the Minister to adopt a precautionary attitude in the face of the uncertainties about the risks due to low doses of radiation. Moreover, the Minister of Civil Protection took a leading role in co-ordinating and centralising information, something that in itself denotes a case of civil emergency.

As regards the social factors, the antinuclear movement was very active in organising demonstrations and debates on the risks of nuclear power and could rely on experts able to challenge the view of those governmental and non-governmental scientists who argued that there was no danger from the fallout in Italy. The mass media provided extensive coverage of the news on Chernobyl, thus rendering 'visible', through words and images, the invisible radioactivity. In this context, and because those most at risk were children, concerns over the possible consequences of the fallout were widespread among lay people. This was taken into consideration by politicians in need of legitimacy.

Federal Republic of Germany

In the FRG the first news on the Chernobyl accident also came on 29 April. In the afternoon, the Federal Minister of the Interior stated, after a meeting with the Radiation Protection Commission –Strahlenschutzkommission (SSK) – that there was no danger for the FRG because Chernobyl was far away. However, he asked the federal and state monitoring institutions to measure radioactivity concentrations. While monitoring was being undertaken, a highly politicised debate (extensively covered by the media) started on the consequences of Chernobyl. The most controversial issue was not so much the possible health and environmental consequences of the fallout, but the necessity and desirability of continuing or ending the production of nuclear power in the FRG. This debate – which was particularly heated also because of the nearness of elections –influenced the decisions on the countermeasures to be taken against the Chernobyl fallout and the different evaluations of the suitability of such measures.

On 2 May, the federal authorities decided, on the advice of the SSK, to control and limit the imports of certain foodstuffs from Eastern European countries, excluding the German Democratic Republic (DDR). Moreover, the SSK recommended a threshold of 500 Becquerel/litre of iodine 131 for milk. The setting of this and other thresholds did not prevent the authorities in the individual states from applying lower thresholds and implementing stricter measures in comparison with those decided at the Federal level.

These were the first signs of a problem that characterised the Chernobyl emergency in the FRG: the conflicts between the federal authorities and some state authorities in deciding about countermeasures, with the related differences in implementing federal provisions at the local level. This problem was only partially connected with the different levels of radioactive contamination detected in different areas. Political disagreements over the nuclear issue were much more important. In general, the states governed by the Christian Democratic Party (CDU), that is, the ruling party at the federal level, applied the recommendations issued by the federal government, while states governed by the Social Democratic Party (SPD) in several cases adopted stricter measures.

In an attempt to control this situation, the federal government asked the state governments on 8 May to implement the new SSK guideline that suggested maintaining a normal lifestyle and a normal diet. The reassuring statements of the government and the SSK were criticised by counter-experts and the Greens.

In the meantime, the federal government's information policy was heavily criticised by the SPD and the Greens for being incomplete as regarded the disclosure of data on the fallout and for being too reassuring about the 'absolute' safety of German nuclear plants. The SPD argued in favour of a moratorium and for a gradual abandonment of the German nuclear programme, while the Greens suggested an immediate 'Ausstieg' (exit) and the antinuclear movement organised several demonstrations asking for the closure of all German plants. The Minister of the Interior and Chancellor Helmut Kohl (both members of CDU) defended the federal management of the Chernobyl emergency and the overall German nuclear policy.

On 4 June 1986, 40 days after the Chernobyl accident, the establishment was announced of a new Federal Ministry for Environment, Nature Protection and Nuclear Safety. This Ministry was given the task of dealing with the consequences of the Chernobyl fallout and with environmental problems in general. Thus, the worries and debates caused by Chernobyl produced, among other things, a new institution.

The German case presents some similarities and some differences with the Italian one. With regard to the way the problem was defined in the two contexts, the following points can be made. In both cases the fallout was regarded as a domestic as well as an external problem, to be dealt with by public authorities and in both cases health protection concerns were at the core of the definition of the problem and of the related measures decided upon by public authorities. These similarities can be attributed to the presence in both countries of scientific advisory institutions advocating precautionary action, as well as a strong antinuclear movement that asked for measures to be taken, and mass media coverage of the fallout contamination and of the debate on nuclear risks within the two countries.

A major difference between the Italian and German cases was over the definitions of the relation between the scale of the problem to be faced and the level of action to be taken. In Italy some contrasts emerged between central and local authorities, but the definition of the problem as a national emergency to be primarily tackled by national authorities was generally accepted. In the FRG, controversies over the proper level of action and responsibility characterised the management of the Chernobyl fallout, with the federal authorities emphasising the national dimension of the problems and the state authorities stressing the local differentiation of contamination and especially the states' responsibilities for dealing with nuclear emergencies. This difference between the German and Italian cases reflects the influence of different administrative systems (centralised *vs* federal) in shaping the framing of unexpected events.

Different social and institutional conditions caused a very different definition of the Chernobyl problem to prevail in France.

France

Chernobyl did not reach the French newspapers until 30 April. Side by side with the first news of the accident, the papers reported the opinion of some French experts who maintained that there was no risk of radioactive contamination in France. On 2 May an editorial in *Le Monde* commented on Soviet information policy and stressed the necessity for transparent information. Criticisms on the attitude to secrecy, regarded as a peculiarity of the Soviet system, were repeated during the days that followed by French authorities and journalists.

During the first week of May, the countermeasures decided upon in some Western European countries like Italy and the FRG were reported on. These measures were attributed by French commentators to panic and to pressure from the Greens.

Regarding the situation in France, the Central Laboratory for Food Hygiene asked its regional sections to 'double their level of attention' in analysing radioactivity levels in food, but no particular countermeasures were taken. The Central Service for Radiological Protection (SCPRI) centralised all the monitoring data.

In the meantime a less than heated debate on the safety of French nuclear plants began. The Greens (not represented in the Parliament), some environmental groups and the CFDT (trade unions linked to the Socialist Party) criticised the declarations made by the safety inspector of EDF (the state-owned nuclear industry), which claimed that accidents similar to that at Chernobyl could never happen in a French plant. But neither the ruling Socialist Party nor the opposition parties showed any doubt regarding the continuation of the French nuclear programme.

In a TV programme on 10 May, the director of SCPRI showed maps of the radioactivity levels in France between 30 April and 5 May. He declared that the radioactive fallout in France had been much weaker than the contamination detected in other European countries, thanks to favourable winds.

Over the following days, the information policy of the French authorities was harshly criticised by environmental groups and several journalists. The accusations previously addressed against the secretive attitudes of Soviet authorities were now levelled at the French ones. Furthermore, signs of widespread distrust in the public authorities started to appear; for example, sales of certain vegetables dropped sharply within a few days, even though no recommendations on this point had been issued by official sources.

Central authorities tried to remedy this situation. On 14 May, the Minister of Industry announced the establishment of an interministerial information structure on nuclear energy. He also decided to forbid the selling of spinach from Alsace. But this last measure raised even greater suspicions about the grounds on which precisely Alsatian spinach had been 'incriminated'.

News of minor accidents which had occurred in French nuclear plants in 1984 and May 1986 rekindled the debate on the French nuclear policy. However, only about 5000 people participated in an antinuclear demonstration in Paris on 24 May.

The most striking feature of the French case is the almost total lack of response, in terms of policy measures and social reactions, in comparison with the Italian and German cases. Evidence shows that this was not due to objective differences. Certain areas of France (Corsica, Var basin, Moselle valley) were as highly contaminated as certain areas in the neighbouring FRG and Italy. Different social and institutional factors favoured the construction of the problem as an 'external' one, and as a non-problem within French borders. These elements include the centralised structure of expertise and data gathering, the less precautionary attitude of French radiation protection authorities in comparison with the German and Italian ones, the relative weakness of the French antinuclear movement (which used to be one of the strongest in Europe in the 1970s) at the time of Chernobyl and the almost unquestioning acceptance of government statements by the French media for about two weeks. It should also be remembered that the nuclear industry provides about 80% of France's electricity. While this situation does not represent an explanation by itself (the German nuclear programme is also economically important), it did contribute to the shaping of the French response to Chernobyl.

Summary

As is clear from the different responses to the Chernobyl fallout, several social, institutional, economic and political factors shaped the framing of one and the same event as a different issue or non-issue in different contexts. It is worth pointing out that the uncertainties related to the risks due to low doses of radiation were differently perceived and used and this made an important difference with regard to the actual measures being taken. In Germany and Italy, influential actors emphasised these uncertainties and advocated the need for precautionary action. In France, the same uncertainties were either downplayed or used to criticise the adoption – on the basis of indecisive evidence – of countermeasures in neighbouring countries. Thus, the Chernobyl fallout proved to be a social construct as well as an actual dramatic event.

3.6 Conclusion

This chapter has discussed and illustrated the reasons why environmental problems should not be seen as given but as socially constructed. Some of the most influential conceptual instruments developed in the social sciences have been introduced and referred to in the context of specific examples.

We started by asking ourselves how something comes to be regarded as a problem, and why. In the discussion we stressed that the way an event is dealt with points to the social conditions that allow something to be seen as a problem at all. The definition of the nature of the problem is also socially constructed. The interface between science and policy has been focused on since it represents an important element in the social construction of environmental problems.

Important factors influencing the framing of environmental issues have been addressed, such as the features of the relevant institutions and political systems, the place of certain issues on policy agendas and priority lists, the communication patterns between different sectors of society, the economic interests at stake and the resources available in different social groups and countries.

A more detailed examination of political and economic factors shaping environmental problems and the formulation and implementation of their solution is provided in the following chapters.

---

*The views expressed are those of the author and do not necessarily represent those of the European Commission.

4

Environmental problems in their political context

David Potter

4.1 Introduction

Environmental problems have 'physical' properties addressed by the natural sciences, and they are shaped by social processes within an international context. These important ideas are elaborated in the first three chapters of this book. Environmental problems also have a political context, another important consideration that has been referred to earlier. In Chapter 1, for example, there is reference to the political difficulties of solving environmental problems through international decision-making processes dominated by 'sovereign' states. Of course there is more to the 'political' than decision making, as will rapidly become clear in this chapter.

Two main questions are addressed in this chapter. The first is: 'What are the main features of the international political context of an environmental problem?' This is a complex question, not least because to answer it requires making clear the meanings of a number of rather abstract concepts like 'political' and 'power'. For this reason, the chapter starts with an example of one environmental problem (section 4.2) which is then used to illustrate the general discussion about main features of the international political context (4.3). We then move on to other examples of environmental problems and their varying and changing political contexts (4.4). The second main question considered in this chapter is: 'What is the significance of the "sovereign" state in relation to environmental problems?' In this context we discuss the theory of sovereignty and look at the state as one of the most important environmental change agents (4.5).

4.2 An environmental problem at Lake Toba

An environmental problem is defined in Chapter 2 as a change in the physical environment brought about by human interferences which are perceived by people to be unacceptable with respect to a particular set of commonly shared norms. What has happened at Lake Toba since 1989 is an example of the development of an environmental problem.

Lake Toba is in North Sumatra (Indonesia), an area known for the rich cultural life of the local Batak people and the great natural beauty of the surrounding countryside and its forests. Since 1989 the area has changed in at least four main ways. (What follows in this section is based on WALHI, 1992.)

First, tropical forests have been degraded or destroyed. Ageing stands of indigenous *Pinus merkusii* (planted during the Dutch colonial period) and mixed hardwoods have been logged extensively. In some cases, the forest has been clear-cut and replaced by fast-growing eucalyptus plantations intended to supply wood for the pulp and paper industry. The former Harianboho Protection Forest near Lake Toba consisting of old-growth trees and a rich biodiversity has been divided by a logging road; on one side are lush natural forests full of animal and plant life and on the other side is a dry, silent eucalyptus plantation. The microclimate has already begun to change; particularly around the plantation, the air and soil are becoming noticeably drier, increasing the area's vulnerability to forest fires.

Second, landslides are becoming more common. The watershed around Lake Toba is mountainous and erosion-prone; the forests are extremely important in preventing siltation in the lake and checking erosion in the mountains. Since 1989, landslides have increased with deforestation. Villages and ricefields have been buried and people killed. On the advice of forestry officials, Batak people in some villages have moved from the traditional multiple-family homes to single-family houses in the Javanese style, and in so doing have had their community life disrupted or destroyed.

Third, the water and the air in the region have become polluted. The colour of the River Asahan began to change in 1989 to dark brown, and the river began to stink due to a pulp and paper factory having commenced operations there. One consequence has been that nearby wells have been polluted, and women and children in the area have had to travel further from their homes to obtain drinking water. Fish populations have declined sharply, threatening livelihoods. Officials in the factory have expressed concern that the stench so nauseates their employees that it affects their work.

Fourth, livelihoods of the local people more generally have been adversely affected. New laws enabled logging companies to 'own' former community forests, as on Samosir Island; local people were then forbidden to enter the forests and wood carvers found they had to 'steal' from 'their' former forest to keep up their traditional craft and means of existence. Basic family needs in Hutagalung village were threatened because the rattan (stems of climbing palms used to make wickerwork, thongs, etc.)culled from the nearby forest by women and then sold in local markets was no longer available. People in Habinsaran village who used to gather incense from the community forest were no longer able to do so.

Clearly, then, this is an example of a developing environmental problem in the sense that there were human interferences in the physical environment perceived by local communities as disrupting commonly shared norms related to work patterns and livelihoods more generally.

What was causing the problem? For the local Batak people what was most visibly disrupting their livelihoods were the men who were cutting down the forests and planting eucalyptus trees. These people worked for a local commercial pulp and paper company called the Perseroan Terbatas Inti Indorayon Utama Ltd or Indorayon for short. Indorayon was one of 30 such companies owned by the Raja Garuda Mas Group chaired by Sukanto Tanoto, the 'timber king' of Sumatra. Tanoto had rapidly made a fortune through his companies. In 1989 Indorayon alone made profits of $53.6 million; this was helped by the fact that production costs at $226 per ton of pulp were the lowest in the world. International bankers and investors had supported Indorayon from the beginning; a consortium of foreign banks provided commercial loans to aid the original investment and the Swiss Bank Corporation in 1992 approved the issue of convertible bonds worth $43.4 million to provide the finance needed to build Indorayon's pulp and rayon plant on the Asahan River near Lake Toba. Tanoto benefited; so did the banks.

People in the Forest Department and other government officials in the Lake Toba area broadly supported the activities of Indorayon. Such commercial activity was consistent with the broad strategy of the Indonesian government to pursue development for the country principally by providing infrastructure to enable the dynamism of capitalist enterprises like Indorayon to flourish. The results of this strategy prior to developments at Lake Toba had been impressive from the government's point of view.

Plate 4.1 Lake Toba, Sumatra, Indonesia. Photo: Randy Topp/Lineair

The average annual growth in Indonesia between 1965 and 1988 had been 4.3% (GNP per capita), one of the highest rates in the world at the time (World Bank, 1990). One aspect of that strategy had been to invite private concessionaires, both domestic and foreign, to 'open up' the forests in 1965. Basic Forestry Law No. 5 of 1967 created vast logging concessions and the concessionaires moved in. By 1979 Indonesia had become the leading exporter of tropical logs in the world, with 41% of the market. Logs were also processed into plywood; by 1985 Indonesia was the world's largest supplier of plywood. The forest business attracted international capital needed to spearhead Indonesian development in other spheres. It also provided foreign exchange to service the mounting debt owed to international, commercial and official institutions. The government's national forestry plan was also linked and shaped by the Tropical Forestry Action Plan sponsored and funded by the World Bank, the UN Food and Agriculture Organisation, bilateral donors including the British government, and others. In all this, the social problems of the indigenous people who had been making a living from the forest received a low priority.

Village people in the Lake Toba region protested to local government officials at the loss of their customary rights of access to the forest and its products, but received little response. They also managed at one point to take Indorayon to court, and, unsurprisingly, the court ruled against them. KSPPM (the Community Initiative Study and Development Group), a local non-governmental organisation (NGO), had worked with some of the local people trying to assist them in their struggle. KSPPM was one of hundreds of local NGOs in Indonesia linked to a national umbrella NGO in Jakarta called WALHI (Indonesia Forum for the Environment). WALHI in turn was linked to international NGOs like NOVIB in The Netherlands, Friends of the Earth (with international headquarters in Amsterdam), which worked to shift the forest policies of powerful organisations at international, national and local levels. Local NGOs in Indonesia have had a tough time against a powerful corporation supported by an authoritarian political regime. KSPPM at Lake Toba, for example, was closed down without explanation by the Indonesian government for six months in 1991 and 1992 and was only allowed to resume its activities on condition that it ended its legal aid programme to the local Batak people.

There are many other people involved in this story of the environmental problem at Lake Toba, some of whom are referred to later.

4.3 Main features of an international political context

What are the main features of the international political context of an environmental problem like the one at Lake Toba? Such features can be derived from a consideration of what the concepts 'international' and 'political' mean.

The word 'international' conventionally refers to engagements or interdependencies involving more than one nation state, at a level 'above' the nation state. The word is also used more generally to refer to both international and *transnational* interactions and associations. An international agreement is an agreement between nation states.

Transnational linkages can be said to bypass governments because they are society-to-society relations, many of which are more or less beyond nation state control. There is an incredible array of such transnational relations, from Shell Oil Company to the International Confederation of Free Trades Unions, the World Council of Churches and the International Red Cross. Some people are beginning to refer to a global politics (McGrew et al., 1992) that includes both international and transnational behaviour. Environmental politics involves both.

There is an ambiguity in the idea of the international context being 'above' the nation state. International contexts of environmental problems include the international/transnational, the national and the local *and the linkages between these different levels*. The environmental problem at Lake Toba brought this out clearly. International processes can also have a spatial dimension; they can press down more or less firmly on different localities at different times.

The key concept in the main question is 'political'. How one uses the concept is of paramount importance in determining what the 'main features' are. Although there is no agreed definition, one can say that, broadly speaking, the political aspect of social life is grounded in the antagonisms and conflicts that are more or less part of any set of social relations and it is about the ensemble of practices, structures, relationships and discourses which establish and maintain some sort of 'order' in such circumstances. Within that general context, for our purposes here, the word 'political' can be said to refer to four main aspects:

○ *steering and choosing*
○ such steering and choosing are determined more or less by *conflicting interests and values*
○ they involve *power relations* within and between *agents*, such as organisations, groups and individuals
○ and they are shaped by *structures of power* – economic, social, ideological, cultural.

Defining 'the political' that way suggests that a description of the international political context of an environmental problem can be framed in terms of these four main features. We consider each of these four in the following sections.

Steering and choosing

The international context of an environmental problem involves steering or governing. The word 'governing' comes originally from the old French *guvernor* which is from the Latin *gubernare* (to steer, pilot, govern), which in turn derived from the Greek *Kybernan* or *kubernao* (which means 'to steer'). Plato, for example, referred to the process of governing as similar to steering a ship at sea ('the ship of state'). Steering a ship at sea requires a number of things, like trying to stay in control in the midst of turmoil, charting a course and trying to achieve an objective (reach a destination). All these are important aspects of political leadership and to that extent Plato's analogy is quite suggestive. But the people being led are missing from this elitist analogy (rather typical of Plato). We prefer the analogy that has been around in Asia for a long time, of the ruler or political leader being like a person trying to ride a tiger in a particular direction, the tiger being the more or less obedient masses who must be coaxed along and who may, if goaded too hard, turn on the ruler and make big trouble. Steering the tiger involves a series of choices over time. If the tiger starts to become agitated, then the leader may choose to slow the pace for a while (e.g. delay action or amend legislation), let the tiger wander temporarily from its intended trajectory (e.g. compromise with the opposition), feed the tiger (e.g. bring out a 'people's budget' just before an election) or get out the whip (e.g. use the police and/or the army to force the people to accept the direction of the leadership). Steering processes are always part of the political context of any environmental problem.

There are always several different sets of organisations, each engaged in processes of steering in accordance with their interests and values, whose actions over time affect the environmental problem in various ways. Three such steering processes were indicated in the Lake Toba case sketched earlier. First, there was the network of institutions (the World Bank, the FAO, the Indonesian government, local government) engaged in trying to steer Indonesian society along a particular course of economic development, the consequences of which were affecting the forests and lifestyles of the Batak people at Lake Toba. Second, there was the network of Swiss Bank, Raja Garuda Mas, Indorayon, and loggers and pulp mill workers steering in accordance with their interests. Third, there was the Friends of the Earth International, WALHI, KSPPM, and local village people who were trying to steer developments in a somewhat different direction.

Steering involves a series of choices over time. Choosing is indeed central to steering. Any agent trying to steer in a certain direction, be it to maintain the status quo or to bring about change, is choosing all the time as it is swept along by the constraints and opportunities that confront it. To choose to steer in one direction inevitably means choosing not to steer in another, and those choices are political because they benefit some people more than others. A set of choices by an organisation, or a network of organisations and groups, over time amounts to a *policy*, defined here as a deliberate course of action by an organisation designed to achieve an objective. Identifying the political context of an environmental problem requires, amongst other things, trying to locate both the relevant agents whose actions or policies affect the problem and the constraints and opportunities that influence the policy choices made.

Conflicting interests and values

Politics is not just about processes of steering and choosing at different levels. The content of any particular environmental policy or course of action by an agent and its supporters usually entails a political project or purpose of some kind that expresses the values and interests and ideologies of those doing the steering, and that may or may not be shared by those being steered. The best way to get at the conflicting interests involved in any political context is to ask: who benefits? In whose interests is that particular environmental policy? Any course of action by a powerful agent that bears on an environmental problem is going to be more advantageous to certain interests and less advantageous to others. For example, take the content of the Indonesian government's policy regarding the forests. Indonesia has the third largest tropical forest area in the world, and the Indonesian government has chosen to use the forests as an important springboard of national development by encouraging policies of large-scale

90

exploitation of the forests for timber with little regard for the economic value of non-timber forest products like rattan and incense or the value of intact forests as a biodiversity bank. The government's policy is to convert the tropical forests into large-scale concessions for commercial exploitation by wood-processing firms. Who benefits? Commercial loggers, industrial wood-processing industries, the banks, urban elites in the cities, others. Who loses? People who have depended on non-timber products from the forests, perhaps eventually people in the North and South who will be affected by global warming, future generations denied the biodiversity inherent in tropical forests, others. The matter is not that simple, and this example can be elaborated considerably; the illustration is only meant to underline the important political point that some benefit from the content of dominant courses of action, or policies, more than others. The political context of an environmental problem always involves manifest or latent conflict between the interests of those who benefit greatly and those who benefit less or not at all.

Conflicts of interest can also divide the North from the South. On the issue of tropical forests, governments in the South are increasingly expressing the view that the North, having historically devastated their own forests and grown rich in the process, are now demanding that the South preserve their forests and stay poor. North-South international conflicts of interest are now a major aspect of the political context of environmental problems. Such conflicts shape policy debates in many settings. For example, at the annual meeting in 1992 of the International Tropical Timber Organisation, comprising representatives of the main producing and consuming states accounting for over 95% of the international trade in tropical timber, there were major disagreements between northern and southern states over a proposed policy to regulate the cutting of timber. The South wanted an 'all-timber' agreement affecting northern and southern forests, the North wanted only a tropical timber agreement.

Political processes of steering and choosing at different levels are shaped by the conflicting interests of those involved. Ultimately, such processes are informed by values. Values are preferences and moral assumptions about what is good or desirable. Any course of action related to an environmental problem is going to reflect certain dominant values and not others. The course of action pursued by the Indonesian government *vis à vis* the forests at Lake Toba rests on a whole set of value preferences which have to do with competition, economic efficiency, the free market, and so on as the desirable way forward for national development and well-being, and at bottom the whole strategy may be said to rest on some moral conception about the value of individual freedom for entrepreneurs and others. Another strategy of development with rather different environmental consequences for the Lake Toba region would de-emphasise such values and give much more weight to sustainable forestry, collaboration, grassroots empowerment, the rights of local communities, and so on. This would amount to a different political project grounded fundamentally in a more egalitarian moral premise.

Naturally, political leaders and others involved in political processes will 'claim to be taking all factors into account when trying to reach a reasonable trade-off between conflicting values and interests' (Goldsworthy, 1988). They will say they are of course 'for' both freedom and equality, 'for' both enterpreneurial enterprise and grassroots empowerment, and so on. But no course of action can be anything like optimal for all the individuals, groups and social classes involved. What is optimal depends on the values you entertain and these differ between agents. Therefore, biases in favour of certain people and not others are necessarily embedded in environmental policies. That is why the environment is an intrinsically political subject.

Differential power of political agents

Various organisations and other political agents inhabit the international political context of an environmental problem. Each agent is engaged in processes of steering and choosing as framed by conflicting interests and values, and each is also more or less powerful.

Power is like the air we breathe; it is everywhere and invisible. There is no universally agreed definition. There are instead a range of related but different definitions (Lukes, 1986, pp.1–4); Robert Dahl, for example, defined it as the ability of A to get B 'to do something that B would otherwise not do' and Nicos Poulantzas said it was 'the capacity of a class to realise its specific objective interests'. What these different definitions share perhaps is the sense that individuals or organisations have power if they have the capacity to shape action. We shall use the word 'power' in this general way in this chapter.

Notice the word 'capacity'. A may have the capacity to shape the action of B, but A may actually do nothing; B's actions are nevertheless shaped by A because of what B thinks A could do. For example, a motorist, B, stops at a red light; the action of the driver is shaped by the power of the state, A, as represented in various ordinances and laws. No police or other state officials are in sight, the state does not act, but the power of the state nevertheless shapes the action of this motorist because of what the motorist thinks might happen if he or she breaks the law. This is what Poulantzas implies when he suggests that the structures of society can give a social class or other social organisation like the state the capacity to realise its objectives without actually 'doing' anything.

In any social context all agents, individuals and groups, may have some power, but of course some have more than others. The more powerful usually have more, or easier access to, political resources, e.g. physical strength, arms, wealth, information, expertise, organisation, charisma, legitimacy, sanctions that can be applied to others, and so on. Measuring precise amounts of power is virtually impossible, but general evaluations of the relative power of any individual or organisation in relation to political resources are feasible.

Political organisation and other political agents

The international political context of an environmental problem will comprise an extravagantly complex array of agents at various levels whose power, and the interests and values that give it direction, impinges on the problem. These agents comprise groups or organisations which either impact directly on the problem or shape the actions of others who are also directly involved. Moreover, these agents are located at different levels throughout the world and linked together by complex networks of communication and affiliation. Some organisations, like the World Bank, are fairly durable whereas others, for example the Rio Earth Summit (though not the subsequent so-called 'Rio-process'), are more transitory. Some have full-time employees organised in bureaucratic hierarchies (e.g. governmental departments), others are informal groupings of volunteers animated by a common concern (e.g. Earth First! in the USA, the Chipko movement in India). There are also influential individuals who belong to no group or organisation.

To identify and delineate the relative power relations between all the individuals and informal groupings and organisations throughout the world that impinge directly or indirectly on environmental problems is beyond the capacity of anyone's political understanding, even in principle. However, it is possible and important to be able to identify prominent features of the international political context of any particular environmental problem.

A useful approach to understanding the international political context of an environmental problem is to start by trying to identify prominent organisations and groups and their relative power at local, national, and international levels and to notice the interdependencies between them. Each organisation or group will be steering and choosing in accordance with their particular interests and values, the consequences of which bear directly or indirectly on the international problem. At each level one should

Plate 4.2 Member of the Batak tribe in the rainforest of Palawan Island, Philippines. Photo: Ron Giling/Lineair

start by locating relevant organisations or groups in at least four different worlds: the world of government organisations; the world of business – industrial, financial and other economic organisations; the world of NGOs – organisations that are non-governmental and non-profit; the world beyond formal organisations, e.g. environmental movements, protest groups, voters.

The local level

Take Lake Toba. At the local level, organisations and groups in all four worlds were pursuing courses of action, in co-operation or conflict with each other, that shaped the problem there. From the world of business, Indorayon steered a course of action in pursuit of their interests in making profits from their logging, pulp and paper activities. Indorayon's interests were in conflict with the interests of local people wanting to use the forests in other ways. Indorayon was able to shape local activities to its advantage in this conflict because it had more power due to its command over substantial political resources in comparison with the limited resources of the unorganised Batak people. It also had the support of the state. Local officials of the Forestry and other departments of the Indonesian government administered the law, including Law No. 5 of 1967 making legal the forest concessions which Indorayon were using to their advantage. The local district court and the High Court ruled in favour of Indorayon when local people brought a case against them. The local police moved in and closed down KSPPM, the local NGO working for the local people against Indorayon, thereby tilting the balance of power even more to Indorayon. Understanding the local political context, and the power relations involved helps to explain why the forests around Lake Toba were being adversely affected.

The national level

Such actions, conflicts and power relations that make up the political context locally do not take place in a vacuum. They are shaped by power relations of the four different worlds of organisations and groups at national level. For example, Indorayon's power locally is much enhanced by its being one of the companies in Tanoto's larger Raja Garuda Mas Group. The government of Indonesia's broad economic strategy, backed by the considerable power of the state apparatus, provides a favourable context for the Group's activities and Indorayon's actions at Lake Toba. The government of Indonesia, however, is not a monolith. It is a very large organisation, or rather set of organisations, and there are conflicts and inconsistencies within it. Thus, Emil Salim, a well-known Minister for Population and Environment for many years (until 1993), used to express himself fairly freely in Cabinet on behalf of environmental concerns, and, although he was highly regarded, he was also regularly overruled by the Ministers for Forestry, Industries and others. Some progressive environmental legislation gradually found its way into the statute books. Emil Salim actually had good connections with all the environmental NGOs in the country, sometimes supporting their activities, at other times disagreeing sharply with them. Such national level tensions and inconsistencies between different Ministries within the government had an effect locally and compromised somewhat the overall power of the local state.

Two NGOs in Jakarta were also prominent at the national level of the political context. One was SKEPHI, a forest-specific NGO. The other was WALHI, an umbrella organisation linking hundreds of local NGOs throughout the country; one of these local NGOs was KSPPM at Lake Toba. WALHI, represented by the Indonesian Legal Aid Foundation, brought a court case against Indorayon, the national Ministries for Population and Environment, Forestry and Industries, the National Investment Co-ordination Board and the Governor of North Sumatra arguing that the Indorayon factory had been licensed without completing an Environmental Impact Analysis required by Indonesian law. WALHI lost the case, but won the right to stand for the environment, thereby setting a useful precedent in environmental law. Through these and other actions by local and national NGOs, the local Batak people could be said at least to have some representation in the Indonesian political arena.

Such representation, even if only rather marginal, is important given the authoritarian character of Indonesia's political regime. Indeed, WALHI and SKEPHI and other NGOs are tolerated by the Indonesian state as useful 'pressure valves' enabling middle class people to let off steam and ventilate their grievances; they are useful precisely because the Indonesian state does not permit competitive elections enabling voters from time to time to shape the composition of the government. Also, civil and political rights appropriate to democratic regimes are severely compromised in Indonesia. Individual citizens have difficulty forming associations of like-minded people to lobby the government. Most people at Lake Toba, in short, have little influence, and this is an important aspect of the distinctive political context of the environmental problem there. Indorayon and the state do not rule supreme, but their capacity to shape action locally to suit their interests is impressive. The political context of, say, a local forest problem in a more democratic setting might look a little different.

The international level

Indorayon and the Indonesian state also do not reign supreme because their actions are shaped by the power of organisations at the international level. Indorayon's behaviour at Lake Toba, for example, was shaped by the need to service the loan from the Swiss Bank Corporation; and the Indonesian state forest policies that affect Lake Toba so profoundly are shaped by a large and complex array of organisations and processes in the international arena. The most important international processes affecting the national state and the company relate to international debt, trade and aid.

As for debt, the data in Table 4.1 show that Indonesia owed over $53 billion to external creditors in 1989 (see column 5); of the ten main rainforest countries in Asia, only India, because of its great size, comes out in the table as more heavily in debt.

The problem for the Indonesian government of servicing that debt jumped substantially between 1980 and 1989 as columns 6 and 7 of Table 4.1 suggest. The Indonesian government has had to find a way to earn foreign exchange to repay rising debts. One thing the government has done is to exploit the large tropical forest (see columns 1–4) for timber and timber-based products, for which there is a substantial demand internationally. Overexploitation is the more appropriate word; Indonesia's deforestation rate of 12,000 square kilometres per year (see column 1) was by far the highest in Asia, and indeed in the world after Brazil. The connection between deforestation and

Table 4.1 Deforestation and debt service ratios in some Asian countries: the 1980s Source: FOE (1992), p. 13. Note: the debt figures were taken from World Bank (1991). The figures related to forest loss are from Myres (1989).

Country	Annual deforestation rate (square kms) 1989	Forest already lost (square kms) 1989	Remaining forest (square kms) 1989	Percent original forest remaining 1989	Total external debt 1989	Debt as a percentage of exports 1980/1989	
Burma (Myanmar)	8,000	225,000	245,000	52%	1,761	25.4	30.4
India	4,000	1,435,000	165,000	10%	62,509	9.1	26.4
Indonesia	12,000	360,000	860,000	70%	53,111	13.9	35.2
Kampuchea	500	53,000	67,000	56%	nd	nd	nd
Laos	1,000	42,000	68,000	62%	949	nd	15.6
Malaysia	4,800	148,000	157,000	51%	18,576	6.3	14.6
Papua New Guinea	3,500	65,000	360,000	85%	2,496	13.8	34.3
Philippines	2,700	200,000	50,000	20%	28,902	26.5	26.3
Thailand	6,000	361,000	74,000	17%	23,466	18.7	15.9
Vietnam	3,500	200,000	60,000	23%	nd	nd	nd

debt has been widely acknowledged; for example, the EC said in 1989 that 'international debt obligations… can lead developing country governments to accelerate the rate of forest exploitation in order to earn needed foreign exchange' (reported in FOE, 1992, p.12), and the Forest Principles agreed at the Earth Summit at Rio in 1992 recognised 'the importance of redressing external indebtedness'. Others dispute that there is a causal connection between international debt and deforestation.

The Indonesian government's rising debts are owed to private creditors, commercial banks, other governments (bilateral debt) and international organisations like the World Bank (multilateral debt). These organisations do not tell the Indonesian government to destroy the tropical forests, but the political leverage they have through Indonesia's debt obligations and the conditions attached to loans shapes the policies of the Indonesian government in the direction of exploiting a primary natural resource valued in the international market. Such international organisations are part of the international political context that affects the thinking of Indonesia's political leadership when they consider the forests in relation to national development strategy.

The Indonesian government also has had to contend with the politics of the international trade in tropical timber governed by the General Agreement on Tariffs and Trade (GATT), the ITTO (International Tropical Timber Organisation), northern governments and intergovernmental bodies. For example, in the decade or so after the

Indonesian government promulgated the Basic Forest Law of 1967, many of the forest concessions from which logs were exported were dominated by large multinational corporations, e.g. Weyerhauser, Georgia Pacific, Sumitomo, Mitsubishi. The economic benefits of these activities for the Indonesian government were modest. In consequence, the government decided in 1980 to ban the export of raw logs from 1985 onwards; they wanted to reap more benefit from the logging industry, build up their pulp and paper industries (which led to the establishment of Indorayon), and capture a larger share of the world plywood market. They also said the ban was environmentally sound. Fewer logs would be needed to earn the same amounts of hard currency. Most of the multinational companies left Indonesia in the next few years for easier profits in Papua New Guinea or eastern Malaysia.

Indonesia's plywood business boomed, most of it involving indigenous companies. In 1987, however, the EC complained to GATT that Indonesia's ban on the export of certain tropical hardwoods violated GATT rules. Eventually, the Indonesian government had to reverse its policy, notifying GATT in 1992 that the ban had been revoked and at the same time announcing also higher taxes on exports of raw timber. Once again, we see the national government's policies in relation to the forests being shaped by the power of international organisations and processes.

As for international aid, probably the most significant instrument affecting the Indonesian government's forest policy has been the TFAP (Tropical Forest Action

Plate 4.3 Commercial exploitation of tropical rainforest, Kalimantan, Indonesia. Photo: Ron Giling/Lineair

Plan) under the direction of the World Bank, the FAO (United Nations Food and Agriculture Organisation), UNDP (United Nations Development Programme), and the WRI (World Resources Institute – a think tank in Washington DC). TFAP is a global mechanism meant to address the problem of deforestation by identifying priorities for action in individual developing countries that aid donors (including foreign governments) can target. About $8 billion was to be spent on such projects from the mid-1980s. Each national plan was to be worked out over a period of time by consultation between foreign experts and international donor agencies together with government officials in the country concerned. The Indonesian National Tropical Plan has not been made public but it is known that the main assumption of the plan is that the forest people, like the Batak at Lake Toba, are targeted as the main problem, not logging companies. There is no mention of the fact that the Batak people have been engaged in sustainable use of the forests for centuries. Here we have an example of international aid flowing in support of a particular view of the environmental problem in the forests that shapes and reinforces the national government's view of it. Such processes are therefore also part of the international political context.

NGOs, North and South, are also part of the international political context affecting national government policy and the actions of companies and corporations working in the forests. Reference was made earlier to such NGOs in the Lake Toba case, e.g. NOVIB in The Netherlands and FOE (International). NGOs and North-South coalitions have continued to press for changes in environmental policy at international levels. They have, for example, been critical of TFAP, e.g. 'the plan not only is failing dismally to meet its objectives, but will actually accelerate the already catastrophic rate of forest loss world wide' (Lohmann and Colchester, 1990, p.92); and 'an ecological Frankenstein has been unleashed' (Rich, quoted in Ekins, 1992, p.150). NGOs have also proposed alternatives, e.g. TFAP should be a bottom-up process involving centrally the people who live in the forests, not a top-down process controlled by northern and southern elites. NGOs lobby at meetings of GATT, ITTO, the World Bank, northern governments. They attempt to shift the activities of companies and corporations; RAN in San Francisco, for example, regularly demonstrates against the Mitsubishi Corporation at trade fairs in the USA, drawing attention to destructive practices of Mitsubishi companies in tropical forests. Such NGOs and NGO coalitions have fewer political resources than governments and corporations and are therefore less powerful, but they do have some influence at times in limiting damage or hastening environmentally friendly decisions which would otherwise have taken longer.

Structures of power

The previous sections have emphasised that the international political context of an environmental problem involves the *actions* of four worlds of political organisations (government, business, NGOs, social movements) and other political actors who, as agents, are more or less powerful at international, national and local levels. This aspect can be referred to as the *agency* of power – the actions of specific organisations or groups that shape behaviour and choices affecting the environment. Dahl's definition of power, referred to earlier, is mainly about this aspect of power – 'the ability of A to get B to *do* something that B would otherwise not do'.

There is, however, another aspect of power. The contemporary international political context of an environmental problem involves structures of power inherited from the past, accumulated legacies of past practice and beliefs and past privilege. Poulantzas' definition of power – 'the capacity of a class to realise its specific objective interests' – is more in keeping with this aspect. He is implying that the structure of society generally can enable a social class, e.g. a capitalist class, to benefit without it actually 'doing' anything. Identifying the international political context of an environmental problem requires being alive both to the agency and structure of power relations bearing on the problem.

Structure and agency are intimately related. Political organisations and groups as agents adopt policies, pursue courses of action, co-operate or run into conflict with each other. Their actions as agents are shaped by structures of power or underlying processes of a more enduring kind over which they have little or no control. For example, WALHI and SKEPHI in Indonesia pursue policies meant to safeguard the tropical forests there and the interests of people who live in them. These NGOs are in conflict with other political organisations and groups, like Indorayon and the Indonesian government, in ways which also have consequences for the forests and the people in them. But this interorganisational activity does not take place in a vacuum. It is framed by structures of power which help to determine the outcomes of political struggles between the groups and organisations by being more favourable to some groups than others.

Four dimensions of power structure can be identified: the economic, the social, the ideological and the political:

○ *Economic structure of power.* All political struggles inhabit, for example, a global economic structure of power, a dynamic world of global capitalism dominated by private ownership, production for profit, the accumulation of profit, competitive struggles between large corporations and companies, reliance by such organisations on wage labour and continuing tensions between owners and workers in such organisations. The Indonesian state is powerfully influenced to manage its economy within that context for that is the world it inherited from the past and inhabits now. Its policies in relation to its tropical forests are shaped profoundly by the constraints of that economic structure. Also, capitalist organisations like Indorayon using the forests for capital accumulation and profit are, broadly speaking, advantaged by that economic structure more than environmental NGOs (which are non-profit) and local people using the forest for their own needs.

○ *Social structure of power.* That general way of organising economic production tends to create and sustain particular social structures of power – class, gender, ethnic and other interlocking inequalities which are relatively entrenched. Powerful interests are served by, and organised in relation to, these structures from which they benefit. By enhancing their power, the social structure enables such interests to have a disproportionate influence on environmental policy.

○ *Ideological structure of power.* Dominant ideologies – sets of collective beliefs – can also be said to form a structure of power. Such ideologies help people to make sense of, and accept, the prevailing social structure from which ruling groups and other powerful interests benefit. There can also be counter-ideologies which question the existing structure and serve the interests of subordinate groups (Ekins, 1992). Environmental movements and NGOs representing them may be said to be advancing new ideologies – new ideas about the forests, for example, which see them not as a resource to be plundered for profit by the few but as a precious asset to be sustained for all for the benefit of present and future generations.

○ *Political structure of power*. Environmental policy makers also must work within the constraints and opportunities provided by political structures of power. An environmental NGO, for example, is confronted by an international system of nation states and other international organisations; even if many NGOs get together they cannot immediately get rid of that system and replace it with, say, an environmentally-friendly world government. Governments, corporations, NGOs and other political organisations and groups must work within that political framework and understand its particular configurations of power in order to advance their particular interests. Similarly, within particular societies, politicians and other political actors inherit a political structure and set of political processes which they cannot do much about, at least not immediately.

Summary

So far it has been suggested that identifying the international political context of an environmental problem requires paying attention to four main features:

○ There are those general processes of steering and choosing by governments, economic organisations, NGOs and other political organisations at international, national and local levels. Such processes produce, amongst other things, environmental policies or courses of action by organisations that cause or otherwise affect the environmental problem.

○ There are the interests and values expressed in the content of such policies affecting the environmental problem and other conflicting interests and values not expressed there. Identifying a political context means comprehending such conflicting interests and values related to the policies of various powerful organisations, and recognising whose interests are better served by those policies.

○ There are the myriad political organisations and other political agencies whose actions affect the environmental problem, each of which is more or less powerful. They can be grouped roughly into the worlds of government, business, NGOs, and social movements at local, national and international levels.

○ There are more enduring structures of power that shape the power and actions of political organisations, determine whose interests and values prevail, and frame the processes of steering and choosing at different levels.

4.4 Political contexts: variation and change

The story of the deforestation at Lake Toba sketched in section 4.2 provided illustrations of the four abstract features of the political context of an environmental problem. Of course, deforestation is only one environmental problem. All environmental problems have political contexts containing processes of steering and choosing at different levels, conflicting interests and values and relations of power. But each political context has distinctive features. In the following section a wider array of examples is used to demonstrate four different dimensions which help differentiate the political context of environmental problems:

○ *Scope and scale of the environmental problem.* First, political contexts vary depend-ing on the scope and scale of the environmental problem. Some problems are global, e.g. depletion of the earth's ozone layer (as discussed in Chapter 3); others are local, e.g. pollution of Brighton beach in southern England. The political context of the former is distinct from the one at Brighton beach because of the sheer number of political agencies involved and the greater complexities of reaching agreed courses of action due to the wider array of values and interests that need to be accommodated. What makes ozone a global environment problem (and pollution at Brighton beach not a global problem)? One of two criteria must be satisfied (Porter and Brown, 1991, p. 15): either the environmental consequences of an economic activity (e.g. producing CFCs and halons) are global or the political actors (state and non-state) involved transcend a single region of the globe. Deforestation at Lake Toba is therefore also a global environmental problem because the political actors involved certainly tran-scend a single region and the consequences of the activity there have at least a mar-ginal impact on the loss of biodiversity and global warming.

○ *Control of the environmental problem.* Political contexts also vary depending on whether or not the activity producing the environmental problem is considered to be under the control of a nation state. Some activity takes place in areas not under such control, like the atmosphere, the oceans and the deep sea bed. Such areas are part of the so-called global commons, and there are distinctive political features of international efforts by so many states to manage the commons (Vogler, 1992). The political context of such problems in the global commons is distinctive by virtue of the relevant conventions and protocols that have been agreed or by the efforts to reach such agreements. We will come back to such agreements in a moment. Other global environmental problems not part of the commons are more firmly under the jurisdiction of nation states. Tropical forests and land degradation are examples. The political context of such problems is distinguished by the greater prominence of states trying to insist on their 'sovereign' right to control their forests or land for their own benefit rather than necessarily in accordance with the interests of some global constituency.

○ *Advancement on the environmental agenda.* Political contexts also vary depending on the extent to which the environmental issue has advanced on the global environ-mental agenda. That agenda has now been agreed, at least in principle, by virtually all of the nation states when government leaders accepted Agenda 21 at Rio de Janeiro in 1992 (see Chapter 1 and Box 1).

Some of the issues in Agenda 21 are further advanced than others, in the sense that they are the subject of multilateral conventions and protocols among at least some nation states. (For detailed discussion on conventions, protocols and other legal instruments, see Chapter 5.) Furthest advanced, perhaps, by the mid-1990s was ozone; fairly tough multilateral agreements had been reached. Other issues were less well advanced. For example, there were no agreed conventions or protocols on freshwater resources and water quality, land degradation and desertification or deforestation and degradation of forests; and there was only a Framework Convention on Climate Change, agreed at Rio. Once conditions and protocols are agreed,then there are implementation stages involving monitoring and verification and political actors working to bring other relevant actors into the agreements in order to strengthen them. The political context of environmental problems can vary depending on whether multilateral agreements are strong, weak or non-existent. Explaining why an environment issue moves from one stage to another involves identifying and analysing its political context, including the transnational political processes relating to that issue.

○ *The 'level' of democracy*. Lastly, the political context of an environmental issue can vary depending on whether the political regime involved is more or less democratic (see Box 2).

Democratic regimes may be more open and less secretive, with more independent and outspoken media, and are therefore more willing to accept the monitoring and verification procedures that are an essential element in implementing and ensuring the credibility of multilateral environmental agreements. Democratic regimes are also more likely to enable environmental NGOs to flourish, and to be allowed to participate in environmental policy making. Democratic regimes, however, do not necessarily always provide environmentally advantageous political contexts. Also, environmental disasters may be so palpable that they will achieve prominence on the political agenda regardless of whether a regime is democratic or not. Despite such ambiguities regarding the general relationship between democracy and the environment, it is clear that the political context of an environmental problem, including the relative power of different political organisations and groups, will look somewhat different depending on whether relevant political regimes are more or less democratic.

Environmental issues in Agenda 21

Agenda 21 is a long document but one can say that there are broadly ten issues on the global agenda:

○ atmosphere pollution
○ ozone depletion (in the stratosphere)
○ climate change
○ marine pollution
○ freshwater resources and water quality
○ land degradation and desertification
○ deforestation and degradation of forests
○ loss of biological diversity
○ environmental disasters
○ environmentally sound management of toxic, hazardous and radioactive wastes.

See: Tolba (1992).

What is a democratic regime?

Democratic regimes are distinguished by at least the following: rulers are accountable to the ruled through representative assemblies and governments formed at regular intervals through competitive elections based on universal adult suffrage involving multiple political parties providing reasonable choice for the voters; there is a diversity of power centres within the state and in society generally; there are guarantees in law of civil and political rights and freedoms; there is political participation by people throughout society in collective decisions that directly affect their lives. Democracy has historically been about lessening the unequal distribution of power, about the empowerment of subordinate classes and groups through the vote, representation and increased political participation in the collective concerns of society (Rueschemeyer et al., 1992).

Changing political contexts

A point which needs to be emphasised is that political contexts change through time. Take, for example, in reverse order the four points just made about the variability of political contexts.

First, political regimes can change as authoritarian regimes move in a more democratic direction, a process of political change called democratisation. In the 1990s democratisation has been occurring in a number of countries in Eastern Europe, Asia and elsewhere, and there have been a number of attempts to explain this phenomenon (e.g. in Held, 1993). It is possible that the potential for more effectively tackling environmental problems in these regions may be enhanced as democratisation proceeds. Then again, it may follow that environmental problems will not be tackled, at least not at first.

Second, political contexts change when conventions and protocols are agreed. Parties to such agreements then begin to meet on a more regular basis to discuss both the implementation of the environmental agreement and strategies for getting other relevant political actors to join. Changing legal and other constraints also changes the political context. For example, the Montreal Protocol on Ozone in 1987 committed signatories to specific reductions in CFC and halon manufacture. The 1990 London Conference then tightened these regulations, committing developed country signatories to a complete phase-out by the year 2000 and the possibility of economic sanctions in cases of non-compliance. The political context of the ozone problem by the mid-1990s had changed considerably from what it was only ten years previously.

Third, political contexts of environmental problems in the global commons change as the technological capability to exploit the commons increases. For example, traditionally the ocean commons were open to all for use beyond the famous 'three mile limit', the reason being that the prevailing technology was such that anyone's cannon shot could not travel further than about three miles. More recently, new technologies have changed the nature of the ocean commons and the uses made of it, some of which are polluting, and these dangers have stimulated multilateral conventions and protocols regulating activities at sea, e.g. the 1972 Convention on the Prevention of Marine Pollution by Dumping of Wastes and other Matter; the 1976 Convention for the Protection of the Mediterranean Sea against Pollution, and several related protocols.

Fourth, the political context of environmental problems is changing as the scope and scale of economic and technological activity, and its adverse environmental consequences, are increasingly globalised. This has led to the increasing globalisation of environmental politics. One consequence of this is that there has been a marked increase lately in co-operative endeavour by states and international agencies in the form of agreed conventions and protocols, which are seen as necessary to deal effectively with many contemporary environmental problems. In short, political contexts are changing as 'sovereign' states acting alone find themselves unable to cope with environmental problems having global causes and consequences. This leads to the subject of the final main section of this chapter.

4.5 Sovereignty and the state

The nation state (and its power) has figured importantly in the discussion so far. Notice that the state's power is conditional (see Box 3). The state *seeks* predominance and *aims* to institute binding rules. What this underlines is that the state's predominance may be strong and effective, but it may also be weak and reflexive, so weak indeed that the state's power may really be of little consequence beyond the walls of the political leader's compound.

Conventionally allied to the idea and reality of the state, but distinct from it, is the theory of *sovereignty*. This amounts to a claim by the state to supreme authority over the people within its jurisdiction and over the course of events (both social and physical) within its domain (Camilleri and Falk, 1992). This claim by each state is legally recognised in principle by all the others, creating a world partitioned into separate domains with (in principle) uncontestable physical boundaries, each sovereign state having supreme authority over its particular society, economy and ecology.

3

What is the state?

The state is an ensemble of political institutions – coercive, administrative, legal – distinguished from other organisations in society in 'seeking predominance over them and in aiming to institute binding rules over the activities of other organisations within its boundaries' (Azarya, 1988, p.10). Each state also aims to provide security from foreign intervention for people within its boundaries by conducting relations, both peaceful and warlike, with other states. A state also seeks continually to promote a sense of national identity and common citizenship in order to have its rule accepted by the people (or at least some of the people) as legitimate, and in doing so to define away or suppress competing ideologies subversive of the state's rule and what the state defines as 'the national interest'. This process of legitimation is central to the reproduction through time of any state form.

The theory of sovereignty not only sharply delimits space in this way; it also presupposes that the state's supreme authority extends indefinitely backwards and forwards in time. State leaders have regularly proclaimed their 'sovereign right' historically to such control, free from 'outside interference' in the country's internal affairs. Over time, these ideas have become an important ingredient of the state's political consciousness, invoked frequently by political leaders to explain and justify state policies and actions and widely believed in society more generally.

Despite the power of the idea, the theory of sovereignty has always been a legal fiction. Historically, powerful states have intervened repeatedly in the affairs of weaker states; and the legal sovereignty of a state has always been more or less compromised in practice by transnational economic and social processes. Although thoughtful observers have always recognised the 'tensions between interdependence and sovereignty in world politics' (Di Muccio and Rosenau, 1992), by the 1990s the mismatch between the theory of sovereignty and the political reality of the modern world was becoming increasingly obvious. President Bill Clinton remarked in his Inaugural Address in January 1993 that 'there is no clear division today between what is foreign and what is domestic'. In Europe in the 1990s, it has been argued that 'all *significant* societies are either larger or smaller than the nation state' (Mulhern, 1993, p.199). The mismatch is nowhere clearer than in the difference between the description of reality implied in the theory of sovereignty and the dynamics of the environment.

It is transparently clear that environmental problems, their causes and consequences do not come tidily packaged within the confines of states. The previous three chapters have made this abundantly clear when considering the depletion of the ozone layer, acid rain, and many other environmental problems. Even the problem at Lake Toba, seemingly a very local affair within a nation state, is seen upon careful examination to be shaped by an international political context. States rarely have 'supreme authority' over environmental problems, as the theory of sovereignty presupposes, because their environmental policies are determined more or less by international debt obligations, international trade arrangements, other international economic agreements and conditions, international security arrangements, international environmental conventions or protocols and broader class structures as well as domestic political considerations.

This does not mean that state power is of no consequence. Indeed, states are still more or less autonomous and powerful within the international political context and what they do or fail to do can have major positive or negative impacts on environmental problems. But states are not sovereign even though state leaders still like to proclaim that they are. Even with regard to those environmental problems, where the state apparently rules supreme, the theory of sovereignty is misleading (see Box 3).

Nuclear power provides a good example. This would appear to be pre-eminently a matter in which each state has had 'supreme authority' (sovereign power) to opt for a nuclear industry, develop it, control crucial aspects of the nuclear fuel cycle even after transferring some aspects of it to private companies, defend nuclear power by obscuring from public view its environmental hazards, and so on. Yet even nuclear power has an international political context. For example, the apparent freedom of the state to determine a 'need' for nuclear power has often been shaped by strong pressure from external nuclear vendor companies, who work with international banks to provide low-interest loans to enable states to purchase nuclear reactors on favourable terms. Such foreign technologies, once obtained, can lead to the receiving state relying increasingly on international vendor companies for expert advice, replacement parts, maintenance, and so on (Camilleri and Falk, 1992, p.189). Attempting to understand the causes of state decisions about nuclear power is not helped by a theory of sovereignty which ignores the international political and economic context in which the state acts.

Nuclear power also provides a classic example of how the theory of sovereignty fails to cope with environmental consequences. As Chapter 3 shows, when the Chernobyl reactor near Kiev caught fire on 26 April 1986, it spewed clouds of radioactive gases into the air for ten days which drifted easily across many states in Europe and elsewhere causing significant increases in radiation levels and threatening the lives of state citizens. It was a stunning demonstration of the mismatch between the theory of sovereignty and the reality of modern technologies which can pose environmental risks beyond the control of any one state.

Implications for the theory of sovereignty

Generally, then, the theory of sovereignty is a poor guide to the role of the state in environmental problems. More than that, it is actually misleading because it can obscure both the causes and the consequences of such problems. In addition, according to Camilleri and Falk (1992, Ch.7), there are at least three other implications to be drawn from the theory of sovereignty that have adverse consequences for environmental problems and political efforts to cope with them.

First, the theory insulates the state from the international environmental consequences of its actions. Each state claims the 'sovereign right' within its domain to make decisions on complex environmental problems. Such decisions may have appalling environmental consequences for people living beyond the state's domain, but the theory of sovereignty enables that state to defend such decisions as legitimate choices by a sovereign power with supreme authority. Furthermore, other states in principle respect their sovereignty.

Second, the world being divided into many sovereign states, each respecting the sovereign right of others, makes for a formidable impediment to concerted action to meet environmental challenges transcending state boundaries. Anyone who has been involved in trying to orchestrate interstate agreements in the form of environmental conventions and protocols can attest to the difficulties posed by representatives of states insisting on not compromising their 'sovereign rights' over activities within their domain. The history of such agreements that have been reached has been marked by efforts to overcome what can be called the discourse of sovereignty. For example, the negotiations between France, The Netherlands and Germany on measures to protect the Rhine against pollution eventually had to rise above the sovereignty discourse; according to that discourse, France, for example, could do what it liked in relation to a river flowing through its domain. As one expert remarked after an interstate agreement about the Rhine had been reached, 'legal developments concerning protection of the Rhine against pollution show that nothing can be done in this field at the national level. Pollution control in Europe requires international co-operation ...' (Kiss, 1985, p.637).

Third, a collection of many sovereign states each with their own laws and regulations enables organisations whose activities are polluting or otherwise environmentally damaging to move from countries that adopt strict environmental controls to other countries whose laws are less strict. In this way, the theory of sovereignty serves the interest of a transnational polluting industry, for example, by enabling it to argue that the state to which it has shifted its operation has the sovereign right to decide what laws and regulations are best for its particular domain, and that we, the polluting industry, are merely pursuing our legitimate interest within the laws of that state. An example is Union Carbide locating one of the dirtier aspects of their pesticides business in Bhopal, India, where enforcement of national legislation to regulate safety measures at pesticides factories was not rigorous. In 1984 an emission of lethal gas at the Union Carbide plant in Bhopal killed an estimated 3000 people (at least), injured at least 200,000 more, and had devastating environmental consequences (Shrivastava, 1992).

The theory of sovereignty – that states have 'supreme authority' within their boundaries – is both a legal fiction and a powerful idea with important environmental consequences. It is fiction because the state has never had such supreme authority and people and environments within states have always, and increasingly today, been affected by transnational processes over which states have little or no control. It is still a powerful idea, however, because many state leaders regularly proclaim as real their sovereign right to determine the destiny of the national community (even though they know better), many people still actually assume (without really thinking about it) that states have such supreme authority, and leaders of other states continue to respect (or at least pay lip service to) the claim because it strengthens their own claim and sense of self-importance. As the 20th century draws to a close, the charade of sovereignty is being increasingly exposed by global economic processes of production and exchange beyond state control, by global political processes that shape what states can and cannot do, by modern technologies that 'shrink the globe' and ignore the state, by environmental problems whose causes and consequences implicate many states, and by other globalising processes.

It does not follow from this exposé of the theory of sovereignty that the state itself is becoming increasingly unimportant. The idea of the state and the theory of sovereignty are two quite separate things, as was made clear earlier. States are not sovereign but they are powerful, and in some settings very powerful, within international political contexts. Indeed, a smaller or weaker state may actually become more powerful or influential when it abandons the pretext of sovereignty and joins other states in forming interstate agreements binding on all of them.

Within international political contexts the state can be profoundly important in relation to environmental problems in three general ways. First, the state as a *powerful agent* in society can adopt and implement policies nationally or locally that directly cause environmental problems or exacerbate ones that already exist. The British government during the 1980s and early 1990s, for example, pursued a policy (pressed on it by the Central Electricity Generating Board) of not fitting antipollution equipment to its largest power stations. The possible effects on trees in Norway, Germany and other European countries downwind of these power stations had been widely publicised for years. Less well known until recently was the effect on British trees; a joint survey in 1993 by the EC and the UN Economic Commission for Europe reported that the proportion of trees moderately or severely affected by ' blight' was higher in Britain than in any other of the 34 European and former Soviet countries surveyed, and that virtually all scientific and other experts in Europe (apart from the state-owned British Forestry Commission) were now almost certain that the 'blight' throughout Europe was caused principally by that noxious brew of pollutants to which the British power stations made such a significant contribution (Lean, 1993).

Of course, the state as a powerful agent in society can also adopt and implement policies that directly contribute to the solution of environmental problems or result in distinct improvements. For example, the implementation of the Clean Air Act passed by the British Parliament in 1956 contributed (along with changes in central heating fuels, fewer sources of industrial pollution and lower density developments) to the gradual reduction in levels of coal dust that had hitherto afflicted the people of London.

Second, the state can deliberately provide an *enabling structure* for other organisations and groups in society whose actions directly affect environmental problems. One such enabling structure is the particular content and character of the law and of law enforcement agencies administered by the state which non-state economic organisations, NGOs and others can use in various ways which have direct consequences for the environment. Another enabling structure may be said to be the set of economic policies favourable to capitalist accumulation, including policies to control the labour force, which provide essential infrastructure for capitalist economic development which may or may not be environmentally sustainable. An illustration from this chapter of how important both these enabling structures in combination can be is the way in which the Indonesian government in 1967 created vast logging concessions in much of the country's tropical forest which enabled private capitalist logging companies to move in and make huge profits with devastating environmental consequences at Lake Toba and elsewhere.

Third, the state can be a *structural obstacle* blocking advances towards more environmentally sustainable forms of development. In this aspect, the state neither deliberately creates enabling structures nor actively makes environmental policy. Instead, it does nothing (structural power), but its sheer presence blocks avenues of advance for people whose livelihoods are threatened by disturbances of physical resource upon which they depend and who want to do something about it. When the state is perceived by ordinary people – peasants, workers, others – as such an obstacle, then forms of collective struggle may be generated which combine defence against further threats to their livelihoods with resistance to the structures of the state and the power of capitalists and landlords who benefit from those structures (see Box 4 for an example).

This example of Chipko shows that the three aspects of state power are not mutually exclusive; through time the Indian state moved from being a structural obstacle to initiating as an agent a particular course of action. Furthermore, a state can even be simultaneously a powerful agent regarding environmental problem A, provide an enabling structure for environmental problem B, and be a structural obstacle for environmental problem C. Whatever the combinations, it is clear that the power of the state in relation to environmental problems is such that it can both be a major part of the problem and provide a major part of the solution. The state through its actions or sheer presence can do great environmental damage, but state policies can also be

---

4

The emergence of Chipko Aandolan (literally translated as the 'hugging' movement) in the foothills of the Garhwal Himalaya

In India in the 1970s, in response to growing threats to their livelihoods from logging operations and growing dissatisfaction about the distribution of profits from forest resources to forest contractors through the 'contract system' maintained by the state, village people, especially women, began to hug trees identified for the chop and these actions were so successful that they spread more widely in the Himalaya and elsewhere in India (Khator, 1991; Guha, 1991). The targets of the movement included state officials, who were perceived as in alliance with the contractors. Chipko became an environmental movement, a struggle against economic exploitation, and more generally an effort to undermine the structural obstacle of the Indian state. Eventually, in 1980, the state stopped being an obstacle and acted (a little). The Prime Minister (Indira Gandhi) declared a temporary ban on logging in the Garhwal Himalaya.

---

environmentally beneficial and when international environmental protocols are agreed to control certain activities having adverse environmental consequences, it is currently only the state which is in a position to enforce such agreements.

4.6 Conclusion

This chapter has dealt with two main questions:

❍ What are the main features of the international political context of an environmental problem?
❍ What is the significance of the 'sovereign state' in relation to environmental problems?

In approaching the first question it was necessary to define the word 'political' and then to use the definition to suggest that an environmental problem always has a political context because it is affected by processes of steering and choosing which are favourable to certain interests and values (and not others) and which involve relations of power. In dealing with the first question it was suggested that the tough business of identifying the international political context of an environmental problem means paying attention to those four main features in the definition of the word 'political' as they relate to the problem. The example of the environmental problem at Lake Toba was used here.

As for the second question it was argued that states are not 'sovereign' in the sense of having supreme authority over people and events within their boundaries, even though many people still believe that states are sovereign and this belief has environmental consequences. But although not sovereign, states are certainly more or less powerful and autonomous within international political contexts, and they have the capacity to affect environmental problems positively or negatively in profoundly significant ways by virtue of their power as agents and structures.

So what? Does knowing about the political context of environmental problems actually matter to anyone besides academic people who write chapters in books? The answer is that it matters very much to anyone wanting to understand who or what is causing an environmental problem. If people in an NGO, for example, understand that the causes are at least partly political, and if they perceive correctly who or what they are up against politically and who or what to target, then they are more likely to work collectively in ways that may result in their being more successful in achieving their objectives.

Acknowledgement

This chapter is based in part on research supported by the Economic and Social Research Council of Great Britain under its Global Environmental Change Initiative Phase II, which financed an Open University research group (of which the author was a member) during 1993–95 working on the subject 'Setting environmental agendas: NGOs, democracy and global politics'.

5

Principles of international environmental law

Menno T. Kamminga

5.1 Introduction

In the foregoing chapters we have seen that adequate protection and improvement of the environment, and the achievement of sustainable development on a global scale, will require a considerable amount of international regulation. Whales cannot be saved and CFCs are unlikely to be banned as a result of spontaneous domestic action alone. This is why there is a need for international environmental law. International law is the body of rules which are legally binding on states in their intercourse with each other (Jennings and Watts, 1992, p. 4). International environmental law is the corpus of international law relevant to environmental issues (Birnie and Boyle, 1992, p.1). A lawyer's answer to the question, 'What are international environmental problems and why are they important politically?', might be as follows. International environmental problems are those over which conflicts of interest are arbitrated and reconciled by the development of international legal agreements between contending parties.

This chapter provides a perspective of international environmental law as it has developed so far. As we shall see, the typical lawyer's approach is to identify and help to create relevant standards and also to contribute to the implementation and enforcement of those standards.

The history of international environmental law stretches back to the beginning of the 20th century. At that time, states began to find it convenient to conclude international agreements on environmental matters that could not be adequately dealt with on a purely national basis, such as transboundary water pollution and the protection of certain migratory species (whales, seals, birds). However, until the late 1960s, attempts to respond to environmental problems through international law and international institutions remained limited to ad hoc responses to certain issues. The development towards a more integrated legal approach to the management of the biosphere owes much to the political push generated by two major international conferences.

The 1972 UN Conference on the Human Environment held in Stockholm is rightly regarded as the starting point of the development of modern-day international environmental law. The Conference marked the worldwide recognition of the environmental crisis as a matter of international concern, requiring an integrated international response. The Conference adopted a Declaration on the Human Environment containing principles which, although not binding by themselves, subsequently inspired or explicitly found their way into a large number of binding international instruments.[1]

Two decades later, the 1992 UN Conference on Environment and Development (UNCED), held in Rio de Janeiro, constituted the second major milestone in the development of international environmental law. This Conference focused on the linkage between environment and development and the need for sustainable development, as set out in the 1987 Brundtland Report. This approach was reflected in the Rio Declaration on Environment and Development, containing 27 principles, which may be regarded as the successor to the Stockholm Declaration.[2]

These international conferences stimulated the development of international environmental law. This chapter gives an impression of the most important institutions dealing with lawmaking (5.2), describes the main features (5.3) and considers the general principles of international environmental law (5.4). Our discussion is guided by the question: 'What progress has been made and what has been the actual result?'.

5.2 International institutions

The absence of international institutions with effective legislative and executive powers has encouraged a tendency for international law generally to develop in a haphazard, unco-ordinated manner. International environmental law is no exception to this. States have so far resisted the establishment of an effective international agency with overall responsibility for dealing with environmental issues. The United Nations Environmental Programme (UNEP), set up in the wake of the Stockholm Conference, is not a UN specialised agency but merely a 'programme', without executive powers and with a budget that is to a large extent dependent on voluntary contributions from states. UNEP's main purpose is to promote better co-ordination between existing UN programmes in the field of the environment, rather than to develop its own programmes. Nevertheless, UNEP has gradually managed to carve out a useful role for itself by taking the initiative on such issues as the control of transboundary movements of hazardous waste and the protection of the ozone layer.

The need for the co-ordinating role performed by UNEP becomes evident if one considers the large number of international agencies that contribute to the creation of international environmental law. The International Maritime Organisation (IMO), the key organisation with responsibility for the protection of the marine environment, has promoted the adoption of numerous conventions in this field. The Food and Agriculture Organisation (FAO) has been active on subjects such as deforestation and conservation of fisheries. The World Meteorological Organisation (WMO) plays a key monitoring role in the field of climate change and global warming. The International Atomic Energy Agency (IAEA), although not initially much concerned with environmental issues, has begun to adopt conventions on the subject in the wake of the

Chernobyl disaster. Similarly, the World Bank or International Bank for Reconstruction and Development (IBRD) has in recent years begun to pay more attention to the environmental side effects of its lending policies.

One important outcome of UNCED was the establishment in 1993 of the UN Commission on Sustainable Development. The Commission consists of 53 member states elected for a period of three years. It reports to the UN Economic and Social Council (ECOSOC) and its mandate is to monitor the implementation of Agenda 21 (UNCED's programme of action). This means that issues relating to environment and development have now been provided with a much higher profile within the United Nations organisation itself.

Outside the UN system, regional organisations which have adopted significant legal instruments in the field of the environment include the Organisation for Economic Co-operation and Development (OECD), the Conference on Security and Co-operation in Europe (CSCE) and the Organisation of African Unity (OAU). The environmental policy of the European Union is in a category of its own and will be discussed in more detail below.

Non-governmental organisations (NGOs) frequently have consultative or similar status at international conferences, and may have a considerable impact on the proceedings, depending on the quality of their research and the sophistication of their representations. NGOs which have had such impact include the International Union for the Conservation of Nature (IUCN), Friends of the Earth (FOE) and Greenpeace International. For example, Greenpeace played an important part in ensuring the ending of sea dumping of nuclear waste in 1987.

International disputes relating to environmental issues tend to be resolved through ad hoc negotiations between the parties concerned. In principle, states are free to resolve such disputes by whatever peaceful means they find appropriate and they are not bound to accept any compulsory settlement procedure. Accordingly, the International Court of Justice in The Hague does not have automatic jurisdiction to adjudicate international environmental disputes but can only do so with the consent of the states involved. In an apparent attempt to attract more environmental cases the Court recently decided to establish a standing specialised chamber composed of seven judges to deal specifically with such cases.[3] One environmental dispute pending before the Court is that between Hungary and Slovakia, regarding Hungary's decision to abandon, on ecological grounds, the Gabcikovo-Nagymaros dam project in the Danube. Slovakia maintains that Hungary has thereby breached its treaty obligations (see Box 1).[4]

The European Union as an international institution

The European Union is a peculiar type of international entity. The extent to which it can still be qualified as an international organisation is debatable. However, for our purposes it is sufficient to recognise that environmental measures taken by the European Union and its predecessor, the European Community, share many characteristics with international environmental law produced by other international institutions. It is no coincidence, for example, that the European Community's first environmental action programme was adopted in 1973, one year after the Stockholm Conference.[5]

If success is measured by regulatory output alone, the European Community's

---

The Gabcikovo-Nagymaros dam dispute

I

In 1977, Czechoslovakia and Hungary concluded a treaty which provided that they would jointly build a system of dams and locks in the Danube between Bratislava and Budapest. The purpose of the project was to improve navigation and irrigation, to generate electricity, and to provide better protection against flooding.

In 1989, Hungary suspended all construction activities relating to the project because it had become convinced of its undesirable ecological consequences. Several rounds of negotiations followed in which the two governments failed to reach agreement. In 1992, Hungary formally terminated the treaty.

In 1993, Hungary and the Slovak Republic decided to jointly submit their dispute to the International Court of Justice in The Hague. They agreed to accept the judgement of the Court as final and binding. The key question put to the Court was whether Hungary was entitled to suspend and subsequently abandon work on the project.

Hungary's main legal argument is that there have been fundamental and unforeseeable changes in circumstances since the treaty was concluded in 1977. First, the two countries no longer have communist governments and the treaty's objective of 'socialist integration' no longer pertains. Second, the importance attached to ecological considerations has increased dramatically since 1977. These two factors (communism and the absence of ecological considerations) constituted an essential basis for the consent of the parties. Because they no longer apply, the parties should no longer be bound by the treaty.

The dispute therefore highlights a conflict between two opposing interests of the international community: stability in international obligations on the one hand and flexibility in adapting to new circumstances on the other. The Court has not yet pronounced on the dispute.

---

environmental policy has been a great success indeed. More than 200 binding instruments, many of them very specific, have been adopted so far, covering literally all aspects of environmental policy (see Freestone, 1991, pp. 135–54; Krämer, 1991, pp. 151–84). This has had a major domestic impact on member states of the European Union. Their room for manoeuvre in the field of environmental policy is largely determined these days by what has been decided in Brussels.

Remarkably, much of this has been achieved without a proper legal basis. Although environmental protection was not among the objectives included in the 1957 EEC Treaty, the EC's Council of Ministers decided in 1973, when adopting the first environmental action programme, that the objectives contained in Article 2 of the EEC Treaty, in particular a harmonious development of economic activities and a continuous and balanced expansion, could not be achieved without a proper environmental policy. The lack of explicit provisions on the environment in the Treaty of Rome was therefore not considered a decisive impediment to Community action in this field. Specific environmental provisions were added to the EEC Treaty only in 1986 by way of the Single European Act[6] and in 1992 by way of the Treaty of Maastricht.[7]

Against this background it should cause no surprise that in striking a balance between economic and ecological objectives EC environmental policy has long

---

Economic versus environmental objectives: two examples

2

In the Danish bottles case, the European Commission argued that Denmark had violated Community law by creating a system whereby beer and soft drinks could only be marketed in reusable containers that had been approved by the Danish authorities. In the view of the Commission, this unduly restricted the free movement of goods into Denmark. The Court ruled that while the deposit-and-return system was acceptable in itself, the fact that only approved containers could be marketed was disproportionate to the objective pursued. The Court did not accept the Danish argument that, for the system to work effectively, it was necessary to restrict the number of different bottles to about 30.[8]

In the Wallonian waste case, the European Commission maintained that by prohibiting the importation of waste into the region of Wallonia, Belgium had acted contrary to Community rules providing for free movement of goods. The Court decided that the prohibition was justifiable with regard to ordinary waste but not with regard to dangerous waste. The Court argued that a blanket ban on the import of dangerous waste was incompatible with the regime laid down for this type of waste in a directive adopted by the Council of Ministers. No similar directive had been adopted with regard to ordinary waste.[9] Understandably, this paradoxical finding was strongly criticised by environmental groups.

---

suffered from a bias in favour of the original goals and methods of the European Community, particularly economic growth and the free movement of goods. Accordingly, although environmental policy has blossomed in comparison to some other EC policies, it has long remained an isolated sector. Environmental considerations have so far failed to be sufficiently integrated into other EC policy sectors, such as agriculture, transport and energy (Kamminga, 1994, pp. 23–5). Characteristically, for example, the question of whether more stringent domestic environmental measures are acceptable is still being decided these days by considering whether they do not disproportionately affect the common market. The question is not approached by applying the test the other way round, i.e. by wondering whether certain EC measures aimed at establishing the internal market do not disproportionately affect the principles of sustainable development. The dilemma is illustrated by the two cases in Box 2 in which the European Court of Justice attempted unsuccessfully to steer a middle course between environmental and economic demands.

In spite of this built-in antienvironmental bias, it should be recognised that much of what has been achieved by the European Community in this area over the past 20 years could not have been achieved by its member states individually. On the whole, it is probably true that EC environmental policy has done more to encourage the laggards than to hold back the leaders (see Freestone, 1991, p. 148).

Recent trends in the development of international environmental law

A number of general trends can be distinguished in the development of international environmental law.

Initially, its focus was on the transboundary effects of environmental degradation. The issue here was how to reconcile the sovereign right of the upstream state to pollute with the sovereign right of the downstream state not to suffer undue harm. In the 1930s, an arbitrary tribunal set up jointly by the United States and Canada was asked to resolve a dispute concerning severe air pollution caused by a zinc smelter plant in the Canadian town of Trail. The plant's fumes were damaging crops across the border in the United States. The tribunal coined the famous ruling that:

'Under the principles of international law, as well as the law of the United States, no State has the right to use or permit the use of its territory in such a manner as to cause injury by fumes in or to the territory of another or the properties of or persons therein, when the case is of serious consequence and the injury is established by clear and convincing evidence.'[10]

It was not surprising that the tribunal felt able to arrive at this sweeping conclusion, in spite of a total lack of relevant precedents in international law. The tribunal had been specifically permitted to rely on precedents in United States law and, at the start of the proceedings, Canada had already admitted liability. These peculiar circumstances should have limited the relevance of the ruling to the case in question. Nevertheless, as will be seen below, the ruling has enjoyed an enduring popularity and has evolved into the most frequently quoted basic principle of international environmental law.

In subsequent years, the emphasis of international environmental law has gradually moved away from a preoccupation with state responsibility for the effects of transboundary pollution towards a more general emphasis on the integrated management of natural resources. States have found this easier to accept, however, with regard to resources in areas beyond national jurisdiction (the so-called 'global commons') than with regard to areas within their own jurisdiction. Accordingly, the most recent codification of the Trail smelter dictum, incorporated in Principle 2 of the Rio Declaration on Environment and Development, still implicitly admits that states are free to cause environmental damage to areas within their own jurisdiction:

'States have, in accordance with the Charter of the United Nations and the principles of international law, the sovereign right to exploit their own resources pursuant to their own environmental and developmental policies, and the responsibility to ensure that activities within their jurisdiction or control do not cause damage to the environment of other States or of areas beyond the limits of national jurisdiction.'

The two basic elements of this principle, the freedom to act at home coupled with a duty not to cause damage beyond national borders, represent the fundamental compromise between the developing states on the one hand and the developed states on the other. This principle had already been agreed upon, in almost identical terms, in Principle 21 of the Stockholm Declaration. The Rio Conference merely added the words 'and developmental', which did not change the meaning of the principle. A strict distinction between the 'domestic' and the 'foreign' environment is of course highly artificial and ultimately untenable from an ecological point of view. It is, however, a convenient diplomatic device rooted in the old international legal concepts of state sovereignty and the prohibition of interference in the internal affairs of another state.

As a matter of fact, international environmental law reflects a continuing struggle between competing interests. The most important of these contradictions is of an economic nature. Countries from the North and the South tend to strike a different balance when it comes to choosing between environmental and developmental priorities. Another basic contradiction is caused by geographical differences. In international river law, downstream states tend to be more concerned about the environment than upstream states. In the law of the sea, coastal states tend to be more preoccupied with pollution, while flag states (states in which vessels are registered) tend to be more preoccupied with freedom of navigation. States which belong to two competing groups can often play an important bridge-building role. For example, the United Kingdom has a strong interest both in protecting its long coastline and in maintaining freedom of navigation for its large fleet.

In spite of these competing interests, international environmental law has in recent years moved well beyond the generalities of the Trail smelter variety. The emphasis is no longer on state responsibility for environmental damage but on the setting of international standards in an attempt to prevent harmful consequences. An impressive number of international legal instruments (see Box 3) was prepared in the run-up towards UNCED, dealing with various aspects of environmental protection. These developments can be summarised as the formulation of ever more specific international obligations and the adoption of these obligations in the form of legally binding rules rather than merely as 'soft law' (recommendations). Rules contained in binding instruments, such as treaties, conventions, and protocols, have gradually become the main source of international environmental law. As a result, state sovereignty in this area is slowly but steadily being eroded.

3

International legal instruments

International legal instruments can be divided into two fundamental categories: binding and non-binding .

Binding instruments may be called *treaties* or *conventions*. *Protocols* are binding instruments by which parties to a treaty or convention may undertake additional obligations. Whatever label has been chosen, the essential point to keep in mind is that a treaty, convention or protocol is only binding on states that have specifically agreed to be bound by its provisions. States are not bound by majority decisions unless they have specifically agreed to do so (this has been done, for example, in the European Union). States can express their consent to be bound by an international instrument by way of ratification or accession. States that have ratified or acceded to a particular instrument are called parties.

Non-binding instruments may be called *resolutions*, *recommendations* or *declarations*. Again, whatever the label, the essential point is that these instruments are not legally binding, even for states that have voted for them.

5.3 General features of international environmental law

International environmental law can be analysed in two basic ways: in terms of the main *features* of individual subject areas (water, air, noise, etc.) or in terms of *general principles* (remedies, liability, etc.). Since neither of these approaches offers a complete picture, both will be adopted in this chapter.

The main features of international environmental law can be identified by reference to five areas. These are:

○ pollution of international watercourses
○ marine pollution
○ atmospheric pollution
○ international transfers of hazardous waste
○ the risks of nuclear energy.

These will be dealt with in this section. From the analysis five basic principles of international environmental law will be deduced and discussed in the following section.

Pollution of international watercourses

A comparatively well-developed area of international environmental law is that concerning international watercourses (see Nollkaemper, 1993). Relevant general rules may be found in the draft articles on the non-navigational uses of international watercourses adopted in 1994 by the UN International Law Commission.[11] These draft articles are likely to serve as the basis for a future framework convention on the subject. With respect to Europe, more specific rules may be found in the 1992 Helsinki Convention on the Protection and Use of Transboundary Watercourses and International Lakes (not yet in force).[12] The rules contained in this convention are particularly relevant for those international rivers in Europe for which no specific treaty regime has yet been agreed. They played an important role, for example, in the recently concluded treaty negotiations for the protection of the Meuse and the Scheldt.

In Europe, the most sophisticated legal regime applies to the River Rhine (see Lammers, 1989, pp. 440–57). Three legal instruments are particulary relevant: the 1976 Chlorides Convention[13], the 1976 Chemical Pollution Convention[14] and the 1987 Rhine Action Programme. With regard to pollution by chlorides, a protocol to the Chlorides Convention was adopted in 1991 which should provide a practical solution to a problem which has proved intractable for decades. The protocol provides that France will reduce discharges by its potassium mines whenever the concentration of chlorides at the German-Dutch border exceeds 200 mg/l. At the same time, The Netherlands will reduce discharges of saline seepage water into Lake IJsselmeer. The combination of these measures should ensure that the IJsselmeer water remains suitable for the production of drinking water.

In response to the chlorides pollution of the Rhine by the French potassium mines, legal remedies have been employed under both public and private international law.

While governments were continuing to negotiate a satisfactory solution, Dutch market gardeners who were suffering damage to their crops decided to sue the potassium mines for damages. In 1976, the European Court of Justice, in a landmark decision, decided that the market gardeners could sue both in the place where the tort had been caused (Strasbourg) and in the place where the harmful event had occurred (Rotterdam).[15] The market gardeners thus found themselves in a much more favourable legal position than the American victims of pollution by the Trail smelter, who could sue neither in the United States nor in Canada, but were dependent on action taken by the US government on their behalf. In 1988, the case was settled when the potassium mines agreed to pay the market gardeners 3.75 million Dutch guilders. The extent to which this lawsuit influenced the intergovernmental negotiations which resulted in the 1991 protocol remains uncertain.

The method adopted in the Rhine Chemical Pollution Convention, the setting of limit values for discharges of individual substances, has turned out to be extremely cumbersome. In practice, limit values have so far only been agreed upon with respect to a handful of substances. The convention's approach has now in effect been replaced by the approach contained in the Rhine Action Programme, i.e. the adoption of a global target of a 50% discharge reduction of certain priority substances by 1995. This approach owes its popularity to the fact that it leaves the riparian states a great amount of leeway to decide on the manner in which they wish to achieve the 50% reduction. What is interesting from a legal point of view is that, unlike the convention, the action programme is not a legally binding instrument. Its adoption therefore goes against the trend identified above, viz. towards ever more binding international standards.

Marine pollution

Marine pollution may be caused by land-based activities, by shipping, by dumping and by sea-bed activities. All these sources of pollution are covered in more or less detail by the 1982 UN Convention on the Law of the Sea (UNCLOS)[16] (see Churchill and Lowe, 1988, pp. 241–87).

By far the most important source of marine pollution is land-based activity (this includes pollutants transported through the atmosphere). Surprisingly, therefore, this is not the area which has been subject to the most detailed international regulation. UNCLOS itself refers to land-based pollution only in the most general terms and it has in effect been left to regional conventions to establish relevant rules and regulations. The most advanced regime may be found in the 1992 Paris Convention for the Protection of the Marine Environment of the North-East Atlantic (not in force in 1995 when this was written), which also covers dumping and sea-bed activities.[17] Under this convention, the parties agree to adopt programmes and measures to prevent and eliminate pollution in the relevant maritime area. These programmes and measures will be drawn up and their implementation supervised by a commission consisting of representatives of the parties. Similar regimes have been established, inter alia, for the Mediterranean, the Baltic and the Black Sea.

Although shipping is by no means the most important source of marine pollution, the fact that shipping accidents can cause spectacular catastrophes – for example, the disasters involving the Torrey Canyon (1967), the Amoco Cadiz (1978) and the Exxon

Plate 5.1 In March, 1989, the Exxon Valdez hit the rocks off the coast of Alaska. The impact on the marine and coastal environment was disastrous. Before the Gulf War of 1991, this accident was the world's largest oil spill. Photo: Alan Levenson/Sunshine

Valdez (1989) – has contributed to the creation of one of the most sophisticated legal regimes in international environmental law.

The applicable UNCLOS provisions strike a careful balance between the interests of coastal states and port states, which are not to be subjected to pollution, and the interests of flag states in freedom of navigation. On the whole, these provisions reflect customary international law, which means they are also binding on states that are not parties to UNCLOS. The provisions make a distinction between prescriptive jurisdiction (the right to prescribe rules) and enforcement jurisdiction (the right to enforce rules).

With regard to prescriptive jurisdiction, the basic principle is that flag states must ensure that their ships comply with pollution regulations which are at least as strict as those adopted by the competent international fora (in particular the IMO).[18] The coastal state, in turn, may impose additional regulations for ships passing through its territorial sea, but only as long as these regulations 'do not apply to the design, construction, manning or equipment of foreign ships unless they are giving effect to generally accepted international rules or standards'.[19] The same principle applies in a coastal state's Exclusive Economic Zone (EEZ), which may be up to 200 miles wide, but in this case the additional requirements must also be approved by the IMO.

With regard to enforcement jurisdiction, the flag state again has the primary responsibility to enforce compliance with antipollution regulations applicable to ships flying its flag. However, the more serious the pollution caused by a vessel, and the closer the offence occurred to the coast, the more likely it becomes that the coastal state is entitled to take additional enforcement action. Thus, a vessel navigating in a coastal state's EEZ may be physically inspected by that state if there are clear grounds for believing that it has caused or threatens to cause significant pollution there, and if it refuses to provide the relevant information.[20] A vessel navigating in an EEZ may be detained by the coastal state if there is clear, objective evidence that a discharge by that vessel in the EEZ has caused or threatens to cause major damage.[21] As a matter of fact, it will often be difficult to apprehend an offending ship while it is still in the EEZ in which it has committed the offence. Significantly, therefore, a port state, i.e. the state of the port in which a vessel finds itself, may also detain a ship for such an offence if it has been committed *outside* that state's territorial sea or EEZ. Such a measure may be taken at the request of another coastal state whose EEZ has suffered as a result of such an offence.[22]

Atmospheric pollution

As regards the protection of the atmosphere, treaties have so far addressed three major problem areas: long-distance air pollution, depletion of the ozone layer and climate change. The relevant treaties here are all framework treaties. This means that they are quite different from UNCLOS, which encompasses all aspects of the law of the sea, but took 14 years to negotiate and 12 years to come into force. Framework treaties tend to have more modest objectives. They aim to take a first step, to test the waters with a view to further co-operation, and to enable the adoption of possible further measures through the adoption of protocols containing additional obligations. In general, this incremental approach appears to be more suitable for tackling environmental problems.

Rising concern about the effects of acid rain in Western Europe caused by long-distance air pollution contributed to the adoption of the 1979 Economic Commission for Europe (ECE) Convention on Long-Range Transboundary Air Pollution.[23] This convention does not in itself provide for specific antipollution measures, but it does create a general forum for the exchange of information and for consultation on further measures. More specific commitments were subsequently included in four protocols to the convention. A protocol on sulphur dioxide (SO_2) adopted in 1988[24] resulted in the projected 30% reduction of SO_2 emissions by 1993. A protocol on nitrogen oxides (NO_x) was concluded in 1989[25], a protocol on volatile organic compounds (VOCs) in 1991[26], and a further protocol on SO_2 in 1994.

Similarly, the 1985 Vienna Convention for the Protection of the Ozone Layer, prepared under the auspices of UNEP, is a mere framework convention providing a forum for research and for consultation on more specific measures in the future.[27] However, this convention acquired real teeth with the adoption of the 1987 Montreal Protocol on Substances that Deplete the Ozone Layer[28] (see Benedick, 1991). This protocol is significant for several reasons. First of all, it contains specific obligations to reduce the production and consumption of CFCs in phases. These measures were taken even though there was still considerable scientific uncertainty about the precise

Plate 5.2 Atmospheric pollution: steel factory located on the beach at IJmuiden, The Netherlands. Photo: Mark Edwards/Lineair

effects of CFCs on the ozone layer. This is a clear example, therefore, of the application of the precautionary principle (see below). Moreover, the protocol provided that parties could decide to revise these figures by a two-thirds majority vote of parties representing together at least 50% of the total consumption of the substance in question. This possibility was used for the first time at a conference of the parties in London in 1990.[29] Further revisions, providing for a total ban on the consumption and production of CFCs by 1996, were agreed in Copenhagen in 1992.[30] Thus, a worldwide decision on a phaseout of CFCs was decided upon in a few years' time, without conclusive scientific proof that this was necessary and without cumbersome ratification procedures.

A third framework treaty is the 1992 UN Convention on Climate Change.[31] Again, the specific obligations contained in this convention are relatively modest. Importantly, however, it lays down the ultimate objective: the stabilisation of greenhouse gas concentrations in the atmosphere at a level that would prevent dangerous anthropogenic interference with the climate system. It also provides for a detailed system of international accountability on measures taken to control emissions of greenhouse gases. This by itself could have a beneficial effect. Clearly, however, this is a much more controversial subject which will take much longer to tackle than the reduction of CFCs.

International transfers of hazardous waste

The key treaty governing international transfers of hazardous waste is the 1989 Basel Convention on the Control of Transboundary Movements of Hazardous Wastes and

Their Disposal, concluded under the auspices of UNEP.[32] This convention provides essentially that hazardous waste may only be transferred from one state to another with the prior informed consent of the latter. While this is obviously a step in the right direction compared with the free-for-all situation existing before, the convention's approach has been criticised by environmental groups. They have argued that there can simply be no good reason why hazardous waste should be transferred from industrialised states to developing states at all. Moreover, it has been suggested that in practice it will often not be too difficult in a poor country to find an official who will give the required consent. Environmental groups have therefore argued in favour of a total ban on hazardous waste transfers to developing countries.

While such a total prohibition could not be included in the Basel Convention, it was included in two subsequent conventions with a more limited regional scope. The 1989 Lomé IV Convention between the member states of the European Community and some 80 states in Africa, the Caribbean and the Pacific (ACP) provides that the Community shall prohibit all export of such waste to the ACP states.[33] The 1991 Bamako Convention on the Ban of the Import into Africa and the Control of Transboundary Movement and Management of Hazardous Waste within Africa, concluded under the auspices of the Organisation of African Unity (OAU), also provides for such a total ban.[34] The two conventions are a reflection of widespread African concern at 'dumping' on their territories of hazardous waste coming from industrialised states. Unfortunately, the result of these selective bans might be that hazardous waste flows would simply be redirected to parts of the world where they could be disposed of with less difficulty. Significantly, therefore, the parties to the Basel Convention decided in 1994 that transfers of hazardous waste from OECD to non-OECD countries were to be halted.

Another problem with the Basel Convention is that radioactive waste has been explicitly excluded from its scope on the assumption that international transfers of this particular type of waste could be better dealt with under the auspices of the IAEA. However, the IAEA in 1990 merely adopted a non-binding Code of Practice on the International Transboundary Movement of Radioactive Waste.[35] While non-binding instruments are not necessarily less effective than binding ones, this has created the unfortunate impression that the IAEA is not particularly concerned about these transfers.

Risks of nuclear energy

So far, the environmental risks of nuclear energy have not given rise to the development of many binding rules of international environmental law. Typically, the Statute of the IAEA reflects the belief that the use of nuclear power should be encouraged and that this will bring 'peace, health and prosperity' to all. Accordingly, international regulation of the nuclear industry has tended to focus on the need to control the proliferation of nuclear weapons rather than on the need to protect the environment. The scope of the more radical international standards and procedures adopted by the IAEA, such as on-the-spot fact-finding by IAEA inspectors, is limited to non-proliferation aspects. Because relevant international regulation has remained the virtual monopoly of international organisations such as the IAEA, the nuclear industry

Plate 5.3 Dumping chemical waste, Kandy, Sri Lanka. Photo: Ron Giling/Lineair

has remained virtually untouched by the principles of international environmental law which have been emerging in other sectors. One reason for this sorry state of affairs is that within the IAEA the major nuclear powers tend to run the show. Non-nuclear states (who naturally have a stronger interest in environmental aspects) tend to have little impact on the proceedings.

One area in which the IAEA has played a pioneering role, however, is civil liability for nuclear damage, which has been the subject of four early, detailed conventions. The two most important ones are the 1960 Paris Convention on Third Party Liability in the Field of Nuclear Energy,[36] adopted under the auspices of the OECD, and the 1963 Vienna Convention on Civil Liability for Nuclear Damage,[37] adopted under the auspices of the IAEA. Only the Paris Convention has been widely ratified. The first principle reflected in these conventions is that liability is absolute, i.e. that it is not necessary for the claimant to demonstrate fault or negligence. The second principle is that only the operator of the nuclear installation is liable, i.e. that the claimant need only address the operator. The third principle is that there is a ceiling to the amount of liability, enabling the operator to obtain insurance. The underlying ideas of this system are obvious: on the one hand, to facilitate access to damages for the individual claimant and, on the other hand, to avoid the potentially extremely high costs of a nuclear accident for the nuclear industry. This system later inspired the system established for civil liability for oil pollution damage by ships.

The Chernobyl disaster has contributed to some change of emphasis. The IAEA reacted almost immediately by adopting two conventions dealing with the aftermath of nuclear catastrophes. One was the 1986 Convention on Early Notification of a Nuclear Accident, which spells out the obligation of states to inform other states if an accident has occurred with a nuclear installation on their territory that may have transboundary consequences.[38] The other was the 1986 Convention on Assistance in the Case of a Nuclear Accident or Radiological Emergency.[39] None of these conventions has very far-reaching consequences. On the preventive side, a Convention on Nuclear Safety, providing safety rules for nuclear installations, was adopted in 1994. This is aimed mainly at the still existing unsafe installations in Eastern Europe.

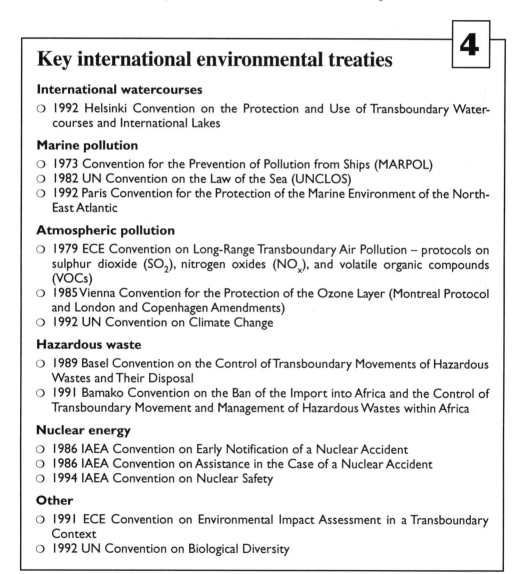

4

Key international environmental treaties

International watercourses

○ 1992 Helsinki Convention on the Protection and Use of Transboundary Watercourses and International Lakes

Marine pollution

○ 1973 Convention for the Prevention of Pollution from Ships (MARPOL)
○ 1982 UN Convention on the Law of the Sea (UNCLOS)
○ 1992 Paris Convention for the Protection of the Marine Environment of the North-East Atlantic

Atmospheric pollution

○ 1979 ECE Convention on Long-Range Transboundary Air Pollution – protocols on sulphur dioxide (SO_2), nitrogen oxides (NO_x), and volatile organic compounds (VOCs)
○ 1985 Vienna Convention for the Protection of the Ozone Layer (Montreal Protocol and London and Copenhagen Amendments)
○ 1992 UN Convention on Climate Change

Hazardous waste

○ 1989 Basel Convention on the Control of Transboundary Movements of Hazardous Wastes and Their Disposal
○ 1991 Bamako Convention on the Ban of the Import into Africa and the Control of Transboundary Movement and Management of Hazardous Wastes within Africa

Nuclear energy

○ 1986 IAEA Convention on Early Notification of a Nuclear Accident
○ 1986 IAEA Convention on Assistance in the Case of a Nuclear Accident
○ 1994 IAEA Convention on Nuclear Safety

Other

○ 1991 ECE Convention on Environmental Impact Assessment in a Transboundary Context
○ 1992 UN Convention on Biological Diversity

5.4 Five general principles of international environmental law

At present, there is no binding international charter which contains general principles of international environmental law. During the preparations for UNCED, attempts were made to draft an Earth Charter which would have served this purpose. However, no agreement could be reached on the desirability of such an approach. In the preceding sections, we have seen how conflicts of interest between rich and poor nations, between upstream and downstream states, between coastal states and flag states, between net exporters and net importers of hazardous waste and between nuclear and non-nuclear states often make it difficult to reach consensus. Nevertheless, there is now such an abundance of international instruments with regard to environmental issues that it is certainly possible to identify a number of basic principles on which these instruments are invariably based:

○ the polluter pays principle
○ the principle of non-discrimination
○ the precautionary principle
○ the principle of common but differentiated responsibilities
○ the principle of intergenerational equity.

Most of these are reflected in the Rio Declaration on Environment and Development. Whether some or all of these principles reflect binding customary international law is questionable. What matters, however, is that they tend to be relied upon, either explicitly or implicitly, when drafting international environmental instruments.

The polluter pays principle

According to the polluter pays principle, the polluter should bear the expenses of carrying out the antipollution measures decided by the public authorities. The costs of these measures should thus be reflected in the costs of goods and services which cause the pollution. This longstanding principle, originally developed by the OECD, attempts to ensure that no distortions occur as a result of subsidies provided by the authorities. The principle has been widely accepted in the developed world and it has been included in recent conventions, such as the 1992 Treaty of Maastricht, the 1992 Helsinki Convention and the 1992 Paris Convention. However, the wording in these 'Northern' conventions is considerably stronger ('shall') than the wording used in the Rio Declaration on Environment and Development ('endeavour to'). This is a clear illustration that developing countries are less committed to the principle. Significant exceptions to the principle have occasionally also been accepted among developed countries, for instance in the instruments dealing with chlorides pollution of the Rhine, which provide that the costs of the measures shall be divided in a manner which bears little relationship to the amount of pollution caused by each individual state.

Principle of non-discrimination

According to the principle of non-discrimination, polluters causing transboundary pollution should be treated no less severely than they would be if they caused similar pollution within their own country. This is a procedural principle, also developed by the OECD, which by itself does not guarantee that the other state will suffer no undue harm. An important principle derived from the non-discrimination principle is that of the right of equal access. This entails that a victim of transboundary pollution should be granted no less favourable treatment than victims in the country where the pollution originated. Accordingly, he or she should have access to administrative and civil proceedings on the same basis as victims in the country where the pollution originated. These principles have been widely (although not necessarily invariably) applied in Western Europe and North America. There is little evidence, however, that they have found worldwide application.

Precautionary principle

According to the precautionary principle, lack of full scientific certainty shall not be used as a reason for postponing measures to prevent environmental degradation. The principle has been widely referred to in treaties concluded during the past few years. One of the clearest examples of the actual application of the principle are the measures taken under the Montreal Protocol on Substances that Deplete the Ozone Layer. After all, the scientific predictions and calculations on the basis of which the decision was taken to phase out the use of CFCs were far from conclusive. In its more far-reaching interpretations, the principle would imply a reversal of the burden of proof: potentially harmful activities could then only be undertaken if it could be convincingly demonstrated that they are not going to be harmful to the environment. Whether many states would accept such an interpretation seems questionable, however.

Principle of common but differentiated responsibilities

According to the principle of common but differentiated responsibilities, states should divide the costs of measures to protect the environment on the basis of the fact that they have made different contributions to global environmental degradation. This was one of the newer and more controversial principles included in the Rio Declaration. One of the clearest examples of the application of this principle may be found in the 1992 Convention on Climate Change. This convention not only accepts that developing countries need to comply with less strict standards than the developed countries; it also accepts that they are entitled to technological and financial assistance in order to help them meet their obligations under the treaty. The convention even acknowledges that developing countries are not required to comply with their obligations if this assistance has not been forthcoming. Obviously, the abandoning of the old rule that all states shall be subject to the same obligations will have far-reaching consequences in the future.

Principle of intergenerational equity

According to the principle of intergenerational equity, states are obliged to take into account the long-term effects of their actions affecting the environment. This principle attempts to emphasise that attention should not only be paid to long-distance effects but also to the long-term effects of human activity. After all, present-day decisions may restrict future uses of natural resources and may force upon future generations considerable clean-up costs. It cannot simply be assumed that future generations will be able to develop the necessary technology for this purpose. Some of the damage may even be irreversible. The principle of inter-generational equity is the key element in the definition of sustainable development. It has been included, for example, in the 1992 Helsinki Convention. One way of operationalising the principle would be to assume that current generations should not impose burdens upon future generations that they would not have accepted for themselves. One of the legal problems is of course that future generations do not yet exist so that it is difficult to take their views into account.

What these five principles have in common is that they try to address what is perhaps the key cause of environmental degradation: the off-loading of burdens. The polluter pays principle attempts to ensure that environmental costs of the production and consumption of a good are adequately reflected in its price, so that they are not off-loaded on the environment. The principle of non-discrimination attempts to ensure that the environmental risks of industrial activity are not off-loaded on neighbouring countries. The precautionary principle attempts to ensure that policy makers do not off-load on scientists the responsibility to take environmental protection measures now. The principle of common but differentiated responsibilities attempts to ensure that countries in the North do not off-load on countries in the South the duty to respond to environmental degradation for which the former bear the primary responsibility. The principle of intergenerational equity attempts to ensure that environmental risks of present-day activities are not off-loaded on future generations.

However, the status of these principles differs considerably. The older ones, such as the polluter pays principle and the non-discrimination principle, are perhaps more solidly established than the others. But then again, this may be too Northern a perspective. In the South, the principle of common but differentiated responsibilities would probably be regarded as the most fundamental. The principles also differ in the extent to which they offer clear guidance to policy makers. Probably the vaguest and least defined is the principle of intergenerational equity. It should also be recognised that some of the principles may be somewhat contradictory, depending on the interpretation that is given to them. For example, certain applications of the principle of common but differentiated responsibilities may be difficult to reconcile with the polluter pays principle. These contradictions are a result of the fact that the principles were developed at different times and for different purposes. They should not be regarded as forming part of a coherent and logically organised system.

5.5 Conclusion

International environmental law has developed into one of the fastest growing areas of international law. In response partly to widely perceived threats to the global environment and partly to the institutional deadlines imposed by the UNCED process, numerous innovative concepts in standard setting have been introduced during the past few years. Some of these new devices have been referred to above. They include the use of framework conventions in combination with subsequent protocols containing more detailed standards; the use of simplified amendment procedures to avoid the need for cumbersome ratification procedures; and the use of incentives by way of financial and technological assistance to encourage more states to join a particular agreement (see Sand, 1990; Brown Weiss, 1993, pp. 675–710).

The question arises, nevertheless, of what has been the actual result of this outburst of legislative activity. Are all these international instruments actually being implemented or have they remained mere pieces of paper? This question cannot easily be answered because the necessary information is generally unavailable (for a rare systematic analysis, see Sand, 1992). International fact-finding procedures in the field of the environment are few and far between. As we have seen above, the IAEA's inspection rights for nuclear facilities are limited to non-proliferation aspects, and a coastal state's right to inspect a polluting vessel is strictly limited in the interest of freedom of navigation.

The supervisory method employed most frequently in international environmental instruments is an obligation of the parties to report periodically on the measures they have taken to comply with their obligations. The information thus obtained is then reviewed by representatives of the parties. However, the quality of the material gathered in this way may vary considerably, and this may make it difficult to conclude with certainty whether obligations have actually been complied with. The value of the peer review method also tends to be limited by the fact that participants are often reluctant to publicly hold their opposite numbers accountable.

The experience of the European Union demonstrates that it certainly cannot be assumed that international environmental instruments are always faithfully implemented. In the EU, the European Commission is responsible for overseeing the implementation of EU legislation. Under Article 169 of the EC Treaty, the Commission is entitled to bring a case before the European Court of Justice if a member state fails to carry out its obligations. In recent years, the Commission has begun to employ this procedure more aggressively. In the environmental sector, the Court found 12 infringements in 1990, 19 in 1991 and nine in 1993 under this procedure (see Macrory, 1992, pp. 347–69). However, in view of the fact that 12 EU member states are expected to comply with more than 200 environmental instruments, these figures are not unduly alarming.

According to Louis Henkin's famous observation, 'Almost all nations observe almost all principles of international law and almost all of their obligations almost all of the time' (Henkin, 1979, p. 47). International environmental law is no exception to this phenomenon. Moreover, law does not lose its significance if compliance is less than 100%. NGOs working in the field of the environment can attest to the fact that international environmental standards play a crucial role as a rallying point for the worldwide mobilisation of shame. Examples include the global bans on whaling, nuclear waste dumping at sea and the production of CFCs. Without continuing pressure from non-governmental entities these bans would probably not have been internationally agreed upon. Once they were accepted, these new standards enabled NGOs to put pressure on individual states to adhere to them and to become parties to the international agreements in which they were included. Without the mechanisms of international law, such worldwide pressure would have been much more difficult to sustain.

However, in spite of the advances that have already been made, international environmental law is still in its infancy. The challenges that remain are formidable. Apart from the problems of implementation and enforcement referred to above, many new standards and procedures urgently need to be developed. Agenda 21, the lengthy programme of action adopted at UNCED, outlines the numerous areas in which further international regulation is required. Thanks to some of the new concepts discussed in this chapter, international environmental law is now in a better position to try and meet these requirements set by the world community.

Notes

1 11 *ILM* (International Legal Materials) (1972), p. 1416.
2 31 *ILM* (1992), p. 874.
3 International Court of Justice, press release No. 93/20, 19 July 1993.
4 International Court of Justice, press release No. 93/17, 5 July 1993.
5 OJ EC (Official Journal of the European communities) 1973 C 112/1.
6 25 *ILM* (1986), p. 503.
7 31 *ILM* (1992), p. 247.
8 Case 302/86, Danish bottles, [1988] *European Court Reports*, pp. 4627–33.
9 Case C-2/90, Wallonian waste, Judgement of 9 July 1992, not yet reported.
10 Decision of 11 March 1941, *Reports of International Arbitral Awards*, vol. III, para. 1965.
11 See Report of the International Law Commission on the work of its 45th Session, UN doc. A/46/10, pp. 161–72.
12 31 *ILM* (1992), p. 1312.
13 16 *ILM* (1977), p. 265.
14 20 OJ EC (1977), p. 240.
15 Case 21/76, [1976] *European Court Reports*, p. 1735.
16 21 *ILM* (1982), p. 1261.
17 32 *ILM* (1993), p. 1069.
18 Art. 211(2), UNCLOS.
19 Art. 21(2), UNCLOS.
20 Art. 220(5), UNCLOS.
21 Art. 220(6), UNCLOS.
22 Art. 218, UNCLOS.

23 18 *ILM* (1979), p. 1442.
24 17 *ILM* (1988), p. 707.
25 28 *ILM* (1989), p. 212.
26 31 *ILM* (1992), p. 569.
27 26 *ILM* (1987), p. 1529.
28 26 *ILM* (1987), p. 1541.
29 30 *ILM* (1991), p. 537.
30 32 *ILM* (1993), p. 874.
31 31 *ILM* (1992), p. 849.
32 28 *ILM* (1989), p. 657.
33 Art. 39, 29 *ILM* (1990), p. 783.
34 Art. 4, 30 *ILM* (1991), p. 773.
35 30 *ILM* (1991), p. 556.
36 55 *AJIL* (American Journal of International Law) (1961), p. 1082.
37 2 *ILM* (1963), p. 727.
38 25 *ILM* (1986), p. 1370.
39 25 *ILM* (1986), p. 1377.

6

Environmental problems from an economic perspective

Jan van der Straaten and Mike Gordon

6.1 Introduction

Many people think that it is the way the economy operates that gives rise to environmental problems – this even being the root cause of the environmental crisis facing the planet. *Economics* is frequently perceived as being at odds with *ecology* and *the environment*. However, are there ways in which economics can assist in the solution of such problems? This chapter sets out to examine the potential contribution of economics to understanding environmental problems and resolving the environmental crisis.

The chapter begins with a brief description of what economics is about (section 6.2). It then looks at the economic functions of the environment and examines the relevance of the laws of thermodynamics (section 6.3). It goes on to outline how economists have traditionally looked at natural resources and the environment (section 6.4). It then discusses the interrelationship between economic systems and ecosystems (section 6.5) and considers the property and access arguments of 'the tragedy of the commons' (section 6.6). Finally it makes some concluding comments on international environmental policies (section 6.7).

6.2 What is economics? Some economic concepts

Economics can be viewed in two ways – in terms of scarcity or material welfare. It can study how choices are made between alternatives in the allocation of scarce resources to fulfil human aims and objectives. It may also examine individual and social action to obtain and use resources to meet material needs and thereby achieve human well-being.

Traditional economics deals with production and consumption. Labour, capital, and natural resources are used in the production process to ensure a sufficient supply of goods and services which can be bought by consumers on markets. On the other hand, there are collective goods such as an army, dikes, roads, infrastructure and education which are provided by the government or by other authorities. Economic goods are scarce, as scarce production factors are used to produce private as well as collective goods. This brings us to one of the most difficult topics in economics, the problem of *value* and *price*, which is particularly important in relation to nature and the environment. Natural resources may have a market price, as, for instance, coal, natural gas, iron ore, and land. However, in many cases, natural resources do not have a price. A country may not have a shortage of water, but the quality of that water is a different matter. Surface waters may be more or less polluted and not suitable for drinking purposes. As long as sufficient water of good quality is available, water does not have a price, but when pollution becomes significant, drinking water will have a price.

Markets and market forces $\boxed{\textbf{I}}$

In most parts of the world, the economic context is one governed by market forces. This term needs to be defined strictly. Market forces come into being, at the level of the whole economy, when the majority of decisions made at the level of individual firms and consumers take place in markets, and there is no one determining the collective consequences. Market forces are thus the overall sum of many millions of separate individual parts.

It is important also to distinguish between *markets* and *market forces*. Market forces are a macroeconomic phenomenon, at the level of the economy as a whole. Markets by contrast are a microeconomic mechanism, operating at the level of individual products, businesses and households. They are defined by the existence of a number of suppliers and purchasers free to choose with whom they trade, where changes in price mediate between supply and demand. Markets can be and are regulated by government intervention, for example through taxes and laws: there are no completely 'free' markets. But even where markets are regulated, market forces can still operate. They do so whenever the overall result of individual decisions made in markets is unplanned. Regulation of markets *may* be designed to plan the overall outcome, but this is not usually the case. In most cases market-regulating laws are introduced simply to prevent certain microlevel occurrences, such as exploitation of workers or consumers. In the case of taxes the purpose is generally to raise revenue for the government.

This is what happens in most sectors of the economy, on both national and international scales. The overall allocation of resources and commodities (energy, raw materials, money, labour, goods and services, wastes) is not planned by a single agency. It is left, rather, to the undetermined, combined result of many different agents' decisions. These decisions are made privately; that is, without reference to others' similar decisions, on the basis of each agent's own interests. In general it is impossible for individual economic agents to take into account the wider effects of their actions, which cannot be known. Added together, market forces thus generate an overall result which no one has determined. This is the 'invisible hand' which Adam Smith argued brought general prosperity.

Source: Jacobs (1991), pp. 23–5.

However, it could not be argued that drinking water only has economic significance when it has a price resulting from pollution. Even before pollution, it is a significant resource in the process of production and consumption. It can be concluded from this example that price is not always a useful indicator of economic scarcity and significance.

As the majority of natural resources do not have a price, a general impression has arisen that nature and the environment are outside the realm of economics. It must be stressed that this is a myopic view. It is not the price which conveys economic significance; this is found in the scarcity of the good and in its possible use in the process of production and consumption. It is irrelevant, from an economic point of view, whether this scarcity has been translated into prices or not. Nevertheless, economics is often associated with prices and not with scarcity. This is based on a long tradition in neoclassical theory, in which the market was and is the focus of interest.

As the supply of particular resources and commodities increases, so their price will tend to fall; this is the simple relationship between supply and demand, as determined by markets and market forces (see Box 1). However, the price of goods may be influenced by other factors including, for example, who controls the resources, the extent of competition between producers of goods, and government intervention in, or regulation of, the market. The combination of all the economic decisions of individuals (that is, unplanned by government or other central agency) brings about the allocation of resources and commodities and – it is argued – general prosperity.

In market economies, increasing production and consumption of goods and services has generally been regarded as 'a good thing' – demonstrating the material well-being

---

GDP and GNP | **2**

Gross domestic product (GDP) is the total value in money terms of all the production in a country in one year. It is measured in three different ways (which should all end up with the same total): through adding the value of the goods and services produced, through adding the expenditure on them, and through adding the incomes received from producing them. Production where no money changes hands – such as unpaid domestic work – is therefore excluded from GDP. Money changing hands where there is no production – such as gifts – is also excluded.

Gross national product (GNP) is GDP plus rents, interest, profits, and dividends flowing into a country from abroad, minus rents, interest, profits, and dividends paid out to people in other countries. GNP therefore measures the total income received by the inhabitants of a country. GNP depends on where the owners are located; GDP depends on where the economic activity is located. In a country with a lot of foreign investment in it but very little investment by its inhabitants in other countries, there will be a net outflow of 'property income' (rents, interest, profits, and dividends). This will result in a GNP much lower than its GDP.

GDP or GNP per capita, i.e. per head or per person, is GDP or GNP divided by the total population of the country. This gives a figure often described as measuring the 'average standard of living'.

Source: Anderson (1991), pp. 19–20.

Types of resources

Non-renewable resources are those which (in a human time-scale) cannot be regenerated by natural processes: fossil fuels (coal, oil, gas), minerals and other materials. Fossil fuels can of course be 'regenerated', but only over a period of several million years. Non-renewables are therefore ultimately in fixed supply: all use depletes the total stock.

Renewable resources are those which, through natural regeneration processes, can continue in supply despite being 'used' by humankind. Plants and animals, of course, reproduce and regrow. But clean air and fresh water are also renewable: the elements oxygen, hydrogen, carbon and nitrogen (among others) are constantly recycled by living organisms in processes such as photosynthesis, respiration, nitrogen fixing and decay.

Continuing resources, by contrast, are inexhaustible. They are those sources of energy the supply of which is unaffected by human activity. They are often called 'renewable', but this is not strictly accurate. The two principal original sources of continuing energy are the sun, which generates solar radiation and wind energy, and gravity, which generates tidal and wave energy and hydropower (though this, dependent on water, is also partly renewable). Some geothermal energy (heat from the Earth's crust) is also a type of continuing resource.

Source: Jacobs (1991), pp. 3–4.

---

of both individuals and society as a whole. In economic terms, these benefits are reflected in measures (or *indicators*) of *growth*, known as gross domestic product (GDP) or gross national product (GNP) (see Box 2).

6.3 Economic functions of the environment and the laws of thermodynamics

Before we begin to look at the development of economic thinking in relation to natural resources and the environment, it is important to consider what kind of *economic functions* are served by the environment, because all of human economic activity depends on the natural environment.

'The biosphere performs three principal functions for the economic activities of humankind' (Jacobs, 1991, pp. 3–5). Jacobs identifies these as provision of *resources*, assimilation of *waste products*, and provision of various *environmental services* (amenities and 'life-support' services). There are three main types of resources: *non-renewable*, *renewable*, and *continuing* (see Box 3).

Jacobs clearly explains how the 'economic functions of the environment are related in quite specific ways, by the first two *laws of thermodynamics*' (see Box 4).

Having established the important implications for environmental policy of the laws of thermodynamics, Jacobs contrasts two models of the economy, the diagrams reproduced here as Figures 6.1 and 6.2.

The relevance of the laws of thermodynamics

4

The laws of thermodynamics are the physical rules which govern the behaviour of matter and energy. The *first law* is very simple. It states that matter and energy cannot be either destroyed or created. There is a fixed total, which is always conserved in some form or another. This law has a rather profound bearing on economics, because it calls into question what exactly economic activity does. Clearly, for all the effort that goes into production, nothing 'new' is actually created. All that happens is the *transformation* of materials and energy from one state into another. Every quantity of resources which enters the economic process must emerge at the end as the same quantity of waste. The *quantitative* relationship between the first two environmental functions (provision of resources and assimilation of waste products) is therefore straightforward. The more resources are used, the more wastes need to be assimilated. Resource depletion and pollution are essentially the *same* problem, two sides of one coin.

But the relationship has a *qualitative* dimension to it as well. The transformation of resources into wastes follows a specific path dictated by the *second law* of thermodynamics or 'entropy law'. Entropy can be understood as a measure of the 'disorderedness' or 'unavailability' of matter or energy. Thus a lump of coal has low entropy; it is concentrated in form and the energy it contains is available for use. But once the coal is burnt it has high entropy, becoming dissipated as heat and carbon dioxide, neither of which is available for use. The example illustrates the workings of the second law, which states that (so long as there are no external sources of energy) entropy always increases. Entropy is thus indeed a way of defining resources and wastes: the former have low entropy, the latter high entropy. In turn economic activity may be thought of as a process by which low entropy materials are converted into high entropy ones, while useful services are derived from them en route.

It is here, however, that the third function of the environment (the performance of environmental services) enters the picture. For it is not quite true that entropy always increases. Note that the second law only insists on this if there are no external sources of energy. This is of course the case with respect to the universe as a whole. But it isn't so for the Earth. On the contrary, the biosphere is powered by a continuous flow of energy from the sun. And this enables the flow of entropy within the biosphere to be reversed. This 'circular' activity is made possible and carried out by the performance of environmental life-support services.

The three economic functions of the environment are therefore clearly linked. Resources and wastes are ultimately the same quantities. They differ only in entropic value; but high entropy is constantly being converted back into low entropy through the life support services which the environment performs.

It will be apparent that these connections increase the complexity of the environmental crisis. It might be thought possible, for example, to reduce the problem of resource depletion if wastes could be recycled faster or more efficiently. But the damage being done to life-support services actually reduces the ability of the environment to assimilate wastes and recycle them; an increasing quantity simply gets stored as pollution. More recycling could be done by the economy but the entropy law tells us that this can only be done if additional energy is applied, which, if it comes from fossil fuels, only adds to the pollution problem.

Source: Jacobs (1991), pp. 11–13.

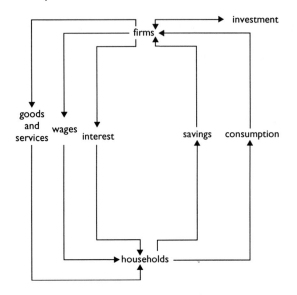

Fig. 6.1 The orthodox model of the economy. Source: Jacobs (1991), p.13

Figure 6.1 shows the traditional view of the economy as a circular flow of money. This ignores the physical environment, matter, wastes and energy, which physical description is illustrated in Figure 6.2. The latter integrates the environment into the view of the economy.

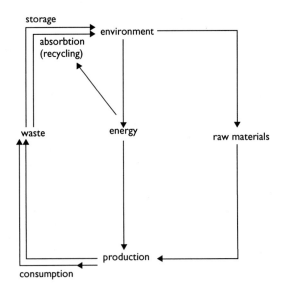

Fig. 6.2 A simple thermodynamic model of the economy. Source: Jacobs (1991), p.14

6.4 Economic theory, natural resources and the environment

In traditional economics, natural resources are only dealt with to the extent that they are traded on a market. The deterioration of Nature and the pollution of the environment are outside the scope of economics as long as these phenomena cannot be defined in terms of prices. Traditionally, therefore, economic growth has been defined as an increase in production and/or consumption, without any attention being paid to the disruption of Nature and the environment (see Box 5).

Environmental problems and property rights

Prices cannot be seen as given facts. They are closely related to the definition of *property rights* with regard to natural resources. If the property right to a natural resource is not well defined, the resource can be used by many economic actors. A lack of property rights to natural resources will result in these resources not having a price and overexploitation will often be the consequence. Society can control the use of natural resources either by means of prices or by a system of regulations.

5

Natural resources and ecosystems

Economics has a long tradition of distinguishing between the production factors of labour, capital and natural resources (either Nature or land). Labour and capital have received abundant attention, but this cannot be said for natural resources. This chapter uses a broad definition of *natural resources*, which is not restricted to natural resources bought and sold on the market. Furthermore, natural resources are taken into consideration insofar as they are important in the process of production and consumption. Thus, deposits of minerals and fossil fuels in the Earth's crust are natural resources, but the fertility of the soil, the attractiveness of landscapes for recreational activities, the biodegradation capacity of certain ecosystems, the energy of the sun, as well as the generating capacity to form new living organisms can also be defined as natural resources relevant for humanity. Furthermore, pollution may be absorbed or buffered by certain mechanisms within the ecosystem; these absorption capacities are natural resources as well.

The term *ecosystem* is used with reference to the great variety of living organisms and the abiotic forces which influence them. Ecosystems can be defined at different geographical levels, for example, rivers, oceans, the Alps or the globe. Ecosystems include flows of materials such as oxygen, water, and nutrients. The term *ecocycle* or *ecological cycle* is used to describe these flows. Both ecosystems and ecocycles are used in the production process. Beyond a certain level of disruption, however, they can no longer be used in the economic system. This level is known as the *carrying capacity* of the ecosystem. It is the maximum level of utilisation which allows a lasting use of natural resources.

This problem of the definition of property rights and an appropriate use of natural resources has international implications. Many environmental problems, such as the greenhouse effect and the hole in the ozone layer, have to be seen in a global context. Global problems can only be solved by global measures. Many environmental problems are transboundary; the costs of environmental pollution are off-loaded by one country onto another. The benefits of a polluting production process go to the producers of the product, located in the polluting country. In the case of transboundary pollution, the costs related to the pollution are shifted to adjacent countries. This type of problem makes an international approach unavoidable.

The off-loading of the costs of pollution on others is not restricted to geographical shifts. Many environmental costs are off-loaded onto future generations. In a market economy, however, only current market forces can influence the outcome of the market. Future generations cannot play a role in the process of reallocation of scarce resources.

Current proposals for solving environmental problems with the help of economic concepts are generally based on economic theories which were developed a considerable time ago. Hence, it is necessary to look at these early theories to see whether they are still relevant in the context of finding economic solutions to environmental problems.

The increasing relevance of markets

Factory production on a mass scale started during the Industrial Revolution. This method of production was accompanied by environmental problems different from those in previous periods. The growing influence of the production processes of the Industrial Revolution increased the importance of the quantitative aspects of the market, a situation accompanied by social changes. The production of goods assumed an increasingly industrial character, which meant that the necessity of trading these goods on international markets also increased.

The Industrial Revolution had a profound influence on economic theories. Production increasingly focused on the relevance of international markets, resulting in increased competition. Labourers worked in factories which were owned by capitalist entrepreneurs. Working conditions in these factories were poor, commonly leading to health problems among workers. Wages were low and many workers lived in unfortunate circumstances. It could therefore be argued that environmental problems in this period centred around the working conditions in the factories and the residential areas around these factories. Marx saw this development as an inherent characteristic of capitalist production, with the labourer being exploited by the capitalist. Although Marx was fully aware of the relevance of natural resources for the production of goods, he did not analyse the relationship between natural resources and other production factors. He concentrated on the relationship between labour and capital. In doing so, he excluded natural resources from his analysis.

The same can be said of the theories of Ricardo, a theorist who lived in the early 1800s, when industrialisation was becoming increasingly relevant. Ricardo was a well-known classical economist in this period and he defined Nature as a fixed asset in his models. This meant that in his models an increase in production could never be accompanied by a decrease in the availability of natural resources. Marx's later use of the Ricardian model partially explains why Marx also ignored this topic. It should not be overlooked, however, that natural resources were considered inexhaustible in this period. The use of these resources was low compared to their supply, so that their relevance could be ignored in the analysis of fundamental economic relationships.

The problem of natural resources

In the same period, the concept of *value* in economic theory changed (see Box 6). Classical economists were still of the opinion that the exchange value of a good was determined in an objective way by the number of labour hours necessary for producing that good. More or less simultaneous, but independent, publications by Menger (1968), Jevons (1924) and Walras (1954) heralded a break with these paradigms. These authors were of the opinion that the exchange value of a good could be derived from the satisfaction of the needs of the individual consumer (in other words, the exchange value related to the 'utility' of the commodity – see Box 6).

It was Malthus who drew attention to the importance of the restricted availability of natural resources. He argued that population increases by geometrical progression, but that the total level of 'subsistence' (for our purposes, natural resources) could only increase by arithmetical progression – i.e. by a lower amount than population. Consequently, in his view, a shortage in the total level of natural resources was inevitable and starvation of the human population would be the result. Limiting the number of children born seemed to him to be the solution. However, neoclassical

---

6

The concept of value

In economics value means either value in use or value in exchange. The theory of value and the theory of distribution together form the theory of price. The theory of distribution deals with the determination of the prices of the factors of production; the theory of value deals with the determination of the prices of consumer goods.

The price of a commodity may be defined as its value in terms of money. The theory of value is therefore concerned with the relative prices or exchange values of commodities. Since goods are demanded because they have the power to satisfy human wants, they also have value in use. Water is valuable not because of the price it commands but because it has 'utility', the power to satisfy a human want.

Value in use is not an intrinsic quality of a commodity but rather its capacity to satisfy a human want. For a commodity to have exchange value it must have utility (or more strictly, it must give the promise of utility so that it is desired), and it must be capable of being exchanged.

Value in exchange expresses the amount of one commodity that can be exchanged for another ... .

Source: *Everyman's Dictionary of Economics.*

economists disagreed with Malthus' concept of the shortfall of natural resources. Marshall, for instance, stated quite explicitly (1925, p. 180) that technical developments had proved that Malthus' earlier arguments had been wrong. The result was that no attention was paid to the fact that these highly acclaimed technical developments were based on the large-scale use of non-renewable resources, i.e. resources with a *stock* character, such as iron ore and coal, which can be depleted. Before the Industrial Revolution, the actual use of natural resources was nearly exclusively based on renewable (or – in the case of wind energy, which derives from solar power – continuing) resources, i.e. resources with a *flow* character, which are in principle inexhaustible, such as muscle power, wind energy, wood and wool. Since the Industrial Revolution, the wealth of humanity has been based to an ever-increasing degree on the use of non-renewable resources – resources with a stock character.

This has had two closely related effects. Firstly, one should be aware of the fact that ores and fossil fuels are only available in the Earth's crust in limited quantities. Eventually, these stocks will be exhausted. Secondly, these materials will, after their use in human production and consumption processes, be discharged into ecological cycles, as is the case with metals and alloys, fumes, and synthetics. Such materials are not natural components of the prevalent ecological cycles, at least not in such large quantities. The result is the disruption and, in the worst case, destruction of ecological

Plate 6.1 Exploitation of non-renewable resources: mining bauxite ore (Billiton), Surinam. Photo: Ron Giling/Lineair

---

The problem of sustainable development

7

It is often claimed that sustainable development is inconsistent with neoclassical theories because, with modern-day high levels of production, resource depletion, and pollution, a traditional neoclassical approach would, in the long run, fail to take account of the need for sustainability. The neoclassical approach assumes that substitution of resources and technical development will lead to increased economic accessibility and efficiency of use of natural resources, so that sustainable development is assumed to be the result of the market process. It is now known, however, that this essential assumption in neoclassical analysis will not hold in the long run. It can, therefore, be concluded that sustainable development requires a strict policy implemented by national and international authorities.

---

cycles. In other words: the Industrial Revolution marks the transition from a more or less closed system of production and consumption to an open economic system characterised by an increasing use of natural resources with a stock character, which are then discharged as alien and poisonous materials into the ecological cycles following production and consumption. This dramatic shift did not, however, significantly influence economic theories in this period (see Box 7).

Externalities

Marshall (1925) was the first to introduce the concept of the *external* effect or external economy. He illustrated the idea with the example of an expanding company which creates beneficial effects for other companies in the region such as training for the labour force, stimulating a growing labour supply or attracting other supplying companies. The existing companies receive these *benefits* as if they were free, since no effort, sacrifice or expenditure is required on their part.

Surprisingly, Marshall did not elaborate on the possible external *costs* of an activity. It was Pigou (1952) who first paid serious attention to environmental problems. For this purpose he introduced the concept of *negative external effect* (see Box 8). This is the cost imposed by one activity on others for which no compensation is paid. Thus, the emission of smoke by factories causes negative externalities: 'For this smoke in large towns inflicts a heavy uncharged loss on the community, in injury to buildings and vegetables, expenses for washing clothes and cleaning rooms, expenses for the provision of artificial light, and in many other ways' (Pigou, 1952, p. 184). It should not be overlooked that Pigou was dealing with problems which had been described by Marx as an exploitation of labourers by capitalists. Pigou's externality was a sideline in neoclassical reasoning; the exploitation of labour by the interests of capital was the core of Marx's theories. Basically, however, both authors were discussing the same types of problem.

In Pigou's line of thought, externalities were part of the difference between the social and the private cost price of goods and services. For example, if heavy metals are discharged into a river following production, the discharging producer transfers part of

Negative externalities

8

One of the examples of externalities given by Pigou is that of a train which uses coal as a fuel. Such trains produce sparks, which can cause fires along the railway. If a forest or a house is burned down by these sparks, this is a negative externality caused by the railway company to the owner of the forest or the house. In such an example there is one clearly identifiable economic agent causing the effects, while the victims are, likewise, limited and well defined.

his production costs to society (in this case, the costs of restoring the river to its former condition). If there is sufficient competition, the price to the customer will be too low, since the costs of purification of the river water have not been incorporated in the price. Thus, as we have noted earlier, market prices do not reflect actual scarcity, as the increased scarcity of clean river water is not part of the equation.

According to Pigou (1952, p.192), it is the task of the government to achieve a transfer of externalities to the buyers. He proposed *taxing* the creators of *negative* externalities (such as the producers of polluted waste water) and *subsidising* the creators of *positive* externalities. A government tax on the release of polluting

Plate 6.2 External effects of economic activities: outflow from an aluminium factory in Delfzijl, The Netherlands. Photo: Mark Edwards/Lineair

substances into surface water would have the effect of making polluters pay a higher price for pollution; the polluter would pay for the negative externalities – the negative effects of pollution. This would result in increased costs for the polluting industries, a lower level of pollution, and decreased costs for the victims of pollution. This is often called an *internalisation* of societal costs by the polluting economic agent. Negative externalities are no longer transferred to society.

During the first part of the 20th century, discussion of the problem of externalities took place on the periphery of economic science. Two World Wars, the stagnation of production, and the large numbers of unemployed people commanded most of the attention in this period. Externalities were regarded in the literature as theoretical and without any practical significance. Blaug (1978, p. 404) states that there was 'a common tendency in the interwar literature to regard external economies as economic curiosa'.

After the Second World War, attention in society was primarily directed at the restoration of production capacity, which had been severely damaged during the war in Europe. Furthermore, the prevention of mass unemployment, a common phenomenon in the 1930s, was given high priority. Special attention was given to the publications of authors such as Keynes, which dealt with serious societal problems in the field of unemployment. The growth of production and the maintenance of a high level of employment were the primary aims of society. The aim of maximising the growth of production was also spurred on by the onset of the Cold War. Both Western and Eastern Europe used the growth of production as a strategy with both political and military significance. In this social climate, there was no demand for a discussion about environmental problems since it was thought this could only hamper the growth of production. Questions about environmental problems were marginalised in terms of social importance and discussion.

The acceleration of industrial production which took place in the course of the 1960s, combined with a rapidly changing social climate, led to a fundamental change in these opinions. The increasing growth of production was accompanied by serious environmental problems; eventually, these were perceived by large sections of the population. Air pollution increasingly became a common occurrence. Smog in the Dutch Rijnmond area, the German Ruhrgebiet, London and the British Midlands was the unpleasant side effect of sunny weather. Swimming in lakes and rivers became more and more hazardous. Certain species of flowers and animals decreased in numbers, owing to increasing pollution and intensive farming techniques. In spite of the construction of more and more highways, there was a steady increase in traffic congestion. Industrial and resort areas were being constructed on a massive scale. The rise of the petrochemical industry was phenomenal, increasing the potential for large-scale disasters. In short, a situation arose in which damage to the environment was viewed by many people as an everyday phenomenon. At the end of the 1960s, these developments led to increased scientific interest in environmental problems.

Externalities revisited

Confronted with these problems, economists with a neoclassical background based their thinking on the concept of externalities introduced by Pigou. The concept allowed situations of inconvenience to be satisfactorily described. However, it was not very

Intergenerational effect

Using Pigou's definition, the future exhaustion of fossil resources can be defined as a negative externality which is off-loaded by the present generation on future generations, as these resources are used up in current production and consumption processes.

useful for analysing the problems of exhaustion of resources, as the inconvenience in these cases is not restricted to specific individuals. Exhaustion affects everyone, making it a collective evil or, when prevention of it is the starting point, a collective good. It is significant that the exhaustion of nearly all natural resources is not an *acute* phenomenon. It is future generations in particular who will be the victims of the present excessive use of natural resources. As we do not know the preferences of future generations, the concept of externality loses its meaning. Indeed, all present productive and consumptive actions would be regarded as a collection of externalities. Although future generations are not involved in any of the present market transactions, they will suffer the influences of these transactions on their own potential to produce and to consume. It was for this reason that neoclassical economists initially saw the environmental problem only as one of pollution, and more complex problems such as the exhaustion of natural resources were not taken into account (see Box 9).

Towards the end of the 1960s, increasing numbers of economists began to investigate environmental problems. The Pigovian tradition was a dominant influence in their efforts. The neoclassical tradition, in which economic information can only be found through the market, is a very well-established paradigm in current economics, so the vast majority of the economists confronted with environmental problems after the Second World War began by looking for solutions from within this paradigm (see Box 10).

One of the most remarkable publications was Mishan's polemical book *The Costs of Economic Growth* (1967). Mishan wanted to demonstrate that an increase in production would be accompanied by a decrease in welfare, as a result of the more than

Environmental economics

Most of the academic work done in environmental economics may be described as an attempt to incorporate the environment into the conventional or neoclassical framework of economic analysis. The environment is perceived as a set of commodities (goods and services) valued, like other goods and services, by individuals in society. But because environmental commodities are usually available free (that is, at zero price), this value generally goes unrecognised. The result is that they get overused, leading to environmental degradation. To bring the environment into the economic calculus, prices or monetary values therefore need to be assigned to the various goods and services it provides.

Source: Jacobs (1991), p. xv.

proportional increase in the number of negative externalities. He claimed that it is absurd that the right to pollute is stronger than the right to live in a sound environment in our society. To solve this problem, he proposed the protection of amenity rights, backed by the criminal justice system. In this system, contrary to present rules, a potential polluting producer would buy pollution rights. The price would depend on the value attributed to amenity. If the costs of the required pollution rights are prohibitive, due to a high priority for a clean environment, the planned production will be too expensive. One could conclude that society does not wish to give priority to these polluting products but to the environmental quality that would be sacrificed.

This approach does not solve the problem. Mishan recognised that in most cases it would not be possible to *quantify* negative externalities – that is, express these effects in money terms. Firstly, because of the diffuse character of many negative externalities, they are not concentrated in time or place. Secondly, many negative externalities have more than one cause, which makes it very difficult, and in many cases impossible, to relate a particular negative effect to discrete economic activities. Finally, Mishan expected that effects which could not be quantified would in many cases be more important than those which could easily be quantified. In essence, Mishan provided arguments to show that a calculation of polluting costs to the victims was far from easy and, in many cases, completely impossible.

Hueting (1980) elaborated this problem in further detail. He paid special attention to the way in which the gross national product (GNP) is defined. Hueting argued that the calculation of the GNP is incorrect when environmental matters are taken into account. It includes much expenditure which is only incurred to remedy environmental problems. If, for example, the government constructs purification plants to clean up surface water, the costs will increase the GNP, because the cost of a purification plant can be quantified; it is a normal economic good. Since the GNP is often regarded as an indicator of welfare, an increase in its level due to higher environmental costs would be interpreted as a rise in income and welfare. We can therefore conclude that GNP figures provide incorrect information. According to Hueting, a correction has to be introduced for all costs which are incurred in neutralising negative environmental effects resulting from productive or consumptive activities. This type of criticism was an attack on the concept of GNP accounting, which assumed that all types of production would have the same effect on economic welfare. National statistical offices in Western countries were disinclined to develop methods to correct GNP accounting.

The argument resurfaced at the end of the 1980s, this time receiving broader support. However, attempts to correct national income accounting are far from easy. The point is that the environment does not have a market price, which means that all calculations of this type are accompanied by a number of subjective decisions (see Box 11).

Hueting also addressed the Pigovian problem of constructing an optimal point of pollution, that is, the point at which marginal costs of pollution are equal to marginal benefits from pollution prevention. Hueting elaborated on this topic by focusing on water pollution by organic materials and argued that in practice it will be impossible to find an optimal point of pollution. Firstly, it is particularly difficult to calculate the damage of polluted water because of the absence of a market for environmental damages. Secondly, the value consumers will attach to clean water is difficult to calculate and furthermore, how to express the level of preference of consumers for clean water in

The example of acid rain

A striking example of the problematic relationship between economic activities and environmental pollution, as well as a good example of a negative external effect, is the large-scale deterioration of forests as a result of acid rain. One of the most important causes of acid rain is the emission of large quantities of sulphur dioxide. Some 20 years ago, the first measures were taken in Europe to reduce the harmful effects of sulphur dioxide. These measures included the changeover to natural gas and nuclear energy and the construction of tall chimneys on factories. At first these measures appeared to be adequate, because air pollution in urban areas and industrial regions did decrease. However, the tall chimneys only dispersed the acidifying substances over larger areas of Europe. Acid deposition beyond the industrial areas increased rapidly, damaging forests particularly in Central Europe and Scandinavia. The acidification of ecosystems could probably have been foreseen. Biologists had warned at an early stage that tall chimneys would at best merely shift the problem elsewhere. Society, however, was easily able to dismiss these warnings as exaggerations, because it was not known for certain what the effects on Nature would be.

Source: Dietz and Van der Straaten (1992).

monetary terms? Thirdly, a comparable difficulty is the level of the government's responsibility for clean water. How high is the priority given by the government to clean water and how can it be measured? This brought Hueting to the following conclusion: 'The crucial question "What is Nature worth to us?" cannot be answered by means of the instruments available to us. But in my opinion the study has shown that at the same time another question remains unanswered, namely "What is the worth of goods that are produced and consumed at the expense of the environment?" For when the value of the environment cannot be determined in the conflict between production and environment, the market price of produced goods may no longer be accepted as an indicator of the economic value of these goods' (Hueting, 1980).

Here, Hueting touches upon a fundamental shortcoming of the neoclassical approach. The fixation on priced forms of scarcity, that is, scarcity which arises from the interaction of market supply and demand, excludes unpriced forms of scarcity (see Box 12).

Shortcoming of conventional environmental economics

Conventional environmental economics, we might conclude, is useless as an instrument of environmental management, because the concept of 'externalities' merely hides the inability to put a value on social costs that are shifted to other social groups or to future generations.

Source: Martinez-Alier (1990), p. xiv.

Ecological economics

The problems of measuring externalities give rise to doubts about the possibility of constructing an optimal point of pollution on the basis of Pigovian principles. Recently, some economists have concentrated on the paradigm of ecological economics, in which the *economic system* is seen as a part of a wider system: *the ecosystem*. The challenge of this approach for environmental economists is to elaborate the relationship between the economic system and the ecosystem.

Several authors had already dealt with these problems in the course of the 1970s and 1980s. Boulding (1966), for instance, argued that current economic theories and policies were using natural resources as if they were infinite and inexhaustible. He came to the conclusion that such an approach was strongly related to the American tradition of the frontier state. He defined this type of economy as a *cowboy economy*, using the environment as an infinite entity. In his opinion, natural resources should be used as in a *spaceship economy*, in which resources and the sink function of the environment can only be used up to a certain level. Daly (1977) argued that traditional economic theories failed to cope with problems of absolute scarcity. Scarcity in neoclassical analysis is only a relative issue: some goods and resources are more scarce than others. However, current environmental problems have to do with an absolute scarcity. Hence, it is necessary to consider the concept of the *steady state*, in which natural resources are used only to a certain level.

More recently, Daly has focused on the problem of how to define the limits which Nature and the environment impose on economic activities (Daly, 1991) (see Box 13).

Optimal allocation of resources

The term 'scale' is shorthand for 'the physical scale or size of the human presence in the ecosystem, as measured by population times per capita resource use'. Optimal allocation of a given scale of resource flow within the economy is one thing (a microeconomic problem). The optimal scale of the economy as a whole relative to the ecosystem is an entirely different problem (a micro-macro problem). The microallocation problem is analogous to that of the optimal distribution of a given amount of weight within a ship: once the best relative distribution of weight has been determined, there is still the question of the absolute amount of weight the ship is able to carry. This optimal scale of load is recognised in the maritime institution of the Plimsoll mark. When the waterline hits the Plimsoll mark, the ship is full; it has reached its safe carrying capacity. Of course, if the weight is poorly distributed, the waterline will touch the Plimsoll mark sooner. But eventually, as the absolute load is increased, the waterline will reach the Plimsoll mark even for a ship whose load is optimally distributed. Even optimally loaded ships will sink under too much weight – although they may sink optimally! It should be clear that optimal allocation and optimal scale are quite distinct problems. The major task of environmental macroeconomics is to design an economic institution analogous to the Plimsoll mark to keep the weight, the absolute scale, of the economy from sinking our biospheric ark.

Source: Daly (1991), p. 35.

Other authors using the ecological economic paradigm still hold the opinion that the problems of valuing Nature and the environment can be considerably decreased by means of further research in this area. For example, Pearce (who is, in fact, an environmental economist, more closely associated with the neoclassical school) argues:

'Empirical work on evaluation remains limited, even in the developed world ... . Its importance for the development process is that the revealed economic values for environmental conservation and environmentally improving projects and policies have frequently been found to be large. Valuation demonstrates that there is an economic case for protecting the environment, in addition to any ethical case. Valuation can assist the process of decision-making. In so doing it offers the potential of more cost-efficient public choices, so that limited public income is spent to the best advantage' (Pearce, 1993, pp. 93–4).

Pearce's argument is, of course, correct. Collective decisions should be based on as much economic information as possible. However, it is clear that the Plimsoll mark metaphor used by Daly (see Box 13) cannot be determined by this type of information. The shortcomings of traditional approaches are too significant to make such an approach successful when major environmental problems come up for discussion. Moreover, our understanding of ecological systems is imperfect, to say the least, and our lack of knowledge and uncertainty raise further questions about the attempts to internalise externalities. The next section discusses a model of thinking which is relevant for an improved insight into these complicated problems.

6.5 Economics and sustainable development

Our discussion so far has led us to a preliminary conclusion, namely, that two related economic and environmental problems have to be solved. Firstly, economic theories pay insufficient attention to the complexity of the relationship between the system of production and consumption on the one hand and the environment on the other. An adequate analysis in economic terms of the relationship between the economic system and the ecosystem is needed.

Secondly, it is often argued that the core of the difficulties is in the concept of negative externalities. Although the neoclassical principle of including the social costs of environmental damage in the calculations of economic agents seems straightforward enough, there are many obstacles to such a process. In the first place, the relationship between the emissions and the level of damages in the ecosystem is not clear. For instance, what is the contribution of the emissions of acidifying substances in The Netherlands to the death of trees in the German Black Forest? These types of calculations are almost impossible. Even if it were possible, there is the problem of the great number of Dutch polluters. In the Pigovian approach, there is only one polluter and one victim, and calculations are not so difficult. Such an assumption, however, is far removed from the complex reality of modern societies, with large numbers of polluters and many people suffering from pollution. This makes political choices immensely difficult. Responsibilities must be defined if we are to find a solution.

In trying to internalise negative externalities, complications also arise in the ecosystem itself. In the Pigovian approach, the ecosystem is defined in a straightforward manner, while in reality it may be quite complex. In many cases, for instance, it involves thresholds: pollution becomes apparent only after it reaches a certain level. Another complication is caused by the rather common synergistic effects of pollution. The combined effects of different emissions may cause a higher level of damage than would be expected from the individual effects of the different pollutants. Finally, there are many uncertainties in the functioning of the ecosystem itself. If, for instance, the economic relevance of the greenhouse effect were to be evaluated, the conclusion would be that this does not fit the framework of a Pigovian approach, due to future uncertainties. The interests of future generations, which are relevant to the greenhouse effect, cannot be taken into account in the case of the internalisation of external effects. This leads to the conclusion that the Pigovian approach of internalisation is interesting from an analytical point of view, as it provides insights into the relationship between pollution and costs, but it does not provide us with real tools for solving the problem of external costs. The main reasons are the absence of a market for environmental goods, the complexity of the functioning of the ecosystem and the absence of future generations in the calculations. In order to come to terms with these problems, it is necessary to develop a line of reasoning which might yield better tools for reaching a solution. In this section, a simple model is presented which takes into account the consequences of the shortcomings of the neoclassical approach.

The problems mentioned above played an important role in the Brundtland Commission report (WCED, 1987). The Commission was aware of the shortcomings of a traditional economic approach, and proposed the concept of *sustainable development* as an absolute necessity for solving problems in this field. They defined sustainable development as development in which the use of natural resources to meet the needs of the current generation would not frustrate the ability of future generations to meet their own needs. Natural resources are seen as capital which has to be maintained by current and other generations. In broad terms, this approach was accepted by many governments and environmental economists. In the next paragraphs, this concept will be elaborated on in connection with economic theory.

Sustainable development in economic analysis

The model in Figure 6.3 separates the system of production and consumption from the ecological system, and applies concepts which are commonly used in the description of the functioning of ecosystems. These concepts appear in the righthand section of the model, which outlines the ecosystem insofar as it is relevant to the process of production and consumption. The lefthand section of the figure outlines the system of production and consumption. This includes the economic decisions of economic agents involving ecological considerations, decisions which will have a negative effect on natural resources.

In ecological science, ecocycles are used to describe ecosystems. If the environment is disrupted, it can be ascertained at which point in the cycles the polluting substances are transported and where they decompose or accumulate. The way in which information and energy are transported in an ecosystem is also relevant. The energy in Figure 6.3 comes from the sun. The main problem in Figure 6.3 is how the information

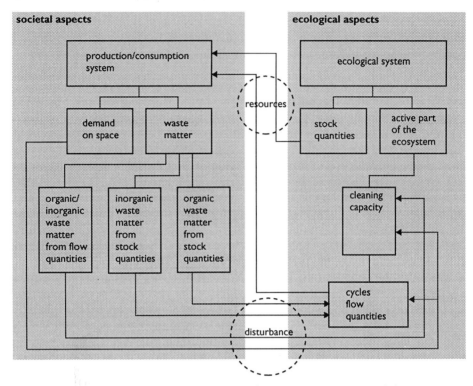

Fig. 6.3 A model of the relationship between the economic system and the ecosystem

which is available in the ecological system can play a role in the system of production and consumption. As was concluded above, the price mechanism cannot work in this respect. The information which is necessary to achieve an optimal allocation of unpriced natural resources will not reach the economic agents. This does not imply that consumers, producers and the government are not informed about environmental disruption. That may or may not be the case. The point is that this information does not reach them through the price mechanism. This leads to a situation in which economic agents acting in a market in which production factors, goods, and services are priced do not have the relevant economic information about the disruption of unpriced natural resources which are, nevertheless, relevant for production and consumption. It is necessary to obtain other types of information, which can help us to make decisions in the allocation of unpriced natural resources. This is only possible if data about the functioning of the ecological system are included. This is a central point in the construction of Figure 6.3.

The model of Figure 6.3 distinguishes between *stocks* and *flows*. It describes the effects of human production and consumption on the ecological system. A system of human production and consumption is based, among other things, on the need to use natural resources from the ecological cycles – the active part of the ecosystem. Such natural resources are, in theory, inexhaustible and therefore go on flowing forever. Around the beginning of the 19th century, however, the large-scale exploitation of fossil natural resources began. But resources such as oil, coal and iron ore are exhaustible; they are defined as stock quantities in Figure 6.3. The fossil part of the ecosystem is hardly, if at all, affected by the flow of waste products originating from the economic system. Pollution of the environment occurs in that part of the ecological system involving cycles, which can be disturbed by the discharge of waste products.

There is a great difference between the dumping of organic materials and the dumping of inorganic and synthetic materials into the ecocycles. Organic materials are normal elements of functioning ecocycles, while inorganic and synthetic substances are foreign to them. These foreign substances include the waste products from fossil resources. If dumped into the ecocycles, even in low concentrations, they cause disturbances, because no mechanisms are available to process or decompose these waste products. On the other hand, the dumping of decomposable organic matter does not necessarily disturb the ecocycles. Such matter is already part and parcel of the ecocycles and can be decomposed by bacteria in the normal way. However, if too much decomposable organic matter is dumped into, for example, surface water, the water's self-cleaning capacity may be overtaxed to the extent that only stinking, rotting and deoxygenised expanses of water remain. The pollution from fossil matter is worse than pollution from organic, decomposable matter. Whereas the latter occurs locally and may be neutralised after a time, pollution from undecomposable stock matter is irreversible. It is almost impossible to restore the cycle in this case. Substances foreign to ecocycles accumulate, with long-term effects for the environment over a large area. Thus, when heavy metals are discharged into the surface water, the flora and the fauna will be seriously affected. Heavy metals do not disappear when the organisms die, but accumulate in the ecocycles.

One category of effects on Nature from human activity has not so far been dealt with: the use of land. Yet this use seriously violates the ecocycles. The process began as soon as people settled in one place, took up agriculture and began to change the natural vegetation. In Europe, this has reached the point where virtually none of the original vegetation is left. Modifications of the vegetation do not necessarily lead to unacceptable changes in the ecocycles, but they do interfere with the cyclical process. Further pressure on the natural vegetation from the construction of houses and factories and of roads and other infrastructural elements has seriously affected the ecosystem. Its effect is different from that of the discharge of waste products, however, in that it threatens the functioning of ecocycles much more rapidly and directly, without complicated intermediary processes. For instance, ecocycles may be changed if natural woodland is turned into arable land or cleared for the purpose of road construction.

Stocks are, in principle, exhaustible. They are the raw materials and supplies of fossil energy which are embedded in the Earth's crust. They are exploited and used in the production process, after which the residuals are released into the environment, leading to disruption of the ecocycles. Arrows in Figure 6.3, starting from the stocks, indicate the route these substances take during the process of being used as a resource, and the release of the residuals as pollutants.

If the goal is ecologically sustainable development, then it is a prerequisite that the ecosystem should be used in such a way that its working will not itself be irreversibly damaged. To a certain extent, this is difficult to achieve. The discharge of materials not natural to the environment and extracted from the stocks should be minimalised or preferably stopped altogether. The discharges of waste products from flows contain materials which are natural to the environment. This does not alter the fact, however, that overloading of the carrying capacity of ecocycles may cause the local or regional disruption of ecosystems. It has been firmly established that the use of space by humanity eventually leads to a disruption of ecosystems.

The speed at which stocks will be exhausted can be considerably reduced by the large-scale introduction of mineral and synthetic recycling. It is impossible, however, to recycle all materials. Some of the materials are 'lost' during the processes of production, consumption and recycling; these materials are discharged into the ecosystem. Technological development should be directed at decreasing the percentage of materials 'lost'. Of course, the best solution would be to switch to renewable or continuing resources. Such resources can be extracted from the ecocycles (using ecologically sound methods) without disrupting them. The same is true of the extraction and use of energy. Fossil stocks of oil, natural gas and coal will sooner or later become exhausted; conversion to the use of energy from flows is inevitable in the long run.

Conversion towards sustainability

A process of conversion to ecologically acceptable methods of production will have a considerable influence on many social relations. Sustainable development will pose a threat to well-established interests as the market process has led to a situation which is far from sustainable. This situation is not the result of the actions of a limited number of individuals. The environmental crisis is, in essence, the result of a spontaneous development of the market. It cannot be expected, however, that reduction of the environmental disruptions will also be a spontaneous process. Such a reduction will only be possible through the introduction of strict environmental policies.

Policies that stimulate sustainable development, however, will not be received with great enthusiasm by the interests which have profited from the present disruption of the environment. Once the ecological limiting conditions for the production and consumption process have been determined, the interests and economic sectors which produce large amounts of pollution will resist the changes which affect them and defend their position. Furthermore, economic sectors may claim that, in addition to creating economic growth and wealth, they also clean up the environment and should therefore not be confronted with strict standards. Well-organised groups of polluting producers such as the petrochemical industry, the transport sector and agriculture may be expected to oppose strict environmental measures or at least to argue for less stringent measures. They do not oppose the aim of sustainable development in general, but the pace at which it is implemented (Dietz and van der Straaten, 1990).

There are, however, limits to the use of ecological space. This implies that all polluting sectors are in competition, each trying to claim a portion of the limited opportunities for pollution. This may well result in a social struggle for the allocation of ecological space to different production and consumption processes. In this social struggle, national authorities will play an important role, as decisions about this allocation will have to be taken on a collective basis. No single instrument can be excluded from the endeavour to attain a situation of sustainable development.

Governments can use taxes, subsidies, controls and regulations to steer the development in the desired direction. Technological development can play an important rule in this process of conversion.

The aim of sustainable development implies that limiting conditions for the production and consumption processes should be formulated from an ecological as well as an ethical point of view. With regard to discharges of waste materials from the stocks, the functioning of the ecosystem itself provides the standards enabling us to set a certain level of discharge which is acceptable from an ecological point of view. Such an environmental policy can be implemented with the help of present-day economic instruments. These would ensure that the polluter pays the full costs of damage inflicted on the environment. In economists' terms the polluter is made to internalise the social costs imposed. In our model, the standards originate in the ecological system, the aim being to achieve sustainable development. In this approach, prices and regulations are instruments for the implementation of previously formulated, ecologically desirable ends. Although the price mechanism can play an important role, it is not the same role it has in neoclassical theories.

6.6 Managing the commons

The tragedy of the commons

Figure 6.3 pays particular attention to the collective decision-making process. Other authors have argued that the solving of environmental problems is only possible if the common natural resources are linked to the functioning of the market. In other words: environmental problems can be solved by privatising common property resources. This school of thought was elaborated by Hardin in the article 'The tragedy of the commons' (1968). He is of the opinion that common property resources such as common pasture land or common fishing grounds in the North Sea are overused, resulting in the degradation of that resource, precisely because they can be used by anyone. There is no pressure on the individual to limit use of the common property resource. This results in a situation in which all individuals repeatedly try to increase their yields, and in doing so, degrade the quality and quantity of the common property resource. Hardin's conclusion is clear: common property resources are always overused. The benefit to a private user of overusing such a resource is always greater than the very small marginal damage each potential user suffers from his own overuse. This results in constant overuse, as every user can gain a private benefit by overusing the resource.

Hardin comes to the conclusion that this is the result of a deficient definition of *property rights*, which can only be solved by privatising the common property resource. After privatisation, the positive and negative results of the overuse will both be the responsibility of the user. The benefits as well as the damages resulting from overuse will affect the owner of the property rights. The owner who is also the user will balance these benefits and costs, and will stop overuse. This argument has received a good deal of attention. In the literature one can find numerous arguments based on Hardin's article about the determined overuse of all common property resources. It should be stated that this approach is completely different from that proposed in the previous section, where it was concluded that a governmental environmental policy was the answer to the environmental disruption of unpriced collective natural resources. Hardin argues that the problem can only be solved by a *privatisation* of *collective* goods.

Open access or common good?

Bromley (1991) made it clear that Hardin's argument ignored the point of *open access*. Hardin assumed that all common property resources have a regime of open access. In many cases of common property there are, however, strict regulations which exclude open access. Thus, according to Bromley, it is not the common property right which creates the problem but a situation of open access. This can be clearly demonstrated by the tropical rainforest in Brazil. These forests were traditionally common property. The Indians living in these forests had built up, in the course of time, an institutional framework guaranteeing sustainable use of these resources. As these forests were taken over by private logging companies, they required private property rights, which can be established in Brazil by applying to the authorities. In the absence of existing private property rights in a particular area, any newcomer can establish such rights. With these private property rights secured, logging could begin in the rainforests, and significant common property resources were destroyed. Here, the establishment of the private property rights led to environmental damage.

On closer consideration, the distinction between externalities and private goods and services based on the intention of the agents is not convincing as a means for understanding environmental problems. If A's paper mill pollutes the river and B becomes ill from drinking the polluted water, conventional theory calls this a negative externality. But if A buys and eats the only bread left at the baker's, as a result of which B goes hungry, no externality is created. The conventional approach to externalities fails to explain why it is any more or less intentional when A eats and B goes hungry than when A produces effluents and B becomes ill.

Externalities point out interdependent relationships between economic agents which in conventional economic theory are seen as 'incidental', that is, as specific and special events. However, as the previous example indicates, there are many situations in which the actions of A affect the well-being of B. Human interdependence relationships are ubiquitous and these relationships constitute the basis of both co-operation and conflict. If two persons are needed to transport the bricks to build a house, they could decide to co-operate. The advantage of co-operation, however, does not mean that a joint effort will be forthcoming. Often, disputes over the distribution of the fruits of joint efforts keep the bricks from being transported at all.

People unavoidably affect each other in situations of scarcity. Scarcity leads to conflict over the control of resources and how this conflict is resolved depends on the structure of property rights in society. Property rights describe the relationship of one person to another with respect to a resource or line of action. As Schmid puts it: 'Rights are the instrumentality by which society controls and orders human interdependence and resolves the question of who gets what' (Schmid, 1987, p.5) .

Internalisation of externalities

In conventional economic theory, externalities are seen as a market failure. Traditionally, *internalisation of externalities* is recommended and it is suggested that internalisation eliminates the externalities concerned. In reality, internalisation procedures do not eliminate externalities. If interests conflict, one or more of the interests must go unmet. Property rights determine which interests prevail, that is, whether A is allowed to affect B or vice versa. Internalisation means a shift in the rights structure. Where formerly the paper mill was allowed to pollute the river, it now either has to pay for effluent discharge, to buy discharge rights (transferable permit) or to install equipment which purifies the effluents before they are discharged. Internalisation reduces the opportunity set (the range of opportunities) of the paper mill, but expands the opportunity set of people living downstream. The interdependence between the paper mill and downstream inhabitants is not diminished, changed or eliminated, nor is the conflict of interests. The change in property rights does not imply that the externality is made internal, it only shifts the externality from one party to the other, that is, the interest of drawing drinking water from the river has been given more weight than the interest of discharging effluents into the river.

In the literature, the impression is created that the establishment of property rights automatically means that the internalisation of externalities can be left to the market. An efficient resource allocation should be independent of the party to whom the property right was given - either the generator or the victim. All that is said to matter is that the parties involved strike an easy bargain in which they agree on the compensation to be given to the rights owner with the aim of reducing the externalities once the rights have been allocated. It should be pointed out that this result hinges on the assumption that internalisation requires no transaction costs, that is, that the gathering of the information needed, the negotiations leading to an agreement and the enforcement of the agreement are without costs. In practice there will always be transaction costs.

In a world with transaction costs, environmental damage is determined primarily by the initial property rights allocation. Mobilising the downstream population to make a bid to encourage an upstream paper mill to reduce its legitimate effluent discharges will result in a more severely polluted river than would be the case if the paper mill had to make a bid to the inhabitants downstream who have the legitimate right to a clean river. Although clearly defined property rights help to solve environmental problems, the most relevant issue is who has the rights and thus who has the effective protection of the state to do as he wishes (Bromley, 1991, p. 35). This, of course, is a political issue: all environmental policies and all definitions of property rights are the result of political processes. Hence, one may conclude that it is this political aspect of environmental problems in particular which is neglected in neoclassical theories. If these theoretical insights are a guide to 'practical' solutions, it is clear that the political barriers will frustrate environmental policies.

6.7 Conclusions: economics and environmental policy

The political context of environmental policy

The above discussion of the privatisation of common resources brings us to the topic of environmental policy as a part of public policy. Environmental policy involves certain measures aimed at achieving a sound environment. It is usually developed in the context of public policy, based on economic theory, which focuses on the level of costs and benefits associated with the implementation of environmental policies.

If strict standards are proposed and implemented by a Minister of Environmental Affairs, certain polluting sectors have to take measures which cannot be achieved without incurring extra costs. Polluting industries are often keen to highlight the likely cost to them of proposed environmental measures. The benefits resulting from environmental policies are extremely difficult to assess. In consequence, the costs of environmental measures are often given more attention than the benefits resulting from the implementation of the policy.

This brings us to the distributional effects of environmental policies. Hardin's argument clearly shows that the definition of the property rights of natural resources plays a significant role. The implementation of strict standards and regulations will

Plate 6.3 Economic industrial development in Minat Itlan, Mexico. Photo: Ron Giling/Lineair

cause a change in the definition of property rights. Industries which have polluted rivers for many decades will be confronted with regulations which reduce their opportunities for using the river in this fashion. Of course, these industries will try to neutralise the effects of this implementation of strict standards. Throughout the process of formulating regulations, polluting industries will try to influence policies.

Polluting industries utilise the uncertainties of environmental science. On the other hand, they emphasise the importance of their production, the employment they provide, and their contribution to the balance of payments. All economic interests and sectors use economic arguments in an attempt to influence environmental policies in a direction favourable to themselves. This demonstrates how weak many traditional economic arguments are, since they can be used by any polluter to strengthen his or her position. Many economists argue that the introduction of economic instruments such as levies, subsidies, and taxes will lead to an efficient implementation of environmental measures. It is often overlooked, however, that all such instruments are part and parcel of the institutions of a country. The institutional framework, of which property rights are an important part, should be taken into account when the implementation of environmental measures is discussed. This is particularly true of the problem of the distribution of the costs and benefits resulting from environmental measures.

As long as pollution problems are mainly national, there is a need for a strong national authority. However, environmental problems are becoming increasingly international or global. As a result, all of the difficulties mentioned above are also present on an international scale. This complicates environmental policies considerably. On the one hand, international co-operation in the fighting of environmental problems is absolutely necessary. On the other hand, different countries have different economic interests. Furthermore, polluting sectors are not evenly distributed among countries. Countries have a tendency to protect their polluting industries, in particular when these industries are relatively important economically. We may now draw some conclusions:

○ Environmental problems can be defined as economic problems. Costs and benefits of environmental policies are relevant. Economic theory can provide us with insights into the complexity of these relationships.
○ Traditional economic theory, which aims to internalise externalities, does not provide real solutions to modern environmental problems. Alternative approaches in which more attention is given to the relationship between the ecosystem and the system of production and consumption will have to be developed.
○ The definition of property rights of natural resources plays a crucial role in environmental economics as well as in environmental policies. The implementation of environmental policies is viewed as a change in property rights by polluting industries. They will defend their traditional right to pollute.
○ Even if one defines environmental problems as economic problems, the distributional effects of the implementation of environmental policies should not be overlooked. Environmental problems are also traditional political problems – at local, national, and international level.

International environmental policies

Many of the above arguments and discussions dealt with national situations. However, all the problems and complications mentioned above are more serious in an international context. This is mainly caused by the fact that in a national context there is a national authority which is able to implement a legal framework with corresponding sanctions. This is hardly ever the case at an international level. In nearly all cases of international environmental disruption, negotiations are the only way to solve the problem. However, a great deal of negotiation is required in order to persuade polluting countries to curb their pollution. This puts the countries suffering from pollution or environmental disruption in a difficult position.

This was the problem at the United Nations Conference in Rio de Janeiro in 1992, of which the Conventions on Climate Change and Biodiversity were the most tangible results. With regard to the Climate Convention, there was an acrimonious debate between countries such as Brazil and the northern countries. From a global point of view, tropical rainforests are extremely important as a sink for carbon dioxide produced by the burning of fossil fuels, a very high percentage of which occurs in northern countries. Hence, northern countries are of the opinion that these forests have to be protected in order to neutralise the greenhouse effect. There were, however, no well-defined cost-benefit analyses available, owing to the many uncertainties surrounding this topic. The external costs of energy consumption could not be defined and the internalisation of these external costs could not be achieved (see Box 14).

The United States government were not convinced that strict measures would have to be taken to decrease the risk of global warming. This opinion was, of course, related to the high energy consumption in the United States, which it is not willing to give up. Countries with large areas of tropical rainforest, on the other hand, argued that developed countries have been destroying their forests for a long time. It would make no sense to say that the developing countries were the only countries responsible for a

---

14

The value of tropical rainforest

The discussion on debt-for-Nature swaps in Brazil reveals the difficulties in valuation of other externalities. A proposal for buying four billion dollars' worth of the Brazilian debt in order to save the Amazonian rainforest was tentatively launched in early 1989 (*New York Times*, 3 February 1989). This 'generous' offer is paltry in the context of Brazil's total external debt, a nominal value of 115 billion dollars. From another perspective, too, the offer looks mean: under one dollar per inhabitant of the world, once and for all, as the price for preserving the Amazonian rainforest. An annual value of, say, 50 billion dollars could be given to the externalities provided to the rest of humankind by preserving the Amazonian rain forest from private exploitation. However, nobody knows how to give present values to the future benefits of preserving tropical biodiversity.

Source: Martinez-Alier (1990), p.xiv.

---

global problem. They felt that developed countries should pay them for protecting their tropical rainforests, as these were to be used to solve global problems.

In this debate, the concept of property rights is a crucial one. Who is the owner of the tropical rainforests? Is it the people living in these forests or the state of Brazil or is it the global community of all countries? Indeed, it is the global community which might suffer from the greenhouse effect, but the developed countries have contributed considerably more to this phenomenon than the developing countries. The developing countries, in particular, harbour the global sinks for carbon dioxide, the tropical rainforests. It may be concluded that the distribution of costs and benefits among different countries is the most relevant problem if a policy on the greenhouse effect is to be established.

The United Nations Conference in Rio de Janeiro functioned as a platform for the debate on global environmental problems. However, this debate has only just started, which implies that the establishment of such an institutional framework will still take much time and effort before an acceptable solution is found. The implementation of global environmental policies is just the beginning!

7

The search for sustainable development

Andrew Blowers and Pieter Glasbergen

7.1 Introduction

The underlying question for this book is: 'What are international environmental problems and why are they important politically?'. We have now examined this question from the different perspectives of the natural sciences, sociology, politics, law and economics. In this way we have emphasised that environmental problems, even those that are ostensibly localised, have an international context that must be addressed through policy arrangements that transcend the national state. The discussion has also focused on environmental problems as both physical and social problems. Consequently, it has been shown that the solving of environmental problems is both a scientific/technical and a social/political matter.

This chapter is a synthesis and development of the foregoing, the emphasis shifting from the environmental problems of the present to the environmental needs of the future. It focuses on the idea of *sustainable development*, which was the *leitmotif* of the Brundtland Report in 1987 and which became the accepted goal of policy makers at the Earth Summit in Rio de Janeiro five years later. Sustainable development is a *concept* that incorporates the problems of environment and development. It is also a *strategy* that informs policy making for both environment and development. In the oft-quoted phrase of the Brundtland Report, sustainable development is development that 'meets the needs of the present without compromising the ability of future generations to meet their own needs'. Thus, sustainability is viewed primarily in terms of human survival.

The concept of sustainable development recognises the natural limits imposed by the ability of the biosphere to absorb the effects of human activities. It also underlines the threat to environmental resources created by the present state of technology and social organisation. Consequently, in terms of present policy dealing with future requirements, sustainability must meet two criteria. First, ecological systems must be protected and maintained in such a way that the existing and putative benefits they contain are not denied to future generations. Secondly, ecological systems should not be altered or interfered with in such a way as to impose risks on future generations.

On the whole, the Brundtland Commission is optimistic in its ideas about the cure. Technology and social organisation can be improved to handle both the problems of the carrying capacity of the environment and problems of poverty and (under)development. Moreover, the Commission states that, far from requiring the cessation of economic growth, a new era of economic growth is necessary. This is an era in which integration of environment and development is required in all countries, rich and poor (WCED, 1987).

Sustainable development is now widely accepted both as a diagnosis and cure for the world's environmental problems. The idea of a sustainable development is, in principle, attractive and as a result has been appropriated by a wide range of often conflicting interests. Business people use it to gild their green image; environmentalists claim it to enhance their credibility; politicians enjoy the free publicity it brings. There is much rhetoric surrounding the simple expression of the idea and it can satisfy many different agendas. The concept of sustainable development can easily be dismissed as 'all things to all people', a concept so vague as to be almost meaningless. Indeed, it has been described as a cliché, a passing fashion, even as an oxymoron. 'Despite the apparent contradiction, creating wealth without destroying the natural resource base is unquestionably an attractive quest, even if it turns out to be something like the Holy Grail' (Friend, 1992, p 157). More sceptical still is the argument that 'sustainable development is in reality a means for the continuing legitimation of "global" strategies of development, which ensure the continued hegemony of the northern, industrialized countries' (Redclift, 1993, p 5). Linking development to sustainability allows one to portray an optimistic vision which suggests that the threats to the environment can be managed by marginal and incremental changes in behaviour, without undermining fundamentally the lifestyles enjoyed by the wealthier nations.

The aim of this chapter is to come to a better appreciation of the meaning and implications for policy of sustainable development. Our main argument, following on the lines of Chapter 1, is that sustainable development should be seen in terms of development and distribution problems that involve conflicts of interest. The present chapter also emphasises the major political and economic constraints to the achievement of sustainable development. The nature of the social changes that will be necessary in order to achieve sustainable development will be indicated and we shall examine the reasons why such changes may be resisted.

7.2 Distribution and development

Sustainable development as a practical concept for international policy making cannot be discussed in isolation from the general structures of the world's economic systems. However, a discussion which starts with this issue is not easy. In one sense it is possible to speak of an international capitalist economic system as the dominant global organisational principle. However, once the relationship between the economy and the environment is introduced, it is clear that there is a complex pattern of contrasting regions and countries in the world. Various categories of countries can be distinguished, for example, the countries of the European Union (EU). But within this category there are various possible subdivisions that reflect major differences in environmental conditions and levels of economic development. The pursuit of uniform environmental regulations reveals the different economic interests. It could be observed that the most developed countries (e.g. Germany, The Netherlands, Denmark) usually take the lead in organising their environmental law. Their attempts at achieving uniform regulations across the EU are hampered by the less developed countries, which want to secure the same level of development first.

At a broader European level, the picture changes dramatically. Although there are economic differences among the formerly communist Eastern European countries, they have all experienced widespread environmental deterioration. This is not to say that there are no environmental problems in the EU countries, but especially in Western Europe, environmental problems are associated with high income and high consumption levels. In other European countries environmental degradation goes hand in hand with low income and low consumption levels. In this respect, the Western European countries are more closely related to other rich parts of the world (USA, Japan, Canada, etc.). They belong to the 20% richest countries which consume 80% of the world's natural resources.

Plate 7.1 Contrast between rich and poor: a shanty town in Bombay, India. Photo: Ron Giling/Lineair

This picture becomes even more complicated when we bring other parts of the world into it. Two more categories of nations can be distinguished. First, there are the low-income countries undergoing rapid economic development, often known as Newly Industrialising Countries (NICs), such as Taiwan, Malaysia, Korea or the Philippines in South-East Asia. Booming economic growth in these countries often goes side by side with neglect of the environmental effects. Secondly, the poorest developing countries, often rich in natural resources, experience low income, low consumption and population pressure, together with heavy exploitation of natural resources.

The process of development in the poorer countries is closely linked with economic growth in the richest countries. Under the current economic system rich countries purchase natural resources from poor countries, allowing economic growth in both the developed and some of the developing countries. However, the resources traded are, for the most part, limited and non-renewable. Furthermore, after trading, the land is usually left scarred and devastated. The income derived from this trading seldom adds much to the welfare of the local citizens. It is, in most cases, the big landowners and multinational corporations who stand to make the biggest profit. This is precisely what is happening to the harvest of wood in rainforests all over the world.

The foregoing is only a rough sketch of the link between environmental degradation and distributional and development issues. Terhal (1992) has made an analytical distinction between 'unsustainability of poverty' and 'unsustainability of affluence', as follows:

○ The first form of unsustainable development is associated with low per capita income and consumption levels, demographic pressure and direct links between

Population, environment and development

A major political conflict exists over the relationship between population and environmental degradation. From a northern, developed perspective it is customary to emphasise the importance of population growth and to urge policies of population restraint on the South. Conversely, southern countries point to the high per capita consumption of resources as the primary cause of environmental deterioration. Both have a point.

On a global scale, environmental degradation is a product of population multiplied by *average* resource use. For illustrative purposes we may use an average per capita energy consumption of 2 kw. Development introduces the problem of inequalities in resource use. For example, per capita energy consumption may be 1 kw in the South but ten times as high in the North. But in terms of pressure on the environment, both population numbers and consumption per head of the population are important. Therefore, neither a policy of population restraint nor one of reduction in per capita consumption is likely to achieve sustainability. A reduction in consumption levels will not compensate for the rapid upsurge in population levels, which are expected to reach a global total of 8 billion by 2025 from about 5 billion in 1990. Both population restraint and a reduction in per capita levels of resource consumption and pollution will be necessary.

resource exploitation and (insufficient) basic needs fulfilment. This results in environmental degradation, which in turn leads to continued poverty.

○ The second form is associated with high per capita income and consumption levels and high levels of investment and resource exploitation, which also leads to exhaustion of resources and large-scale environmental degradation.

In Terhal's view it is of vital importance for the design of 'sustainable development' to recognise the links between the two models, in particular how 'unsustainability of affluence' impinges on 'unsustainability of poverty'. Furthermore, he stresses the danger of the temptation to look for a way out in which the 'unsustainability of poverty' is replaced by the 'unsustainability of affluence' (Terhal, 1992, p. 132–33) (see also Box 1).

It is clear that there are no universal models with universal solutions. Major changes in both types of development, in relation to each other, seem to be necessary, a point to which we shall return.

7.3 The meaning of sustainable development

The previous section has illustrated the complexity of the notion of sustainable development. Sustainable development combines both scientific principles and human values (see Box 2). Once natural processes are affected by human processes, sustainability becomes endowed with social meaning. Once values are applied, sustainable development becomes a matter for interpretation by different groups or interests in society. It acquires ideological overtones as a motivating purpose for society. On closer examination, the concept proves to be complex, demanding careful interpretation of its component parts. The concept therefore has to be interpreted in terms of the interests it serves. And if it is to be a useful concept for policy making, it needs to be clarified in order that objectives can be established, implemented and monitored. This problem of clarification arises with the well-known Brundtland definition of sustainable development as *development that meets the needs of the present without compromising the ability of future generations to meet their own needs*. Within this phrase there are three concepts in particular that require interpretation and more precise definition. These are: development, needs and future generations.

The concept of development

Development is not synonymous with economic growth, though the two are often confused. Economic growth refers to a quantitative expansion of the prevailing economic system. Development is a qualitative concept which incorporates ideas of improvement and progress and includes cultural and social as well as economic dimensions. Furthermore, the concept of development focuses on the relative distribution of scarce resources. This raises two problems. The first is the *problem of scarcity* of resources and its implications for environmental sustainability. A key discussion here is how to measure the cost of using resources in terms of impact on the environment. The second is the *problem of the unequal distribution of resources* and its implications for the achievement of sustainable development. It is here that the

---

Sustainable development: a scientific and social concept

2

Sustainability is a scientific principle indicating the notion of natural systems enduring over time. *Development* is a social science concept relating to the progress of human systems. Taken together, *sustainable development* can be defined as 'a relationship between dynamic human economic systems and larger, dynamic, but normally slower-changing ecological systems, such that: (a) human life can continue indefinitely; (b) human individuals can flourish; (c) human cultures can develop; but in which (d) effects of human activities remain within bounds so as not to destroy the health/integrity of the environmental context of human activities' (Norton, 1992, p. 106). It should be noted, in passing, that this definition is anthropocentric. Sustainable development tends to take a utilitarian view of the protection of species, i.e. their importance tends to be seen in terms of their value (actual or potential) to human survivability.

---

concepts of sustainability and development become intertwined. It is contemporary patterns of economic growth that threaten sustainability and it is the process of uneven development that inhibits the achievement of sustainable policies. How to handle uneven development and the resulting inequality is at the heart of the problem of sustainable development.

The concept of needs

The concept of *needs* also introduces the question of the distribution of resources. The Brundtland Commission is ambivalent on this issue: 'Sustainable development requires meeting the basic needs of all and extending to all the opportunity to satisfy their aspirations for a better life' (p. 44). However, 'basic needs' is a relative concept, since in the richer parts of the world what were once regarded as luxuries are now regarded as necessities. As material standards have improved, so per capita consumption of natural resources and production of pollution has risen. In the poorer countries, meanwhile, the pressure on the environment to meet basic needs creates widespread degradation of natural systems. If the poor are to satisfy their aspirations to a better life, then the burden on the environment will quickly become intolerable. On a world scale, the prospect of maintaining the standards of the rich while improving the conditions of the poor is clearly impossible under present economic systems. This raises, implicitly, the issue of responsibility. The poor nations place responsibility for global environmental degradation firmly at the door of the rich. Consequently, the rich must both reduce their claims on the environment's resources and, at the same time, provide help to the poor to achieve more sustainable practices. Conversely, the rich countries endeavour to promote the idea of a shared responsibility, so that all contribute to ensuring environmental security.

The concept of future generations

Coming next to the concept of *future generations,* we encounter the problem of needs in a different context. Sustainability is essentially about the future and what we should hand on. A pragmatic argument often encountered here is that we pass both benefits and costs down to future generations and that it is difficult to weigh one against the other. For example, how can we balance the benefit of urban parks against, say, toxic waste dumps inherited from the Victorian Age? At its most basic level, sustainability is a concept of stewardship: 'We have a moral duty to look after our planet and to hand it on in good order to future generations' (HMSO, 1990, p. 10). In the more precise terms of sustainable development it is clear that we should not hand on the environment as it stands but strive to improve those areas that are heavily degraded or socially deprived, so that future generations are not burdened by inherited problems. Similarly, we should avoid inflicting irreversible damage or imposing a higher level of risk than we currently experience. Indisputably, we have already breached these criteria by the destruction of species and the production of toxic and radioactive materials which will present risks for generations to come. Our actions in the present may very well deny future generations the resources they need (or might discover they can use). They may also have to devote energy and ingenuity to the safe management of dangerous materials consigned to them. We should not assume that future generations will possess the resources, knowledge or ability to deal with environmental problems inherited from a bygone age (see Box 3).

3

Discounting the future

Discounting is a concept devised by economists and employed by government and business, which expresses future liabilities in terms of present costs. Discounting assumes that money can be invested now and accumulate interest. Consequently, a discount rate can be applied which ensures at least that money invested now will yield sufficient return to defray future liabilities. Anything over this will be profit. To take an example, £1 invested now, at a 5% discount rate, will be worth £1.05 in a year's time.

Discounting reflects the tendency for people to prefer income now rather than later. While it works reasonably well for defined projects over short time spans, discounting over long periods faces major uncertainties. The assumptions of continuing economic growth (hence security of the investment) and of technical capability to deal with liabilities become more doubtful over time. 'Philosophically, discounting the future at a particular annual rate means that the future is treated as progressively less and less important the further ahead we look' (SPRU, 1994, p. 29). For instance, in the case of decommissioning a nuclear power plant, discounting at a low rate of 2% over a century or more may appear reasonable now but it assumes continuing economic growth over the whole period, political and institutional stability and a technical capacity to deal with today's technology by future generations. The future is literally discounted and burdens are bequeathed to future generations who may have neither the resources nor the capabilities for dealing with them.

7.4 Principles and problems for policy making

Once we begin to investigate the social meaning of sustainable development, we find it becomes a very elusive concept indeed. The concept is prey to all kinds of interpretations to support different interests. This makes it very difficult to tie it down in terms of specific policies to achieve sustainability. Conflict is inherent in any attempt to secure agreement on the evidence, the objectives, the instruments and the implementation of policy. The following principles for policy making can be extracted from our discussion so far:

○ Sustainable development requires an emphasis on resource conservation. This necessity has long been recognised for non-renewable resources. It is now recognised that the principle applies to the conservation of the global commons hitherto treated as an infinite resource. This principle involves a fundamental shift from human systems which exploit, pollute and degrade the environment to those which preserve and protect it.

○ Sustainable development requires greater equality of access to natural resources and some redistribution of wealth from rich to poor. Sustainable policies are more likely to be supported if they are seen to be equitable. Under the present economic and political systems some countries are able to exploit global resources while others may be denied the use of resources, even those on their own territory. Redistribution of wealth can be achieved in various ways through the transfer of aid, technology and investment. Aid policies have often, in the past, led to unsustainable forms of development. In the future, redistribution will need to be linked to sustainable development.

○ Sustainable development requires that the present generation desist from those activities which may rob or imperil the future. Contemporary systems of development tend to discount or ignore the claims of the future, particularly the more distant future, which has few claims upon the present.

Taken seriously, these principles present a very radical agenda indeed. They insist that policies for sustainable development should: prevent further destruction of habitats; reduce pollution at least to levels which do not violate the Earth's regenerative capacity; abandon activities which consign to future generations problems of clean-up and risk to health or survival; and, on top of all this, deliver a redistribution of resources that will guarantee a commitment to sustainable development. In short, sustainable development implies a fundamental change in technology, economy and society. New policies and new institutions will be needed if sustainability is to be achieved. But, fundamental changes are only likely to be acceptable if the evidence for policies is scientifically credible and if the alternative forms of institution are politically feasible.

The problem of scientific evidence

Before policies to achieve sustainability can be developed, it is necessary to have some idea of the problems being addressed and the scope of measures to deal with them. But here we encounter the problem of uncertainty and conflict over the evidence, itself a major cause and justification for political procrastination. In the face of uncertainty, scientists have appealed to the precautionary principle. In brief, this means that action

Plate 7.2 A ricefield in Bali, Indonesia: sustainable development? Photo: Ron Giling/Lineair

should be taken now to avoid possible deleterious future impacts, even if the scientific evidence for taking action is uncertain or inconclusive. In the words of the Rio Declaration on Environment and Development: 'Where there are threats of serious or irreversible damage, lack of full scientific certainty shall not be used as a reason for postponing cost-effective measures to prevent environmental degradation'. The principle is, however, difficult to apply, precisely because of the nature of the evidence.

As Chapter 2 has shown, scientists have had a major impact on environmental policy. It can be argued that scientists through their observations have discovered environmental problems in the first place. This is certainly true for ozone depletion and global warming, which are 'invisible' problems. It is also true that science has caused the problems in the sense that applied scientific knowledge has produced processes capable of polluting and degrading natural ecosystems. Furthermore, scientists are often called upon to find the cause of problems and hence suggest appropriate solutions. Such solutions often involve changes in human systems to ensure that natural systems remain intact.

Willingness to change depends in part on the nature and certainty of the scientific evidence that justifies human action. In very general terms we may say that action is most likely to occur when the evidence of cause is conclusive, the consequences are clear and the proposed action is feasible. The example of ozone depletion fits all three criteria. The scientific evidence was sufficiently conclusive both as to the cause (CFCs and other gases) and the consequences (a hole in the ozone layer that would increase cancers and cataracts), so that political agreement on the phasing out of CFCs could be reached. Action was feasible, since the production of CFCs was confined to a relatively few countries and substitutes were available. Even here, however, there are complications, since the substitutes are not themselves entirely environmentally benign, not all countries have agreed to the protocols and it is not clear whether the agreements will have the desired effect in time. The disruption to social systems was very slight. Even so, implementation of the agreements may prove difficult.

It is more difficult to secure change if the evidence of harm is reasonably clear but the probability of occurrence is not. For example, we continue to use nuclear power despite the evidence that, either through routine emissions or through accidents, the consequent radioactivity is harmful to human health. There may be a variety of reasons for this. Perhaps we do not think the evidence of harm is sufficiently worrying or conclusive; perhaps the probabilities of harmful effects are sufficiently low for us to take a gamble on safety; perhaps we believe that the security and safety of nuclear systems are improving; or that alternatives to nuclear energy are not immediately available and are themselves damaging to the environment.

It is much more difficult to bring about social change to protect natural systems when the reasons for doing so are open to question. This is particularly the case when the scientific evidence is uncertain or incomplete. Both global warming and biodiversity illustrate the problem. In the case of global warming the mechanisms responsible and their interactions are not fully understood in terms of sources and sinks. The data are often sparse or lacking altogether (there is, for example, an almost total absence of systematic measurements of greenhouse gases in Africa and Latin America). Consequently, the modelling of the world's climatic systems depends on broad assumptions and generalisations. Based on their predictions from modelling, there is a consensus among scientists on the International Panel on Climate Change (IPCC) that the Earth's temperature is increasing at a rate of 0.3°C (range 0.2–0.5°C) per decade, resulting in the best estimate of a global mean temperature of around 1°C above the present value by the year 2025, and of 3°C by the end of the next century. Beyond that, the predictions become even more speculative. In terms of the distribution of the increase, it is difficult with any certainty to go much beyond saying that rises in temperature will be greatest in northern temperate latitudes. There will be shifts in climatic zones with increasing drought in some areas, more rainfall in others and a tendency towards an increased frequency of more extreme weather. Overall, there will be a rise in sea level mainly caused by thermal expansion of the oceans, but the impacts will vary according to changes in weather, altitude and relative movements of land and sea levels. Given the extreme uncertainties about the scale, distribution and nature of its effects it may seem, in the words of one observer, as if the 'current consensus on the greenhouse effect has raced ahead of the quality and quantity of scientific data on the issue' (Buttel *et al.*, 1990, p. 58).

With biodiversity we are plunged into even greater scientific uncertainty. Of the 4 million to 30 million species currently inhabiting the planet (note the scientific uncertainty already indicated here), some scientists predict that 100 species per day will be driven to extinction over the next 30 years. The current rate of extinction is estimated to be 1000 times higher than that of any other period in history. But at present only 1.4 million species have been classified by biologists (Stead and Stead, 1992, p. 35). The benefits to human beings of species are evident in food, in pollination, in biomass, in pharmaceuticals. The potential is enormous but unknown, and the loss of species cannot be recovered except over unimaginably long time spans.

Scientific knowledge is based on theory which is contestable and evidence which is often a matter of interpretation or even of conjecture. This is especially so in such areas as global environmental change, where the evidence must be derived from trends and forecasts which themselves are often based on experiments or models. As a result, scientific evidence may be provisional and therefore revocable, a condition Yearley describes as 'pragmatic uncertainty'. As he observes about something so complex as global warming, 'we seem to become less certain the more we study it' (Yearley, 1992, p. 136). The scientific evidence on global environmental change is, at this stage, sufficiently qualified to leave room for prevarication over taking the necessary remedial action. However, this is not to say that more conclusive evidence would definitely trigger political agreement. As empirical research on international resource co-operation has sufficiently shown, scientific progress and political progress seldom go hand in hand. It seems that the impact of science alone on environmental policy making is modest unless it is combined with other more influential forces like the tide of public opinion, an increasing level of participation in environmental politics and the integration of the science/politics relationship (Andresen and Wettestad, 1992, p. 281).

The problem of the market

Scientific evidence is crucial in the identification of environmental problems. Whether it is acted upon will depend on the political environment, which is structured by the prevailing form of social organisation in the world today – the capitalist market system. In many countries, whatever their political orientation, the market is encouraged through deregulation, privatisation and the removal of barriers to trade. It should be noted that the market is actually not so free, but is subject to various forms of intervention such as subsidies, price guarantees, regulations, setting of interest rates, etc. But, in principle, the idea that a free market is suited to achieving both economic growth and environmental benefits is pervasive. Without growth, it is argued, the resources that are essential to ensure environmental security would not be created. The present period of history can even be labelled 'the triumph of the market' (Blowers, 1993, pp.789–92) (see Box 4).

At the same time a critique which argues that market capitalism is responsible for environmental degradation is beginning to influence political thinking. The major problem with the market in relation to the environment is that it is concerned with short-term economic criteria which put an emphasis on growth achieved through competition based on comparative advantage. Growth is geographically uneven. Those countries or regions unable to compete become impoverished and their environments deteriorate, while the successful areas also experience environmental degradation through the pollution, waste or resource depletion associated with overexploitation. Another problem with the market is that it fails to take account of externalities (see Chapters 1 and 6). Consequently, unwanted or unforeseen costs are imposed on third parties (individuals, communities or countries). Moreover, the market promotes the private interest over the public and ignores or discounts the interests of future generations. Finally, as Chapter 6 indicates, the market values resources in respect of their

> ## Economic growth and the environment
>
> **4**
>
> The case for economic growth as a necessary condition for environmental protection was put in *This Common Inheritance*, the UK Government White Paper on Britain's environmental strategy, as follows:
>
> 'Economic growth is not an end in itself. It provides us with the means to live better and fuller lives. We should naturally avoid policies which secure growth in the short term at the expense of blighting our broader, longer term ambitions. But we should not be misled. Growth is a necessary though not a sufficient condition for achieving the higher quality of life that the world wants. In countries already beyond the dreams of a generation ago, growth is still needed to provide the resources to clean up the pollution of old industries and to produce the technology to accommodate tomorrow's industrial processes to cleaner surroundings. In countries still miserably poor, growth which will last is essential to overcoming the ruinous impact that poverty itself has on the environment. There is, therefore, no contradiction in arguing both for economic growth and for environmental good sense. The challenge is to integrate the two' (HMSO, 1990, p. 8).

use in production and does not account for the costs of depletion of non-renewable resources. For these various reasons, the market intrinsically cannot deal with the long-term conservation of the environment. Intervention becomes necessary to deal with 'market failure'. Some argue that solutions should be sought through the market. Once a proper valuation of environmental resources is secured, it will, in principle, be possible to devise means of intervention in the market that will ensure patterns of sustainable development. Opponents contend that it would be difficult to value future unknown environmental resources (e.g. forest habitats) or those whose scarcity value increases over time or to recognise the possible changes in the evaluation of resources by different societies over time. These views, of course, reflect a basic disagreement over values which influences practical approaches to policy making (see Box 5). As the problems of achieving sustainability through the market alone have become more apparent so governments have begun to examine a mixture of market and regulatory approaches. A wide range of market-based economic measures (taxes, tradeable pollution rights, recycling credits) is being designed to protect the environment. At the same time, regulatory instruments are adopted as a necessary complement to market mechanisms. The rudiments of a more interventionist approach to the environment are emerging, but there are few signs yet of any willingness to contemplate the fundamental changes in economic organisation that some critics of contemporary capitalism insist are necessary to avoid environmental catastrophe.

7.5 The process of policy making

There is, then, little to indicate that an ecologically inspired process of social change under the heading of 'sustainable development' has been set in motion. The power of environmental policies relative to other sectors of policy appears to be limited. Therefore, a major constraint on policy making is the process of policy making itself (Glasbergen, 1993; Glasbergen, 1995, pp. 6–8).

Weak and strong sustainability

Different approaches to valuing environmental resources are evident in the contrast between so-called 'weak sustainability' and 'strong sustainability'. Weak sustainability allows for the substitution between the various kinds of capital (natural capital and capital produced by human effort) and accepts a dwindling of natural resources if compensated for by extensions of production capital. Advocates of strong sustainability insist that utilisation of a natural resource should always be compensated for by reafforestation elsewhere. In reality it is likely that both positions will prove relevant approaches to specific problems. It is obvious that non-renewable resources cannot be replaced, but some could be substituted. But it is equally obvious that certain resources (notably, atmosphere, water) are essential to survival and must be protected.

If we consider environmental policy's place in society, we observe a peculiar phenomenon. In scores of locations, decisions are made on production, consumption and mobility which impact negatively on the environment. These decisions are inspired by market considerations. Moreover, they are often supported by governments, since the stakes are high. The central and sectoral agencies address the 'priority' agenda of governments – growth, employment, trade, defence, energy, agriculture, industry, etc. Most societies also provide rules and regulations to mitigate or prevent deleterious impacts on the physical environment. In this case, a different sector of government comes to the fore, that of environmental policy making. This sector acts as a legitimate, institutionalised counterforce. After all, the quality of the physical environment is a priority. In its attempt to cross sectoral policy boundaries, environmental policy actually occupies a somewhat isolated position within the interplay of social forces. It is a policy which lacks the support of powerful economic interests. It is a policy with hardly any mandate.

A second factor limiting the effectiveness of environmental policy can be tracked down to the way in which the policy is being made. The conceptual ideas behind the policy merit special notice here. As we saw earlier, the awareness of environmental problems is predominantly based on scientific research. Without this research we would not be familiar with the environmental issues. Scientific research shows us the working of the material world, elucidates the conditions and processes that keep it going and identifies the causes of disruption. Whenever disruptions are observed, there is an environmental problem. Environmental policy is expected to address these problems. A balance must be restored, the scope and nature of emissions and waste disposal must be limited and the exploitation of natural resources must be reduced.

These characteristics of environmental policy show it to act essentially as a correcting mechanism for society. Moreover, it is a mechanism that often operates after the damage has come to light. In its remedial role, government predominantly acts, as it were, as an engineer, controlling the physical system on the basis of its understanding of that system. This environmental policy is typified by a view of social reality as a technical system that can be operated on the basis of centrally defined goals. It is assumed, more or less implicitly, that the policy can rank social objectives according to their hierarchical order and that governments can translate these goals into policy instruments and ultimately achieve these objectives by means of an elaborate plan of action. At times this might be successful, notably where the social effects of environmental policy are not very dramatic. But more frequently, environmental policy gives rise to conflict, which then gets bogged down in deadlock.

Political constraints on policy making

Given the far-reaching implications of sustainable development, it is hardly surprising that there will be resistance to fundamental changes. This certainly seems to be true of the wealthier countries, which already consume a substantial share of resources. Any changes which profoundly affect people's lifestyles are difficult to defend to the public unless actions can be fully justified by the evidence. Put simply, people are hardly likely to forego the enjoyment of comfortable lifestyles, however unsustainable in the long run, if the consequences are unclear and uncertain.

Conversely, the poorer parts of the world have a stake in securing fundamental change. The inequality in resource consumption and pollution provides them with a strong moral position in the debate over global environmental change. Under existing patterns of development, the use of the environment in many parts of the developing world is already unsustainable. The claims of developing countries on the Earth's resources are increasing and these countries will be unlikely to surrender the prospect of the material benefits which they perceive the rich countries to have enjoyed with impunity. At a global level there is an impasse, with rich and poor alike perpetuating unsustainable practices – in Hardin's words, 'we are locked into a system of "fouling our own nest"' (Hardin, 1968, p. 1245).

A switch from unsustainable patterns of development is unlikely to occur without good reason. As we have seen, the evidence for some of the global environmental problems is uncertain. Moreover, the evidence is open to interpretations which can reflect different and conflicting interests. Consider the case of global warming. Added to the scientific uncertainty indicated above is the political complexity, since all countries are implicated both in terms of causes and impacts. Not surprisingly, each country will wish to limit its liability by an interpretation of the evidence which is best suited to its interests. In Chapter 3 we referred to the World Resources Institute (WRI) which compiled a composite index which combined the heat-trapping potential of the major greenhouse gases (CO_2, methane and CFCs). This placed Brazil, China and India among the top six contributors. On the other hand, the United States, though still the largest contributor, produced only 17.6% of the combined total, whereas its production of a single gas, CO_2 from fossil fuel burning, was over a fifth of the total (see Box 6).

An index such as that used by the WRI ignores the inequalities in living standards between North and South. The South has lower living standards and consequently is less able to finance greenhouse gas reduction. It is also more difficult for poorer countries to control the problem. It is technically easier to control the more concentrated emissions of CO_2 or CFCs produced in the North as against the smaller scale and widely dispersed sources of CO_2 or methane in developing countries. Finally, the fact that the greenhouse gases emitted by the North are predominantly irreplaceable fossil fuels is concealed by an index which lumps together all gases.

6

A further look at the WRI index

The WRI index could be criticised as a statistical approach that favoured the rich countries. For example, it overestimated the contribution of deforestation in Brazil by taking the figures for a single year, in which forest burning was exceptionally high; it underestimated the lingering impact of CFCs and the effect of past emissions of other gases produced by the developed countries; and it used data of widely varying quality (data for methane are extremely unreliable as compared to those for CO_2 emissions), which again tended to overestimate the contribution of the developing countries. The WRI index could be used to exonerate the USA and other rich countries from the major part of the blame by implicating the larger developing countries in a shared responsibility for the problem. It enables the USA to claim a reduction in greenhouse gas emissions by the year 2000, in effect masking an increase in its CO_2 output.

The above discussion of the WRI index shows us the different interests of various countries in the debate on international co-operation. The starting points of various countries for stabilising and reducing emissions are different. Andresen and Wettestad have indicated three main obstacles related to these starting points. First, the growing contribution of developing countries to the emissions at stake. Although at this moment it is mainly the industrialised countries which are responsible for the greenhouse problem, in 20–30 years' time, if present trends continue, developing countries will be responsible for more than 50% of the emissions. Most of these countries are understandably seeking rapid economic growth, for example by burning cheap coal. In order to redirect their development paths for global purposes, these countries will demand major economic and political concessions from the developed countries. Secondly, the energy economies of major international actors differ considerably, with fuel resources varying widely. China, for instance, depends heavily on coal, Japan on oil, France on nuclear power. According to Andresen and Wettestad, both the possibilities of fuel switching and the possibilities of energy efficiency measures differ for the various countries. Thirdly, the structural market positions of the major actors differ. Some countries, like the former USSR, are fossil fuel producers and sellers while many other countries, like Japan, are primarily fuel consumers and buyers. Measures to curb greenhouse gas emissions would obviously influence this international market. As a consequence of these factors the various countries will create major obstacles to a simple, uniform approach to the greenhouse problem (Andresen and Wettestad, 1992, pp. 289–90).

The problem of global warming is characterised by the asymmetrical interests and incompatible preferences of nation states. Other global environmental problems show other characteristics. Above and in Chapter 3 we touched on the relative success of ozone layer (CFCs) negotiations. Scientific evidence played an important role in securing agreement, but other factors were important too. Depletion of the ozone layer produces only losers in the short term. Unlike global warming, no nation perceives any short-term benefits from stratospheric ozone depletion. This is one of the reasons why a negotiated agreement to reduce CFCs was possible. Another reason is to be found in the fact that production and consumption of CFCs were concentrated mainly in North

Plate 7.3 Sustainable energy: wind power electricity plant in Flevoland, The Netherlands. Photo: Andy Mason/Oerlemans van Reeken studio

America and Europe. Cuts in production would not seriously disrupt international competitiveness. This is, according to Skjaerseth, further underlined by two important factors. Industry was not heavily dependent on CFC production and CFCs are not critical to the modern industrial economy. Technological alternatives were available and economic uncertainty was reduced by showing that the benefits were far higher than the costs (Skjaerseth, 1992). In most cases (global warming, biodiversity, deforestation, desertification, etc.) global environmental problems pose major and diverse conflicts of interest which will prove difficult to reconcile, however much deference is paid to the precautionary principle.

Economic constraints on policy making

Governments are more likely to pay attention to the immediate requirements of the economy than to longer term environmental goals. Governments depend on the support of business to provide economic growth and wealth and on the votes of workers with an interest in prosperity and jobs. Environmental regulations will, of course, be accepted, but only up to a point. Governments will ordinarily be unwilling, indeed politically unable, to jeopardise present and palpable economic advantage to avoid a future and uncertain environmental cost. They will be resistant to the closure of a plant for environmental reasons, especially if it is likely to result in high levels of local unemployment. They will be particularly unwilling to do so if they fear that others will seize a competitive advantage. The tendency to relieve industry of the burdens of environmental regulation is especially strong in times of recession. On the basis of our discussion we would, in general, expect that the less developed countries and regions within countries would be more likely to accept or endure lower environmental standards. This is because the needs for livelihood and economic growth are seen as overriding development priorities.

We can refer again to the tragedy of the commons discussed in Chapter 6 (where the discussion focused on the issue of property rights). Putting the analogy into the context of modern economic competition, the tragedy theory assumes that companies (and nation states) act as rational free enterprisers, that they have free access to the global commons and that each stands to gain the same benefit from this access. Consequently, it is argued that companies (or nations) will continue to pollute the commons so long as they can gain individual advantage, even though they may do so beyond the regenerative capacity of ecosystems. According to the tragedy, it is only when it is recognised that resource depletion and pollution are beginning to impact on production costs and profits that companies will alter their behaviour, and by then it may be too late. The tragedy suggests that the precautionary principle is unlikely to be applied because nation states act in defence of their own economic self-interest, as the example in Box 7 demonstrates.

In reality the tragedy of the commons is not inevitable. The basic assumptions may be questioned. First, although companies and nations may act in their own self-interest, it is not always clear where their true interest lies. Indeed, there may be a multiplicity of competing, often conflicting, interests, which moreover alter over time. Economic and environmental objectives are not always in conflict. In the long term in particular, economic and environmental survival will be mutually compatible goals. Even in the short run, positive inducements for environmental controls can bring increased economic efficiency and performance. There is sufficient evidence now that stricter environmental controls can force technology and stimulate industries to innovate. There is also a growing market for technological equipment which reduces pollution and waste. Furthermore, as environmental controls become more widely applied, those companies which have introduced appropriate technology will be more competitive.

Secondly, it is not the case that everyone enjoys free access to the global commons. Access is restricted by various agreements to prevent environmental deterioration: bilateral agreements to control transboundary river pollution; international agreements to reduce ocean dumping; and global agreements to reduce ozone depletion, etc. Finally, it is not true that everyone stands to gain the same benefit from access to the global commons. As we have seen, some nations receive disproportionate benefits by using the commons as a dustbin for waste and pollution, while others suffer the negative externalities thus created. Sustainable development rests upon policies which regulate access to the commons, which give precedence to the public and global common interest over private and national interests and which reconcile conflicts of interest over economy and environment. But how can such policies be achieved?

Global warming and the tragedy of the commons

The tragedy of the commons suggests that since the atmosphere is freely accessible, nation states will have no incentive to control the emission of greenhouse gases from their territory. On the contrary, they will calculate that any controls applied unilaterally will penalise industry and the nation's competitive position, while providing only a marginal benefit that will be enjoyed by all countries. Therefore, pollution will continue unabated even though scientific evidence suggests that global warming is the likely consequence if everyone continues to behave as they do at present. Controls will only be introduced when deterioration of the environment becomes so obvious that it impacts on the economy and the quality of life. By that time, it may be too late to avert environmental catastrophe.

This poses a Catch-22 to policy makers. When you are unable to see the problem but could act to prevent it, it is politically unrealistic to do so. When you do see it and are able to act, it may be too late to do so. Thus the tragedy of the commons suggests that the precautionary principle is unlikely to be applied, because nation states act in defence of their own self-interest. On top of this, the differential impact of global warming (with some states enjoying, at least for a time, better climatic conditions or having the resources to defend themselves against the impacts of flooding, drought, etc.) will encourage varying responses to the urgency of the global situation. However, the tragedy of the commons is a special, rather than a general case, as is explained in the text.

7.6 Inequality and the principle of compensation

From the discussion of the elusive concept of sustainable development in this chapter three points can be underlined. The first is that sustainability is a scientific notion concerned with the impact of resource depletion and pollution on the Earth's ability to maintain and regenerate its capacity for supporting life. Since the limits to this capacity are matters of scientific debate it is argued that a precautionary approach to management of the Earth's environmental systems should be taken. The second point is that development is a social construction involving different conceptions of living standards and lifestyles which relate, in part, to values. Taken together sustainability and development become a goal, a strategy even, whereby human behaviour and organisation across the globe are compatible with conserving environmental resources and preventing pollution. But, and this is the third point, the contemporary pattern of social development reveals vast inequalities which must be reduced if sustainable development is to be politically achievable.

If international policies are to be agreed upon and successfully implemented, they will need to be founded on principles of equity and compensation for those communities, countries and future generations who experience the environmental costs of economic development. This necessity was recognised in the third principle of the Rio Declaration: 'The right to development must be fulfilled so as to equitably meet developmental and environmental needs of present and future generations'.

There are three general circumstances in which the principle of compensation could be exercised to ensure environmental protection.

First, where the right to develop is denied or access to environmental assets is limited or prevented. In such cases compensation may be justified for the loss of property rights which creates hardship, but not in cases where compensation would provide a windfall gain. This issue has been controversial in several Western European countries, where compensation has been paid to farmers for not destroying protected features, regardless of the individual circumstances or whether they had any intention to develop. This principle could be applied on a global scale. International agreements to protect rainforests and other global environmental assets deprive communities and countries of the economic benefits of development. Therefore, compensation in the form of aid, debt-for-Nature swaps, technology transfer or direct financial payment would be justified. Conversely, if it is justifiable to withhold certain global assets from exploitation then it is also justifiable to provide greater access to those areas that are exploited. In this sense, environmental resources can be seen as common property rights, not as the exclusive property rights of individuals, companies or countries.

Second, it may also be necessary to compensate those communities or countries that experience the negative externalities of pollution. This applies to communities where polluting activities are concentrated, sometimes called 'pollution havens'. It also applies to countries which are in the path of transboundary pollution. For example, the ageing nuclear reactors in Eastern Europe are recognised as posing substantial risks, and Chernobyl has already demonstrated the potential scale of disaster. But these countries are often heavily dependent on nuclear output for their power supplies and are unable to upgrade, replace or shut down reactors without considerable aid.

Third, under conditions of sustainability there is the obligation of the present generation to the future. This obligation is very difficult to express precisely. Brundtland emphasises not compromising future development by depriving it of natural assets. Other definitions stress the importance of ensuring an environmental legacy that is at least as good as that of today. None of these ideas is very precise. There seem to be two requirements. One is that we should try to avoid imposing environmental risks on future generations. The other is that we should ensure that resources are replenished where possible and conserved where they are irreplaceable. Both sets of requirements have been breached and are, strictly speaking, impossible to meet. Where some deprivation is unavoidable there should be compensation in the form of research and technology designed to mitigate the problems or financial resources sufficient for future generations to manage the problem. In the case of nuclear waste, for example, compensation implies both research into the most appropriate ways of managing waste and finance to support solutions.

7.7 Conclusion: the changing role of the nation state

As the global commons become grossly polluted and as resources are depleted, everyone, developed and developing countries alike, becomes engulfed in gradual environmental degradation. Of course, some regions may initially benefit from a changing climate, while others may have sufficient resources to protect themselves, at least for a while. But, ultimately, none can escape. As global deterioration becomes inescapable, so self-interest is expressed in a common interest in survival. Political response then becomes inevitable.

At present, the political responses which will take place are hard to predict. Unless there is a sudden environmental catastrophe such as would result from a nuclear war, the onset of change is likely to be gradual. It is also possible, as resources become more scarce or climate worsens in some areas, that there will be increasing conflict. Among the likely consequences will be large-scale migration of people as desertification spreads, conflicts over water between countries which share major river basins, and regional wars over diminishing resources. Such conflicts will be likely if contemporary patterns of inequality persist, with the rich countries seeking to maintain their advantage and the poor seeking to secure survival.

Alternatively, precautionary action may be taken through international agreements to prevent environmental deterioration. Such statements – some of which have been signed – would have to be translated into practical and implemented policies. For example, agreements to reduce greenhouse gases which are now tentatively foreshadowed will have to be forged into policies stating targets, time-scales, methods and monitoring which are binding upon nation states. The fundamental changes in development necessary to achieve sustainability thus challenge the prevailing political system based on the nation state, an issue already raised in Chapter 4.

A major political challenge is that of 'political leadership'. Leadership 'provides the initiating stimulus and the pressure for reaching agreement in a context where inertia and conflicts of interests would otherwise be likely to prevail' (Liberatore, 1993, pp. 14–15). In the environmental field, there are only a few cases where leadership was directly provided by an international organisation backed by major powers. As Liberatore observes, leadership is usually provided by one country or a group of countries. In cases such as the international regulation of CFCs or marine pollution, the USA leadership has played a crucial role in promoting and reaching agreement, by providing funds and facilities to international organisations and especially by taking or threatening unilateral action. The USA prodded the reluctant countries into action. At other times, the USA has not been an environmental leader but rather a laggard, as, for example, on the question of biodiversity at the Rio summit. The European Union has occupied a position of leadership especially in the field of the climate change negotiations.

Until now, nation states have been the ubiquitous and most powerful form of political organisation. In principle, they possess sovereign authority over their territory and they have the administrative capacity and coercive power to enforce policies. Sovereignty confers on states the power to permit and regulate the exploitation of resources within their jurisdictions, free from outside interference. In the UK, for example, the peat moors of Scotland's Flow Country can be harvested and afforested. Energy and mineral resources can be exploited, motorways constructed or high-intensity agriculture developed, causing considerable environmental destruction. Within the nation state such developments may be controversial and, as environmental concern has grown, so environmental regulations and controls have been tightened.

As Chapter 4 has shown, national sovereignty in the absolute sense of supreme authority over a defined territory has always been more or less compromised in practice by transnational economic and social processes. In the contemporary world, the transnational corporations (TNCs) wield enormous power over the exploitation of resources. Their investment, production and markets are widespread and mobile. Their control over resources and markets enables them to exert considerable power in many states. And even in the developed countries, TNCs are able to exert influence on a range of policies including environmental regulation. Their size and economic signifi-cance place them substantially outside the control of individual states or international organisations.

State power is also diminished to the extent that international organisations are able to develop and implement binding policies. International environmental action implies some surrender of state sovereignty and a transfer of power to various transnational political agencies and organisations. These include, among others, intergovernmental organisations (IGOs) ranging from those set up to administer, monitor and enforce global environmental agreements to agencies which have an economic remit but which affect the environment, such as the General Agreement on Tariffs and Trade (GATT), the Food and Agricultural Organisation (FAO) or the International Atomic Energy Agency (IAEA). These also include those agencies set up to fund and administer a range of development projects, such as the World Bank.

As well as surrendering power upwards to the supranational level, sustainability also requires an emphasis on the subnational level. It is at this level – regional and local – that commitment to policies must be generated and detailed implementation made effective. Thus the Treaty of Maastricht emphasised subsidiarity as a process 'in which decisions are taken as closely as possible to the citizen', meaning taking decisions at the lowest level compatible with attaining required objectives. International environ-mental policy making is therefore not simply a process of forging agreement between countries, it is also about achieving interrelationships between various levels of policy making, from local right through to global.

Sustainable development indicates a need for structural changes in the political system, notably a transfer of power from the nation state both upwards and down-wards, an increasing responsiveness to environmental criteria in policy making and a willingness to curb the power of short-term economic interests. Our discussion has been more or less abstract and speculative, but it has demonstrated that only the first steps in this direction have been taken.

References

AGARWAL, A. and S. NARAIN (1990) *Global Warming in an Unequal World: A Case of Environmental Colonialism*. New Dehli: Center for Science and Environment.

ANDERSON, V. (1991) *Alternative Economic Indicators*. London: Routledge.

ANDRESEN, S. and WETTESTAD, J. (1992) International resource cooperation and the greenhouse problem. *Global Environmental Change, Human and Policy Dimensions*, **2**(4), 277–91.

ARKEL, H. van (1992) *Het gelijk van het genoeg (Enough is just right)*. Utrecht: Aldie Strohalm.

AZARYA, V. (1988) Re-ordering state-society relations: incorporation and disengagement. In Rothchild, D. and Chazan, N. (eds), *The Precarious Balance: State and Society in Africa*. London: Westview Press, pp.3–21.

BARKER, A. and PETERS, G. (eds) (1993) *The Politics of Expert Advice. Creating, Using and Manipulating Knowledge for Public Policy*. Edinburgh: Edinburgh University Press.

BARNES, B. and EDGE, D. (eds) (1982) *Science in Context. Readings in the Sociology of Science*. Milton Keynes: Open University Press,.

BENEDICK, R. (1991) *Ozone Diplomacy*. Cambridge, Mass: Harvard University Press.

BIRNIE, P.W. and BOYLE, A.E. (1992) *International Law and the Environment*. Oxford: Clarendon Press.

BLAUG, M. (1978) *Economic Theory in Retrospect*. Cambridge: Cambridge University Press.

BLOWERS, A. (1993) Environmental policy: the quest for sustainable development. *Urban Studies*, **30**(4/5), 775–96.

BOJÖ, J., MALER, K.G. and UNEMO, L. (1992) *Environment and Development: An Economic Approach*. Dordrecht: Kluwer Academic Publishers.

BOULDING, K. (1966) The economics of the coming spaceship earth. In Jarret, H. (ed.), *Environmental Quality in a Growing Economy*. Baltimore: Johns Hopkins University Press.

BROMLEY, D.W. (1991) *Environment and Economy: Property Rights and Public Policy*. Oxford: Basil Blackwell.

BROWN WEISS, E. (1993) International environmental law: contemporary issues and the emergence of a new world order. *Georgetown Law Journal*, **81**, 675–710.

BUTTEL, F.H., HAWKINS, A.P. and POWER (1990) From limits to growth to global change: constraints and contradictions in the evolution of environmental science and ideology. *Global Environmental Change, Human and Policy Dimensions*, **1**, 57–66.

CAMILLERI, J. and FALK, J. (1992) *The End of Sovereignty? The Politics of a Shrinking and Fragmenting World*. Aldershot: Edward Elgar.

CHURCHILL, R.R. and LOWE, A.V. (1988) *The Law of the Sea*, 2nd edn. Manchester: Manchester University Press,pp. 241–87.

COMMISSION OF THE EUROPEAN COMMUNITY (1992) *Towards Sustainability: A European Community Programme of Policy and Action, in Relation to the Environment and Sustainable Development, Volume II.* Brussels: EC.

COMMITTEE FOR LONG-TERM ENVIRONMENT POLICY (CLTM) (1990) *Het milieu: denkbeelden voor de 21ste eeuw (The environment: concepts for the 21st century).* Zeist: Kerckebosch BV, pp.5–7.

COMMITTEE FOR LONG-TERM ENVIRONMENTAL POLICY (1994) *The Environment: Towards a Sustainable Future.* Dordrecht: Kluwer Academic Publishers, pp.21–45 and 219–49.

DALY, H.E. (1977) *Steady-State Economics.* London: Earthscan.

DALY, H.E. (1991) Elements of environmental macroeconomics. In Costanza, R. (ed.), *Ecological Economics.* New York: Columbia University Press, pp. 32–46.

DANKELMAN, I. and DAVIDSON, J. (1988) *Women and Environment in the Third World.* London: Earthscan Publications .

DI MUCCIO, R. and ROSENAU, J. (1992) Turbulence and sovereignty in world politics: explaining the relocation of legitimacy in the 1990s and beyond. In Mlinar, Z. (ed.), *Globalization and Territorial Identities.* Aldershot: Avebury, pp.60–76.

DICKSON, N. *et al.* (1992) 'Stratospheric Ozone Depletion in the US: A Historical Perspective of Risk Management'. Contribution to the Project on Social Learning in the Management of Global Environmental Risks (unpublished manuscript).

DIETZ, F.J. and VAN DER STRAATEN, J. (1992a) Rethinking environmental economics: missing links between economic theory and environmental policy. *Journal of Economic Issues,* **XXV1**(1), 27–51.

DIETZ, F.J. and VAN DER STRAATEN, J. (1992b) Sustainable development and the necessary integration of ecological insights. In Dietz, F.J., Simonis, U.E. and van der Straaten, J. (eds), *Sustainability and Environmental Policy.* Berlin: Sigma Verlag.

DOUCET, P. and SLOEP, P.B. (1992) *Mathematical Modeling in the Life Sciences.* Chichester: Ellis Horwood and Simon and Schuster.

DOUGLAS, M. and WILDAWSKY, A. (1982) *Risk and Culture.* Berkeley: University of California Press.

DUTCH MINISTRY OF FOREIGN AFFAIRS (1992) Relatie Noord-Zuid nieuw leven ingeblazen (A new life for the North-South relationship). *Internationale Samenwerking,* **9,** 42–3.

DUTCH MINISTRY OF HOUSING, PHYSICAL PLANNING AND ENVIRONMENTAL MANAGEMENT and DUTCH MINISTRY OF FOREIGN AFFAIRS (1993) V.N. Conferentie inzake Milieu & Ontwikkeling, Rio de Janeiro – juni 1992 (UN Conference on Environment and Development, Rio de Janeiro, June 1992). The Netherlands: The Hague.

EDER, K. (1985) *Geschichte als Lernprozess? Zur Pathogenese politischer Modernität in Deutschland (History as a learning process. On the pathogenesis of political modernity in Germany).* Frankfurt/Main: Surkamp.

EKINS, P. (1992) *A New World Order: Grassroots Movement for Global Change.* London: Routledge.

ELLIOTT, J. (1994) *An Introduction to Sustainable Development. The Developing World.* London:Routledge.

FISCHOFF, B. et al. (1981) *Acceptable Risk.* Cambridge: Cambridge University Press.

FOE (Friends of the Earth) (1992) *Whose Hand on the Chainsaw? UK Government Policy and the Tropical Rainforests.* London: FOE.

FREESTONE, D. (1991) European Community environmental policy and law. In Churchill, R., Warren, L. and Gibson, J. (eds), *Law, Policy and the Environment.* pp. 135–54. Oxford: Basil Blackwell.

FRIEND, A.E. (1992) Economics, ecology and sustainable development: are they compatible? *Environmental Values*, **1**(2), 157–70.

GLASBERGEN, P. (1993) Managing environmental conflicts in an international context. In Sloep, P.B. (ed.), *International Issues in Environmental Science*. Heerlen:Open Universiteit, pp.7–13.

GLASBERGEN, P. (ed.) (1995) *Managing Environmental Disputes. Network Management as an Alternative*. Dordrecht: Kluwer Academic Publishers.

GOFFMANN, E. (1974) *Frame Analysis. An Essay on the Organization of Experience*. Boston: Northeastern University Press.

GUHA, R. (1991) *The Unquiet Woods: Ecological Change and Peasant Resistance in the Himalaya*. Delhi: Oxford University Press.

GUSFIELD, J. (1981) *The Culture of Public Problems. Drinking, Driving and the Symbolic Order*. Chicago: University of Chicago Press.

HAAS, P. (1990) *Saving the Mediterranean. The Politics of International Environmental Cooperation*. New York: Columbia University Press.

HARDIN, G. (1968) The tragedy of the commons. *Science*, **162**, 1234–48.

HELD, D. (ed.) (1993) *The Prospects for Democracy: North, South, East, West*. Cambridge: Polity Press.

HENKIN, L. (1979) *How Nations Behave*. New York: Columbia University Press.

HESSE, M. (1974) *The Structure of Scientific Inference*. London: Macmillan.

HMSO (1990) *This Common Inheritance*, Cm. 1200. London: HMSO.

HUBER, M. and LIBERATORE, A. (1993) 'The EC Ozone Policy: 1977 to 1992'. Contribution to the Project on Social Learning in the Management of Global Environmental Risks (unpublished manuscript).

HUETING, R. (1980) *New Scarcity and Economic Growth*. Amsterdam: North-Holland.

INGLEHART, R. (1977) *The Silent Revolution: Changing Values and Political Styles among Western Publics*. Princeton: Princeton University Press.

JACOBS, M. (1991) *The Green Economy*. London: Pluto Press.

JASANOFF, S. (1987) Contested boundaries in policy-relevant science. *Social Studies of Science*, **17**, 195–230.

JENNINGS, R. and WATTS, A. (1992) *Oppenheim's International Law, Vol. I*, 9th edn. Harlow:Longman.

JEVONS, W.S. (1924) *The Theory of Political Economy* (first published 1871).London: Macmillan.

KAMMINGA, M. (1994) Improving integration of environmental requirements into other EC policies. *European Environmental Law Review*, **3**, 23–5.

KHATOR, R. (1991) *Environment, Development and Politics in India*. New York: University Press of America.

KIERNAN, V. (1993) Atmospheric ozone hits a new low. *New Scientist*, **138**(1871), 8.

KINGDON, J. (1984) *Agendas, Alternatives and Public Policies*. Boston: Little, Brown.

KISS, A. (1985) The protection of the Rhine against pollution. *Natural Resources Journal*, **25**.

KNORR-CETINA, K. (1981) *The Manufacture of Knowledge*. Oxford: Pergamon Press.

KRAMER, L. (1991) Community environmental law – towards a systematic approach. In *Yearbook of European Law*, *11*. pp. 151–84. Oxford: Clarendon Press.

KUHN, T. (1962) *The Structure of Scientific Revolutions*. Chicago: University of Chicago Press.

LAMMERS, J.G. (1989) The Rhine: legal aspects of the management of a transboundary river. In Verwey, W.D. (ed.), *Nature Management and Sustainable Development*. Amsterdam: IOS, pp. 440–57.

LAZARSFELD, P. (1967) Introduction. In Lazarsfeld. P. et al. (eds), *The Uses of Sociology*. New York: Basic Books.

LEAN, G. (1993) Another early autumn for the dirty man of Europe. *The Observer*, 22nd August, 18.

LIBERATORE, A. (1992) *The Management of Uncertainty. Response and Learning Processes following Chernobyl.* PhD dissertation. Florence: European University Institute.

LIBERATORE, A. (1993) *Beyond the Earth Summit: the European Community towards sustainability?* Working Paper EPU, No. 5. Florence: European University Institute.

LIBERATORE, A. (1994) Facing global warming: the interactions between science and policy making in the European Community. In Redclift, M. and Benton, T. (eds), *Social Theory and the Global Environment*. London: Routledge.

LINDEMAN, R. (1942) The trophic-dynamic aspect of ecology. *Ecology,* **23**, 399–418.

LOHMANN, L. and COLCHESTER, M. (1990) Paved with good intentions: TFAP's road to oblivion. *The Ecologist,* **20**(3) .

LOWRANCE, W. (1976) *Of Acceptable Risk. Science and the Determination of Safety*. Los Altos: W. Kaufman.

LUKES, S. (ed.) (1986) *Power*. Oxford: Basil Blackwell.

MAAS, R. (1993) Helpt groei het milieuprobleem oplossen? (Will growth help solve the environmental problem?). InBiesboer, F. (ed.), *Greep op Groei; het thema van de jaren negentig (Getting to grips with growth: a theme for the 1990s)*. Uitgeverij: Jan van Arkel, pp.43–57.

MACNEILL, J., WINSEMIUS, P. and YAKUSHIJI, T. (1991) *Beyond Interdependence. The Meshing of the World's Economy and the Earth's Ecology*. Oxford: Oxford University Press.

MACROY, R. (1992) The enforcement of Community environmental laws: some critical issues. *Common Market Law Review*, **29**, 347–69.

MAJONE, G. (1983) *The Uncertain Logic of Standard Setting*. Laxenburg, Austria: IIASA.

MARIN, B. (1981) What is 'half-knowledge' sufficient for, and when? Theoretical comment on policymakers' uses of social science. *Knowledge: Creation, Diffusion, Utilization*, **3**(1), 43–60.

MARSHALL, A. (1925) *Principles of Economy* (first published 1890). London: Macmillan.

MARTINEZ-ALIER, J. (1990) *Ecological Economics*. Oxford: Basil Blackwell.

MCCORMICK, J. (1989) *Reclaiming Paradise: the Global Environmental Movement*. Bloomington: Indiana University Press.

MCGREW, A. et al. (1992) *Global Politics*. Cambridge: Polity Press.

MEADOWS, D.H., MEADOWS, D.L. and RANDERS, J. (1993) *Beyond the Limits: Global Collapse or a Sustainable Future*. London: Earthscan Publications.

MENGER, C. (1968) *Grundsätze der Volkswirtschaftslehre (Basic principles of Economy)* (first published 1871). Wien:Braumeller.

MILLER, M. (1986) *Kollektive Lernprozesse*. Frankfurt/Main: Surkamp.

MISHAN, E.J. (1967) *The Costs of Economic Growth*. London:Staples Press.

MULHERN, F. (1993) A European home?. In Bird, J. et al. (eds), *Mapping the Future: Local Cultures, Global Change*. London: Routledge, pp.199–204.

MYRES, N. (1989) *Deforestation Rates in Tropical Forests and Their Climatic Implications*. London: FOE.

NIKITINA, E. *et al.* (1992) 'Stratospheric Ozone Depletion: the Ex-USSR case'. Contribution to the Project on Social Learning in the Management of Global Environmental Risks (unpublished manuscript).

NOLLKEMPER, A. (1993) *The Legal Regime for Transboundary Water Pollution: Between Discretion and Constraint.* Dordrecht: Martinus Nijhoff.

NORTON, B. (1992) Sustainability, human welfare and ecosystem health. *Environmental Values,* **1**(2), 97–112.

PEARCE, D. (1993) *Economic Values and the Natural World.* London: Earthscan Publications.

PENG, M. K. K. (1992) as reported in *New Scientist,* 16 May, 38.

PERROW, C. (1984) *Normal Accidents. Living with High-Risk Technologies.* New York: Basic Books.

PHILLIPS, D. (1988) Kinetics of reactions of stratospheric importance. In Coyle, J.D., Hill,R.R. and Roberts, D.R. (eds), *Light, Chemical Change and Life: A Source Book in Photochemistry.* Milton Keynes: Open University Press, pp.128–41.

PIGOU, A.C. (1952) *The Economics of Welfare* (first published 1920). London: Macmillan.

PITARI G., VISCONTI, G. and RIZI, V. (1991) Sensitivity of stratospheric ozone to heterogeneous chemistry on sulphate aerosols. *Geophysical Research Letters,* **18**, 833–6.

PORTER, G. and BROWN, J. (1991) *Global Environmental Politics.* Oxford: Westview Press.

PROKOP, J. (1990) 'Climate Change and Ozone Layer Depletion in the USSR. A Preliminary Policy History'. Contribution to the Project on Social Learning in the Management of Global Environmental Risks (unpublished manuscript).

RAVETZ, J. (1971) *Scientific Knowledge and Its Social Problems.* Oxford: Clarendon Press.

RAVETZ, J. and FUNTOWICZ, S. (1989) *Usable Knowledge, Usable Ignorance. A Discourse on Two Sorts of Science.* Paper read at the conference entitled 'Experts are Categorical: Scientific Controversies and Political Decisions Concerning the Environment'. Arc-et-Senans, France.

REDCLIFT, M. (1992) Sustainable development: needs, values, rights. *Environmental Values,* **2**(1), 3–20.

RENN, O. (1985) Risk analysis: scope and limitations. In Otway, H. and Peltu, M. (eds), *Regulating Industrial Risks.* London: Butterworth.

REYNER, S. and CANTOR, R. (1987) How fair is safe enough? The cultural approach to societal technology choice. *Risk Analysis,* **7** (1), 3–9.

RIVM, National Institute of Public Health and Environmental Protection (1992) *National Environmental Outlook 2, 1990–2010.* Bilthoven: RIVM.

ROAN, S. (1989) *Ozone Crisis.* New York: John Wiley.

RÜDIG, W. and LOWE, P. (1992) *The Green Wave: A Comparative Analysis of Ecological Parties.* Cambridge: Polity Press.

RUESCHEMEYER, D., STEPHENS, E. and STEPHENS, J. (1992) *Capitalist Development and Democracy.* Cambridge: Polity Press.

SAND, P.H. (1990) *Lessons learned in Global Governance.* Washington DC: World Resources Institute.

SAND, P.H. (ed.) (1992) *The Effectiveness of International Environmental Agreements: A Survey of Existing Legal Instruments.* Cambridge: Grotius.

SCHMID, A.A. (1987) *Property, Power and Public Choice: An Inquiry into Law and Economics,* 2nd edn. New York:Praeger Publishers.

SCHWARZ, M. and THOMPSON, M. (1990) *Divided We Stand. Redefining Politics, Technology and Social Choice.* New York: Harvester Wheatsheaf.

SCIENCE POLICY RESEARCH UNIT (SPRU) (1994) *UK Decommissioning Policy: Time for Decision.*

SER (1991) *Economie en milieu. Rapport van de Commissie Economische Deskundigen over economie en milieu (Economy and the environment. Report of the Committee of Economics Experts on economy and the environment).* Publication No. 18.

SHERWOOD ROWLAND, F. (1988) Chlorofluorocarbons and stratospheric ozone. In Coyle, J.D., Hill, R.R. and Roberts, D.R. (eds), *Light, Chemical Change and Life: A Source Book in Photochemistry*. Milton Keynes: Open University Press, pp.142–61.

SHIVA, V. (1988) *Staying Alive: Women, Ecology and Survival in India, Kali for Women*. London: Zed Books.

SHRADER-FRECHETTE, K.S. (1991) *Risk and Rationality*. Berkeley: University of California Press.

SHRADER-FRECHETTE, K.S. (1994) Sustainability and environmental ethics. In Skirbekk, G. (ed.), *The Notion of Sustainability and its Normative Implications*. Oslo: Scandinavian University Press, pp.57–78.

SHRIVASTAVA, P. (1992) *Bhopal: Anatomy of a Crisis,* 2nd edn. London: Paul Chapman.

SKJAERSETH, J.B. (1992) The 'successful' ozone-layer negotiations. Are there any lessons to be learned? *Global Environmental Change, Human and Policy Dimensions,* **2**(4), 292–300.

SLOEP, P.B. (1994) The impact of 'sustainability' on the field of environmental science. In Skirbekk, G. (ed.), *The Notion of Sustainability and its Normative Implications*. Oslo: Scandinavian University Press, pp.29–55.

SLOVICH *et al.* (1982) Facts vs. Fears. Understanding Perceived Risk. In: Kanheman, D. *et al.*, *Judgement and Uncertainty: Heuristic and Biases*. Cambridge: Cambridge University Press.

STEAD, W.E. and STEAD, J.G. (1992) *Management for a Small Planet. Strategic Decision Making and the Environment*. London: Sage Publications.

STRAATEN, J. VAN DER (1990) *Zure regen, economische theorie en het Nederlandse beleid (Acid rain, economic theory and Dutch policy)*. Utrecht: Jan van Arkel.

TERHAL, P. (1992) Sustainable development and cultural change. In Opschoor, J.H.B. (ed.), *Environment, Economy and Sustainable Development*. Groningen: Wolters-Noordhoff Publishers, p.142.

TOLBA, M. (1992) *Saving our Planet: Challenges and Hopes*. London: Chapman and Hall.

TURKENBURG, W.C. (1993) Energy, environment and development. In Bruggink, J.J.C. and Nieuwenhout, F.D.J. (eds), *Energy Co-operation for Development: Options and Obstacles*. DVL/OS, pp.13–22.

VITOUSEK, P.M. et al. (1986) Human appropriation of the products of photosynthesis. *BioScience,* **36**, 368.

VOGLER, J. (1992) Regimes and the global commons: space, atmosphere and oceans. In McGrew, A. et al. (eds), *Global Politics*. Cambridge: Polity Press, pp.118–37.

WALHI (1992) *Mistaking Plantations for the Indonesia's Tropical Forests*[sic]. Jakarta: Wahana Lingkungan Hidup Indonesia.

WALRAS, L. (1954) *Eléments d'economie politique pure* (Elements of pure economics or the theory of social welfare) (first published 1874). Homewood, Ill: Allen & Unwin.

WEINBERG, A. (1972) Science and transcience. *Minerva,* **10**, 209–22.

WORLD BANK (1990) *World Development Report: Poverty*. Oxford: Oxford University Press.

WORLD BANK (1991) *World Development Report*. Oxford: Oxford University Press.

WORLD COMMISSION ON ENVIRONMENT AND DEVELOPMENT (WCED) (1987) *Our Common Future*. Oxford: Oxford University Press.

WYNNE, B. (ed.) (1987) *Risk Management and Hazardous Waste. Implementation of the Dialectics of Credibility*. Berlin: Springer Verlag.

YEARLEY, S. (1992) *The Green Case*. London: Routledge.

Index